gender
2 —

THE QUEST OF
THE WARRIOR WOMAN

D0647155

gender
2 –

THE QUEST OF
THE WARRIOR WOMAN

Women as Mystics, Healers and Guides

CHRISTINA FELDMAN

Aquarian
An Imprint of HarperCollins*Publishers*

Aquarian
An Imprint of HarperCollins*Publishers*
77–85 Fulham Palace Road
Hammersmith, London W6 8JB
1160 Battery Street
San Francisco, California 94111–1213

First published by Aquarian 1994
1 3 5 7 9 10 8 6 4 2

© Christina Feldman 1994

Christina Feldman asserts the moral right to
be identified as the author of this work

A catalogue record for this book
is available from the British Library

ISBN 1 85538 323 3

Printed in Great Britain by Mackays of Chatham, Kent

All rights reserved. No part of this publication may be
reproduced, stored in a retrieval system, or transmitted,
in any form or by any means, electronic, mechanical,
photocopying, recording or otherwise, without the prior
permission of the publishers.

To the countless women who have, over the years, shared with me the joys and sorrows, tears and laughter, of their journeys and their stories—I am grateful. Your courage, vision and compassion are an inspiration.

To Sara, Arran and Mick for always being there— I thank you.

CONTENTS

INTRODUCTION

This book is intended to honour and celebrate the spark of passion and vision that lies within the heart of every woman. Women are not newcomers to the warrior tradition; it is our heritage. Ancient myth and legend give to us the stories of cultures created and guided by wise and courageous women. The goddesses depicted in Buddhism, Hinduism and pre-Christian religion reveal to us a picture of warrior women who held the power to create, to preserve and to destroy. They are portrayed as raging angels—inspired by passion and vision to give birth to and foster communities, civilisations and values rooted in compassion, wisdom and freedom. They are women dedicated to healing and preserving life, dignity and spirit. They are women fearless enough to overthrow and destroy the ignorance, conventions and structures that hinder their journey to freedom.

This book is not about women of the past, but women of the present. Contemporary women breathe life into the epic journey of the warrior. Warrior women of the present have given birth to an authentic vision for women; banishing forever the dark models, structures and conventions which previously condemned women to invisibility and shadows. Women have found new creativity and passion in their own lives; a renewed commitment to healing not only the wounds within their own psyches, but to our wounded planet, our societies and our relationships. This renewal of creativity, passion and clarity rises from the courage of the warrior.

An integral part of every woman's journey to freedom is learning to reclaim the warrior within herself. It is not just in ancient legends and myths that we find the story of the warrior. The heroines of our age are found in the stories of women who live with remarkable dignity and courage in the midst of oppression and exploitation. Women who speak with truthfulness and honour when it would bring more applause to be silent or to conform, reveal to us a fearlessness of spirit. Women who teach their children dignity and integrity in the midst of superficiality and dishonesty bequeath a heritage of freedom. Women who treasure compassion, freedom and liberation more than safety, approval and affirmation embody the warrior spirit. These women are not strangers to us; they are part of our own stories, our teachers, our allies—they are ourselves.

It is not always an easy task for women to reclaim and honour the warrior within. The dominating, destructive, overpowering warrior we are familiar with has wounded and scarred our planet, our communities and our lives with its obsession with winning. We know the dark side of the warrior who is intent upon enemies, power and victory. We know the pain and grief of being disempowered, silenced and devalued. The work of unmasking this defective and distorted warrior has left many women exhausted and frustrated. We may be reluctant to associate ourselves in any way with the warrior tradition, fearing that we will fall into the same patterns of dominance and insensitivity. A generation of women has committed itself to valuing and honouring everything about being a woman: our bodies, sexuality, receptivity, capacity for emotion, sensitivity and openness. For all of this to co-exist with the warrior spirit appears both impossible and contradictory.

The Quest of the Warrior Woman describes the journey of a qualitatively different kind of warrior. The warrior of the spirit is not concerned with the overpowering of enemies and adversaries. She does not include in her arsenal of weapons dominance, control or mastery. Nor is she obsessed with victory, subjugation or conquering. The woman warrior is not intent upon individual gains or possessing the spoils of battle. She is a woman of poise; finely balanced. She knows how to be responsive and clearly focussed. Patience and determination merge happily within her. Strength and gentleness, receptivity and creativity, are not polarised but integrated. She is a woman of passion and creativity, power and healing. This is born of her vision, trust and commitment to freedom, oneness and the end of all dualisms.

The warrior woman is a woman with a calling. Her journey is about the destruction of ignorance, the healing of schisms, the realisation of freedom. Undistracted by the false dualisms of inner and outer, masculine and feminine, spirit and matter, she is not deceived by the promises of empty victories or false defeats. She is a warrior of the spirit, knowing deeply that we can make no difference between outer change and inner transformation. It is a journey which is filled with challenges. The warrior woman embarks on her odyssey inspired by vision and passion, but carrying with her too her own shadows and demons. She must learn how to embrace them with the same skills and balance that she brings to the shadows that she meets in her life. Fear, passivity, distractedness, resignation, doubt, self-negation are demons that will be transformed by the fearlessness, perseverance, courage and creativity that lie within her. Don Juan, an Indian shaman, once said, 'To an ordinary person everything is either a blessing or a curse. To a spiritual warrior, everything is a challenge.' The journey of the spiritual warrior is a journey that involves no enemies; it is a journey of wisdom and transformation.

ONE

SPIRITUAL WARRIOR
TUSHANA'S CHALLENGE

Having spent many years in the company of her sister nuns in the nunneries of the plains, Tushana knew it was time to go into the loneliness of the mountains to continue her search. As a child she had been enchanted by the stories of the great and wise yoginis, who were guided by their hearts to seek for enlightenment. As a young girl she would linger around the gates to the nunnery, hoping to engage one of the great nuns in conversation. Their stories captured her imagination as they told her tales of past and present sages who dwelt in profound peace and knew a true freedom of spirit. Whenever possible she would attend the ceremonies in the temple, fascinated by their mystery. The chanting of the monks and nuns, the burning incense, the ringing bells and the serenity etched on the faces of the participants fascinated her. As she grew older and the time came for her to marry, she found herself unable to accede to her parents wishes. She shuddered at the thought of spending her life churning butter, caring for a husband, gossiping in the market—where the highlight of her days would be the occasional festival. This was not the life she dreamed of.

She slipped out of her parents' home one morning, sought out the abbess of the nunnery and was accepted as a disciple. Her first years in the monastery were spent performing the most lowly of tasks. Preparing the food, caring for the elderly nuns and working in the fields she learnt the craft of patience and humility and her commitment was tested. Many moments she felt disdain for the work she performed, impatient with its mundanity. She complained to the abbess, pointing out that her life in the nunnery bore a close resemblance to the life she would have lived if she had followed her parents' advice and married. Listening to her complaints of drudgery, the abbess would question her: 'And where do you think holiness lies?' Tushana would return to her sweeping. As the years passed by Tushana's grievances grew steadily quieter as she found a greater serenity and calmness in the rhythm of her days. New disciples came into the nunnery and relieved her of her work in the fields and kitchen. She was initiated into the discipline of meditation, had visions, mystical experiences and profound realisations that gladdened her. One day she realised that she was now one of the elder nuns and new young girls had replaced her at the gates of the nunnery, asking her to tell them the story of her own journey.

One day in the midst of recounting her story, telling of the obstacles she had met and surmounted, the difficulties that had challenged her and the achievements she had gained, Tushana was struck by a sudden chord of disquiet. She remembered the vision that had inspired the beginning of her journey—her passion for freedom and awakening and her yearning to follow in the footsteps of the great mystics she had admired. The story she was recounting felt to be only a pale shadow of the vision she had cherished in the beginning of her search. Unable to say another word, she retired to her room, realising that after all the years she had spent in the nunnery, the vision of freedom she had cherished felt as far away as on the first day she entered the gates. She carried with her a burdensome feeling that she had indeed settled for something less than was possible for her.

With a renewed sense of commitment she gathered together her few belongings, bade farewell to her sister nuns and set out for the mountain peaks. After a few days' travelling she found a simple cave in which to make her dwelling. Preparing the cave, she vowed to herself that she would live in solitude until she discovered the meaning of freedom. Strengthened by her resolve, her days settled into a peaceful rhythm—her only companions were the birds and small creatures of the forest; her only work was to gather the wild plants, berries and herbs for food; her challenge was simply to be awake in the deepest way she knew.

After many weeks had passed, Tushana returned to her cave one morning after gathering firewood, only to discover her dwelling inhabited by a crowd of fearsome demons. Some were cackling with glee, others shouting with rage, several were occupying themselves by throwing her belongings about. A few of the demons hung from the roof pulling horrific faces while others taunted and abused her from the shadows. In the face of their bedlam Tushana shivered with fear and doubt. What grievous mistake had she made to summon forth such terrors? How could she persuade them to leave? Determined not to be evicted from her newfound peace by the apparitions that confronted her, Tushana entered their midst to face them.

At first she resolved to ignore them, but her silence served only to provoke them to shriek more loudly. Demanding her attention, they danced around her, pulling at her clothes and hair. Remembering a time in the nunnery when she was sent to serve one of the more fretful, elderly nuns, she slumped into a posture of obedience and smiled at the demons, saying, 'Oh, you are indeed wonderful demons, so strong and powerful. I am not even worthy of your wrath, such a poor, insignificant woman as I am. Why do you not go elsewhere where your magnificence will be truly appreciated?' A few of the demons were sufficiently flattered by her winsomeness to disappear, but the others began to rage even more wildly.

In desperation, Tushana searched for another strategy to rid herself of the demons and she called forth the authority and protection of the teachers and dakinis who had guided her. Facing the demons, she spoke to them. 'You cannot harm me,' she cried. 'I am protected by the power of those more commanding than you. Flee from here before they harm you.' Cowed, several of the demons slunk away, yet still a crowd remained. Searching her heart for a solution, Tushana raised herself into a haughty posture and in an imperious voice scolded the demons before her. 'Who are you to disturb a nun on the path of holiness? Before you stands a successful yogini— one who has conquered and vanquished countless obstacles. Throughout the land I am admired and applauded; I fear no-one and especially not you. Be gone from my home.' Hearing her words, several more of the demons disappeared but three still remained, howling at her.

For a moment Tushana felt overcome by fear and exhaustion and begged the demons to spare her, saying, 'I surrender. Please don't harm me. I recognise my errors and will do my best to serve you, if only you will spare me.' Two of the remaining demons were satisfied with her words and dissolved, but the last demon was the most vicious and powerful of them all. Tushana had no more strategies to rely upon that would please or placate this most fiendish of monsters. It would accept neither her surrender nor her rejection. Knowing there was no way to overcome this most powerful demon, she turned to face its wrath. Approaching the demon, she felt her fear fall away and her heart fill with compassion. Without thought of her own safety, without fear of her enemy, she placed herself in the mouth of the demon. The demon did not devour her or harm her; faced with her courage and compassion it vanished like a rainbow. In that moment Tushana knew there was no difference between the demons she fought and the freedom she sought.

Every great spiritual tradition holds within it the story of the warrior. The image of the seeker setting out on a lonely journey, enduring countless trials and challenges in quest of freedom and truth is an endlessly repeated theme in spiritual parables and mythology. Countless fairy tales repeat the theme of heroines and seekers awakening from sleep, confusion and servitude to discover what is true and free within them. The warrior symbolises the woman who begins a journey in quest of transformation in her life. The warrior goes forth into unknown territory, inspired by a vision of possibility. The warrior is an explorer, an adventurer, a trailblazer.

The warrior of our mythology is a necessary facet in the journey of every woman who seeks to live in the light of inner and outer freedom, to speak with the truth of her own voice and wisdom and to heal the wounds of her planet and communities. Unlike the heroines of our mythology, the warrior woman is no longer content to wait for freedom and truth to be revealed to her by any external hero. She sets forth on her own journey guided by her own vision of freedom. She is possessed of such an unshakeable inner trust that she holds within her the capacity to live as a free, compassionate and wise woman and forsakes all forms of limitation. The vision of freedom that is the guiding light of the warrior woman is vast— she seeks to bring to an end all forms of oppression, exploitation and subjugation that scar her world. She is equally attuned to the rhythms of her own heart and psyche and seeks to disempower her own demons and shadows and the power of conditioning that exile her from freedom. The warrior of the spirit is intent on discovering the freedom to speak the truths she understands, to live with creativity and authenticity and to make choices founded upon wisdom rather than fear.

The vision of freedom that inspires the warrior woman is two-fold. In her journey she seeks to forsake all assumptions, conventions, structures and beliefs that confine her. She is no longer willing to accept conventional assumptions that define her femininity as weakness, passivity, timidity or powerlessness. Nor is she willing to assume roles or identities in her life handed down to her by someone else. The age of the malleable woman whose life is defined only by function or appearance is ended for the warrior woman. Mother, daughter, carer, nurturer may be the forms she chooses to communicate her creativity and freedom—they are no longer identities she feels driven to adopt out of expectation or fear. The warrior of the spirit is equally intent on awakening to what is true about her life and herself. Like Tushana, she turns to face her demons and shadows, embracing them with courage and compassion, transforming her life and herself.

Every woman who begins a journey to understand herself and what is possible for her travels a path that requires a finely-tuned balance. Patience needs the companion of determination, receptivity needs courage, compassion requires focus, and single-mindedness needs humility. The warrior is not without fear; her heart may tremble at the prospect of bringing about radical change in her life and her world, but intuitively she knows that fear is the mother of true courage. Like Tushana, countless women leave behind them the comfort and security of their nunneries to begin new ventures and explore possibilities in their lives. A woman who begins a new career in her middle years, a woman who seeks to forsake years of alcoholic numbness, a woman who ends an abusive relationship—all of these women leave the cocoon of their nunneries. They may well tremble at the prospect of change and the demons they may encounter, yet they are willing to take risks and be alone. They are guided by faith, inner authority and vision: they are warriors.

The warrior needs energy and perseverance—many of the shadows and demons that challenge us have a long history and we may equally have a history of supporting them.

Sharon described herself as a compulsive pleaser—as a child she lived to please her parents, doing whatever was necessary to win their praise. She dressed to please them, was cute whenever they had guests and brought home the badges from school that brought a smile to their faces. She married the man they liked, despite her own misgivings, and proceeded to build a happy life by pleasing him. She couldn't understand her own daughter's refusal to follow in her footsteps. In the midst of rebuking her daughter one morning over her behaviour, it struck her that the voice and words she was using were the voices and words of her own parents. It was an awakening that filled her with shame. She realised how much her daughter was actually living the life she had always wanted to live and recognised the gift her daughter was offering to her.

The warrior woman needs not to have perfected the qualities she needs for transformation prior to beginning her journey—if the perfection of the warrior spirit had been realised it is unlikely that any journey would be called for. The beginning of her journey is marked by her willingness to take the first step of turning towards her demons. The courage, energy and determination of the warrior begins to emerge in the moment of leaving the gate of the nunnery—when we are no longer willing to accept comfort, safety and approval as substitutes for freedom.

The authentic warrior is engaged in a journey and not a battle; is not seeking war but questing for truth. To realise her vision of freedom, to bring about profound transformation, a qualitatively different kind of warrior needs to be born. Success, victory and winning are not among the aims of the authentic warrior. In their absence failure, defeat and loss are also not terrors that haunt her journey. Subduing, conquering, controlling or transcending are not on the agenda of the warrior of the spirit; they are not goals that are compatible with freedom. Invincibility, denial and suppression have no place in the journey of the warrior woman—there are few women who have not travelled these paths or been the victim of them and know them to be vehicles of pain. She forsakes them and seeks to discover the power of her own compassion, vision and wisdom.

The woman on the path of transformation is a warrior who creates no enemies and battles no opponents. Enemies and

7

adversaries are the children of resistance, fear and denial. Yet every woman who treasures freedom is inevitably challenged by shadows and forces that seek to confine or limit the very freedom she treasures: social expectations that demand of women agreeability rather than boldness; political and economic structures that refuse to promote women to positions of authority, and cultural expectations that demand that women make a choice between family and career are all real forces in women's lives that suffocate and debilitate the warrior spirit. Religious institutions continue to covet the power to deliver pronouncements that determine women's lives and aspirations.

None of these challenges or prohibitions are newcomers to the life and journey of the warrior woman. Throughout history these have always been the forces that attempt to forbid, muzzle and silence the voice of the warrior woman—to mould her into a social, spiritual and intellectually acceptable shape. History is also a record of the ineffectiveness of these forces. No matter the culture or environment of a woman, the spark of the warrior continues to burn. In Buddhist history, the life of the wandering woman mystic and teacher was efficiently ended by the introduction of sterner codes that confined women to nunneries under the protection and authority of men. The justification for this code was to protect the nuns' virtue—the effect was to silence them. In Confucian China the introduction of foot-binding for women put an abrupt end to the career of the wandering, teaching nun. For centuries, generations of devout and dedicated women suffered beneath the weight of these constraints, yet continued to nurture their path and their vision. Today we see the fruition of their perseverance—a new generation of women mystics, a strengthened Bhikkhuni order and women with courage and wisdom that have been tempered in the fire of challenge.

We do not have to search deeply the corners of our own world to discover parallel constraints that equally serve to confine the freedom of the warrior: the fashion industry; the legions of authorities that continue to dispense models of acceptable femininity. The unspoken assumption of woman's lack of authority continues to hound the footsteps of the warrior yet the spark of freedom in her heart continues to burn. Taught to be fearful, she exhibits immense courage; taught to be subservient she continues to forge new paths; taught to be humble and self-negating she continues to reclaim and speak the truth she holds to be precious. In the face of threats to their lives and banishment from their families, the women of Ireland took to the streets to speak of peace and confront the weakness of violence. In the face of centuries of disapproval Christian woman continue to expose the fallacy of women's subjugations. They are the visible faces of the warrior woman. Of equal import are the less visible women who, within the arenas of their own lives are refusing to live according to the dictates of another or accept the surrender of their freedom.

Struggling to free herself from confinement and limitation, the warrior woman is wounded through the process of turning a challenge into an enemy. In this transaction she is as much a captive of her own fear as she is of any external challenge. Faced with an enemy, she is tempted to go into battle armoured with traditional weapons carried in the patriarchal warrior lineage—willpower, control and suppression may be effective weapons in the pursuit of subjugation but their rewards are somewhat hollow if she continues to live in the shadow of her own fear.

After leaving home, where she had lived under the shadow of her dominating and abusive father, Trina did everything within her power to humiliate him and make him pay for the years of terror she had suffered. When he was dying she refused to see him despite his beseeching. Refusing even to attend his funeral, she felt she had finally won the battle she had endlessly fought with him. In the years after his death she continued to fight the same battle—every figure of authority in her life was suspect, every suggestion from another perceived as a command, endless possibilities rejected because of her mistrust. Her father lived in her heart, assuming an endless variety of different forms. It took her many years of loneliness and sacrificed possibilities to befriend her own fear of domination.

Emulating the path of the patriarchal warrior, the warrior woman is carrying someone else's weapons and they do not serve her well; travelling someone else's path and its destination possesses an alien flavour. She feels driven to adopt these strategies through desperation and fear. Disenfranchised from the authenticity of her own wisdom and resources through years of denial, she knows of few other ways to break out of the confines of limitation but to adopt the strategies and weapons that have been effective for others or that have been effective in bringing about her own confinement.

In the face of oppression, denial or limitation we feel driven to resort to whatever strategies will alleviate their power. The warrior of the spirit seeks freedom, yet the path of bringing about profound transformation and freedom may be unfamiliar territory to her. Like Tushana, the wounded woman may include winsomeness, flattery, manipulation, defensiveness and defiance in her arsenal of weapons. They are once more weapons of subjugation and control—weapons of war intended to subdue an enemy.

Every time Melissa was forced into a new transition in her life—university, beginning a career, a new relationship—she ensured that everyone she met knew the facts of her horrendous childhood. The people around her felt so sorry for her that they felt they were exceedingly callous if they objected to her inefficiency in her work, her irresponsibility in her relationships or her failure to fulfil her commitments. No one was willing to be the cause of further pain. Wearing her wounds she achieved control of most circumstances in her life. She felt that the sacrifice of respect and creativity was an acceptable loss in the face of the power she gained. Years passed before she awoke to the reality that inhabiting the role of the victim attracted pity but not intimacy and that it was a role that sentenced her to an eternal childhood.

Every war has winners and losers, masters and victims, and leaves behind it a residue of division, pain and resentment. History tells us that peace and freedom are not the legacy of any war; wars leave behind them only the spark of fear and resentment that lies dormant, waiting to be fanned into new fire. Whatever we fear we believe we must control and overcome in order to ensure our own survival. Within us abides an underlying fear that if we do not adopt the strategies of the traditional warrior then we ourselves will be the victims, the losers, the vanquished. In reaction to this fear our lives become filled with enemies that appear to offer us few choices—we must overcome or be overcome; control or be controlled; win or lose.

The enemies and opponents we battle and struggle with lie not just in the world outside of ourselves. Women have become experts, through long training, at naming aspects of themselves as weaknesses and regarding them as adversaries. Our bodies, minds and personalities are judged harshly as being inadequate, not good enough, and turned into opponents to struggle with through control, subjugation and manipulation. We may find ourselves resenting our inner shadows of fear or passivity which are residues of a wounded past, and determine to overcome them. As adversaries, we turn upon our own inner demons and shadows the same arsenal of weapons that we have turned upon outer forces and figures that anger or undermine us. We are at war with ourselves. Blame, denial and contempt become familiar companions in the landscape of our psyche. How to overcome or overpower the subjects of our contempt becomes the preoccupation of our lives.

A young woman living in Los Angeles made a weekly date with her personal retinue of improvement experts. A small lip job one year, a nose alteration the next, an implant here and a reduction there. She explained: 'To be successful in this city, you have to look successful. I can't afford to let myself go.' She could not afford to be who she was. Filled with rejection for our own bodies, minds or hearts, we become intent only on vanquishing what we cannot accept about ourselves. Success is determined by our capacity to subjugate whatever we feel afraid of opening up to; control becomes the measure of our progress. The wounded warrior learns to feel familiar within an inner environment of struggle and war; afraid of surrendering the struggles lest she be overpowered by the force of her own demons.

The greatest challenge for the warrior woman is discovering how to be a warrior without engaging in any war. Learning how to pursue our quest for freedom without battling with adversaries is to travel the path without conflict or remorse. To learn the skillfulness of embracing and moving through forces which limit or confine us, free of contempt or denial, is to learn the art of living without enemies. To bring about changes and transformations within our lives and ourselves without leaving in our wake losers or victims requires immense courage and compassion. To discover freedom in the midst of challenge and difficulty, without ever becoming a master or winner, calls for profound humility and generosity. The warrior of the spirit does not confuse freedom with victory, nor label any challenge an enemy. She knows that it is here that she is offered the opportunity to reclaim the courage and compassion of the warrior spirit that will guide her to freedom.

Throughout centuries the warrior tradition has been the territory of women. The warrior woman is a creator, a preserver, a visionary, a healer, a teacher and a learner. She is the woman who sets forth to plant new seeds in a land ravaged by famine. We have seen her chain herself to the gates of government buildings in protest at inequality; she is the woman who stands vigil in the path of weapons of destruction. She is the woman who defies convention and honours aloneness as a way of most deeply articulating her creativity; she is also the woman who creates a sanctuary of love and peace for her children in the midst of the greatest poverty and abandonment. She is the rape victim who refuses to surrender her dignity and the woman who seeks to begin again in the face of rejection or failure. The warrior woman is rarely seen brandishing weapons or trophies, yet she is guided by the qualities of the warrior. She is courageous and enduring, intuitive and joyous, and in her heart she knows the difference between freedom and limitation. She is compassionate and forgiving; she is equally determined and focussed. Her concerns are truth, healing, wisdom and freedom. Fire is a part of women's deepest nature, the spark of passion that guides her to bond, to celebrate, to mourn, to connect and to envision.

There are many women who feel initially suspicious of the warrior's path. We recoil against the images of violence, aggression, dominance and control associated with the figure of the conventional warrior. The word 'warrior' triggers into our consciousness images of armoured combatants, filled with hostility, intent only on the conquering of enemies. Winning, overpowering, overcoming and suppression are the lifeblood of the traditional warrior. The warriors who have made their mark upon our world are strangers, alien to the awakening woman, who too often has been their victim and their trophy. There are few women willing to adopt the ethics or the goals of the warrior of subjugation.

The warriors most familiar to us have left behind them a legacy of destruction and grief. They have marched behind banners and slogans of justice, liberation, righteousness and equality but have only reaped a harvest of victims, a wounded earth, wounded communities and mourners. Too often women have stood in the ranks of the vanquished, the defeated and the silenced. The warriors we have known from our past and present appear to be cloaked in a mantle of invincibility, a hard-ness of heart that distances them from the tears and the sorrow of the vanquished and the defeated.

These warriors we are so familiar with are not confined to the battlefields of foreign lands. They frequent corporate and political structures, institutions and organisations. They are the figures who reap personal profit and enhance self-interest in decisions, laws and edicts that destroy our planet, deprive individuals of dignity and abandon integrity. Industries are made exempt from pollution controls in the name of econom-ic progress. Single mothers are punished for their solitary sta-tus by depriving them of the funds to live with dignity. The same warriors shadow relationships, bedrooms, families and communities. They appear in the figure who demands sub-servience in exchange for minimal financial support, who finds pride in the capacity to force another to bend to their will, who collects sexual trophies. The armour and the weapons differ, but whenever winning is sought at any price, victory pursued regardless of consequence, or success and power worshipped, the traditional warrior is in action. It is no surprise that so many women feel alienated from the warrior tradition.

Before we banish the warrior entirely from our lives, it may be helpful to pause for a moment and consider whether we may be mistaking the authentic warrior for its shadow. The warrior image women feel so estranged from is but a counter-feit, a poor facsimile of the genuine article. The difference between the counterfeit and the authentic warrior is vast. The counterfeit warrior is compelled and motivated by fear and pride into the battleground. The authentic warrior is compelled and motivated by compassion and courage. The counterfeit warrior desires power, prestige, self-aggrandizement, and is deeply exiled from any true sense of connectedness with the world. The genuine warrior is willing to be visible or invisible but is committed to freedom, healing and understanding and is rooted in a profound sense of interconnectedness. The counterfeit warrior engages in concocted battles and will reap only shallow successes and fraudulent victories. There is no honour in the ability to dominate another, to inspire fear or to over-power anyone or anything in our world. It is not difficult to don the mantle of invincibility, pursue power and create vic-tims in our lives. It requires far greater courage to challenge falsehood, to renounce victory and to live with integrity.

Shallow success cannot nourish our heart; talismans of vic-tory and power cannot sustain our spirit. These truths are hard to accept when our culture and conditioning have done their utmost to convince us that these are the goals that truly mat-ter.

A young woman spoke of her life as a professional athlete. Her talent and potential were spotted in her school days and from that time her whole life was directed towards only one goal—being the best. Her training schedule allowed no time for relationships but she was comforted by the praise of her coaches. The demands of practice meant every moment of her day was spent improving and perfecting, yet her exhaustion was lightened by the promises delivered to her. Work replaced fun and even her concern over the lack of maturing in her body was dismissed as a small price to pay for her improvement. She learnt to close her ears to the tears and anguish of those who lost, to harden her heart towards her own yearning for more ease in her life and her growing anxiety about losing. Her room was filled with trophies, she basked in the praise of win-ning and grew increasingly terrified of losing. In one competi-tion she broke her ankle and was told she would never win again. At first she agonised over the news, blamed herself, blamed her coach. She was forced to care for herself in a dif-ferent way, to learn how to rest instead of to move, to nourish herself instead of feeding on the praise of others. Her world opened and she felt herself blessed in a way she had never experienced before.

Faced with the essential meaninglessness of many of the

trophies in our lives that are a consequence of suppression or overpowering, we at times do our utmost to convince ourselves that the problem lies only in not having quite achieved the goals and successes that truly matter; that will bring us happiness and peace. In accepting this assumption, another cycle of pursuit is initiated, new goals pursued. The counterfeit warrior is seeking salvation through impossible means and in places where it cannot dwell. This is not to imply that the path of the genuine warrior demands abandonment of all thoughts of success, achievement or excellence. The warrior woman knows that all of these are the effects of honouring her creativity, courage and tenacity and not substitutes for them. She runs because she loves to run; she writes because of the wish to communicate her truths; she mothers because she honours life.

There is yet another reason why many women feel reluctant to associate themselves with the warrior tradition. So much courage has been required of women to emerge from the ranks of the silenced and the vanquished. So much effort and energy has been expended by countless women in reclaiming and learning how to honour their innately feminine resources of receptivity, generosity, inner responsiveness and connectedness. So many knots have needed to be untangled for us to learn to value our capacities for relatedness, openness and vulnerability as qualities essential to the survival of our world and communities rather than being liabilities to overcome. Understandably, we are reluctant to forsake this reclamation and renewal, and fear that the warrior tradition threatens the qualities that have become the very foundation of our awakening. We may fear that generosity will be suffocated by boldness, that receptivity will be drowned by focus and responsiveness dulled by single-pointedness.

We are living in an era that abounds with both great confusion and great creativity; immense freedom and the terrors that the possibility of freedom brings. Banished forever are the old and sanctioned stereotypes that defined women's roles and directions—banished with them is the certainty and security they provided. Never before in any other generation have women faced so many choices nor been so alone in being responsible for the choices they make. It is a moment of hope and of doubt; of celebration and confusion.

The warrior woman is concerned with transformation— inner and outer—the cessation of oppression and limitation, the flowering of freedom and possibilities. The legacy of feminism is the freedom to create and guide our own lives, write our own stories instead of living the story of someone else and explore a landscape of possibilities. It is a transformation that has not resulted from patiently waiting for permission or approval to change to be granted from anyone or anything outside of ourselves. In our time we are reaping the harvest of the courage, certainty, discontent, passion and vision of all women who no longer accepted invisibility or limitation as companions in their lives. Free to pursue fulfilment professionally, legally and academically; free to celebrate a spiritual life that honours the feminine, the intuitive, the receptive; free to envision our lives for ourselves—our sense of possibility is vastly expanded. There is celebration; there is also despair.

We grieve for the continuing destruction and pillaging of our planet by cultures and individuals who refuse to heed the urgent calls of women that remind them of our essential interdependence. Despondency is born of the awareness that the freedoms we so gladly embrace remain unknown to countless women in our world. We mourn the revival of oppression that seeks to confine and undermine women that is a reaction to women's visibility. We feel despair when we experience ourselves being so shackled by our inner fears and demons that we are unable to partake of the choices and freedoms that are offered to us. For every woman who sets forth from the gates of her nunnery to seek authenticity there is another who stands at the window looking longingly at horizons she is afraid to explore.

Our hearts are broken by the degree to which the cosmetic and fashion industry, the armies of plastic surgeons, improvement experts and the pornography industry thrive and profit in this climate of women's awakening. The banishment of cellulite has replaced the banishment of dirt as the central focus in the lives of too many women. Once driven to produce the perfect home as evidence of our worth, many women now compel themselves to produce the perfect body, the perfect performance to evidence their worth. More women than ever before silence and numb their confusion and pain in the haze induced by tranquillizers and anti-depressants, while the chaos of eating disorders haunts and destroys innumerable lives. For every woman who walks in the light of her own courage and creativity, there is another who is caught in the shadows. For every woman who dances, there is another who weeps. Choice can become a tyrant in our lives; freedom a demon to be feared. To make wise choices, to explore our understanding of freedom, the warrior spirit is needed.

There is never a time that is right to retire the spirit of the warrior. Even as we celebrate openings and transformations we must be alert to the tentacles of complacency. Even in the midst of despair, we must remember that the spirit of the warrior lies within us, waiting to answer our call. We need to call upon the passion, vision and courage of our warrior spirit to move on in our journeys. We need to ask for the blessing of her faith in our moments of doubt, the benediction of her determination in the moments we stumble. Every woman has faced exhaustion of the spirit in the face of seemingly immovable opposition. Every woman has faced the temptation to settle for something less than she had yearned for when offered the solace of security.

Janine recounted the story of her years of work in the peace movement. She had demonstrated against war, against anti-abortion lobbies. She had been on hunger strikes and picketed draft offices. She had protested at the rain forest destruction and faced down nuclear transports. She inspired countless people to live their lives with integrity but for every shadow of destruction that she managed to face down, a new one arose. Exhausted, she began to feel that perhaps she had done enough; it was time for someone younger to carry the light of peace. She imagined a life of tending her garden, spending time with friends. One day a younger woman came to her and spoke of the inspiration she had blessed others with; how she had spoken the words they'd longed to speak and acted with the courage others had sought for themselves. Again she understood that it was not her successes and failures that mattered, but the integrity of spirit that shone a light for others to follow. The spirit of the warrior brings an integrity that strengthens us in our temptations to compromise and a passion that encourages us in the twilight of exhaustion. She is our guide, our counsel and our healer.

Our lives are marked by the seasons of transition we pass through. The times of childhood and innocence, of puberty and adolescence, of womanhood, of aging and death, are all seasons we share. In the awakening of the warrior, the nurturing of wisdom and the quest for freedom there are equally many seasons and transitions we must pass through. The seasons of the spirit can be wild or benevolent, heart-warming or shattering—they are inevitable in any journey of awakening. In our fairy tales there is a predictable progression to the unfoldment of the story. Life is going to start out tough for our heroine; she is going to be misunderstood and abused. There is also bound to be a fairy godmother or prince waiting in the wings who is going to solve it all so they can live happily ever after with a suitable punishment dispensed to the bad guys. This predictability is unlikely to be found in our own journeys. The happy young girl with the ideal family finds herself faced with the demons of her own addiction to approval in her womanhood. The mature woman who has invested years in creating a life of certainties finds herself abandoned and faced with the need to discover who she is apart from her previously-assumed role. A woman raised in a religious family, filled with faith, faces the darkness of doubt and is asked to question her own understanding of a doctrine she has always taken for granted. In the journey of the spirit there is little predictability and a noticeable absence of princes and fairy godmothers. The warrior is the woman who embraces these transitions and changes in her spirit with a willingness to learn.

Within the cycles of the spirit there is a season of discontent. It can take the form of a tide of depression or a persistent whisper of unease. The jobs, relationships, the lifestyles we have struggled so hard for seem unable to fulfil the promise of richness and happiness we had projected onto them. The thought of beginning yet another round of housework, another day in an unfulfilling job, or searching for yet one more relationship fills us with dread. We may rebel against our own rebelliousness, try to convince ourselves that this is only a passing phase or put it down to our hormones. We may attempt to quell our discontent by filling our lives and minds with busyness, yet discontent seethes within us. In this climate of discontent we find ourselves vulnerable to reactions of rage or sink into lethargy and despondency; decisions loom before us like insurmountable mountains. Something is amiss, something is missing—everything in our hearts and minds, the restlessness of our spirit, the frustration we're experiencing all tell us the same story—but we do not know where to turn to find the answer.

Tamsin finished her art degree and, unable to find a job in her field, took a job in a factory. It was a repetitively mindless job, manufacturing identical component parts which made her body achingly tired. She was surrounded by cheerful working women—to them the factory was a way of life that earned them independence, money and self-respect. They were grateful and happy, she was frustrated and bored to tears. One day, sitting in front of her grimy window, overlooking a rundown industrial site, she saw a butterfly alight inside the window and flutter its wings, trapped by the grime. For her it was a symbol of beauty, freedom, the natural world, and she reached forward to free it from its trap. It was such a simple gesture. At the end of the week she quit her job.

The season of discontent is a crucial time—it is the beginning of a transition, a moment of possibility. The spirit of the warrior is waking up and emerging that intuitively recognises that seasons of discontent invite us to deepen our understanding of ourselves. Different options are available to us in the face of discontent and change. Hopelessness and helplessness tempt us into depression; rage and resentment tempt us into bitterness. We may also choose to listen carefully, to enter into a patient vigilance and an alert receptivity so that we may learn from the winds of discontent that are sweeping through us.

A sage was once asked, 'What is the way to respond to pain and discontent in our lives?' She answered, 'There are those who will meet sorrow and pain as an enemy. Raging at the world, they will find someone to blame, thinking only in terms of fault and blame. There are those who will bewail their fate, saying, "What have I done to deserve this, why am I so unlucky?" There are also those who will blame themselves. Succumbing to guilt, they will believe that their very worthlessness deserves the punishment of suffering. There are also those who will meet pain and discontent not as an enemy but as a teacher. They will follow the path of the wise asking, "What is the root of this sorrow? What is the path to healing and what will I learn from this moment?" '

Sheila's husband committed suicide. It took her totally by surprise. In the morning she had said goodbye to him when she left for work, in the evening she returned to find him dead. She was filled with anger, at him, at herself, at his family, at the pressures of his work. She searched her heart, remembering all the other moments in her life when she had been abandoned and wept at the pain she seemed sentenced to endure. It was a nightmare time filled with unanswerable questions. It took many months of heart-searching for her to understand that she could not take responsibility for his life or his death.

The warrior woman holds a profound faith in the possibility of learning and deepening through sorrow and discontent. She does not celebrate the arrival of pain, neither does she wallow in it nor lose herself in blame. She knows that every moment of discontent or sorrow offers the possibility of renewal. Despite the darkness and chaos found in our seasons of discontent, the voice of the warrior reminds us not to be lost in regret for what is dying away or changing, but to appreciate that in the inevitability of losses in our lives there is also the beginning of new possibilities.

The arrival of discontent is unpredictable, it is rarely chosen. It may be sparked by crisis or loss, it may begin with a single event, it may have no distinctive cause. Discontent may be an inner certainty that we are no longer willing to accept, endure or suffer the unacceptable; be it an oppressive relationship, a life of triviality, or an awareness of an inner impoverishment that no amount of consumption, addiction or distraction can camouflage. This autumn of the spirit is a reminder to us that it is time to move on, to explore new horizons, to discover a sense of renewal, to cultivate a creative sense of vision in our lives.

Naming the sources of this discontent may be an integral part of our capacity to move on. We live in a world peopled by survivors of previously unnamed terrors and violence—physical, sexual and spiritual. Survivors of incest and childhood abuse are discovering the courage to speak their stories. Survivors of alcoholism, of religious oppression, of rape, of spiritual coercion, are finding the needed support to name their abusers. Naming is an important element in emerging from the silence which these terrors has previously decreed and provides an honest foundation from which to proceed in our lives. To acknowledge our terrors is to begin the process of disempowering them.

It would also be difficult to find a woman who is not a sur-vivor—who in her life has not faced humiliation, contempt, oppression—it differs only in degree, not in impact. Naming our demons is a part of healing, an exorcism. It would be a dis-service to ourselves to adopt our demons as an identity, to wear them like a hair shirt that constantly chafes us. Naming enables us to be conscious; frees us to discover who we are apart from our demons. It is not an invitation to create a cult of the survivor that becomes a new description through which we limit ourselves; the warrior rebels against the limitation of all descriptions that confine us to a static identity.

The degree to which we are aware in the process of naming our demons and waking up in our lives will determine whether this process is creative or destructive. Rage, sadness and grief are like autumn gales that howl through us and strip away everything we have previously described and defined ourselves by. We are divested of our certainties and identities, left naked and vulnerable, fearful that nothing will ever grow again in the climate of devastation we feel within.

Sandra grew up in an apparently happy family. Every week her parents would go out, leaving her in the care of her uncle, who systematically abused her over the years. Her hysterics on hearing her parents make plans to go out were dismissed and punished. Her withdrawal at school was ignored, her tendency towards extreme modesty as she concealed herself in unattrac-tive clothes led to beratement. Until she left home she believed that this was the norm in her friends' lives. Confronting the truth of her life meant also confronting the chosen indiffer-ence of her family and teachers. Mistrust, anger and grief overwhelmed her. Through the care of others, through her own reflection, she began to understand that the truth of the events in her life could never describe the truth of herself. Equally, she understood that in confronting the truth of her life she faced a choice of continuing to inhabit the landscape of the past or to step into a present and a future that held both uncertainty and possibility.

In moments of change, in moments of meeting our demons, we need to acknowledge the ways in which new growth is stunted through harbouring rage and bitterness. We are asked to make choices between helplessness and determination, rage and compassion, passivity or courage. The choices we make will determine whether we stay within the confines of the known, even when it is painful, or whether we will make the choice to let go of what has already gone by.

The autumn of the spirit is a season of the dying away of the old: no matter how beautiful or ugly, it has had its season. The renouncing of the familiar and the known is an intrinsic part of every spiritual journey; it is the path of the warrior. In spiritual stories it is symbolised in the figure of the renunciate who goes forth into homelessness. To be naked, to be vulnerable is the fertile ground of new growth and understanding—to embrace uncertainty is also challenging. The degree to which we cling to what we have created and established our identity in—whether it is prestige, roles, attachments, fears or shadows—this is the degree of reluctance we experience in letting go.

A very successful career woman decided to go on a silent retreat to connect more deeply with a sense of spiritual direction. One day she found herself weeping on the toilet because she could not accept being anonymous. Seasons of change and transition are not times for regret, remorse or fantasy. All that we let go of in our lives is not banished; it is the compost where the shoots of renewal will find their roots. To be a conscious participant in the process of change is to be a joyous participant in the creation of our lives, our vision and our renewal.

The faith and wisdom of the warrior tell us that there can be no renewal without the dying away of the old, no beginning without an ending. Courage enables us to embrace uncertainty and open to possibility; compassion enables us to heal and accept the fears and anxieties that arise in the face of change. Patience offers us the restraint we need in our desire to seek new certainties and havens of security in the face of loss or change. The season of change in our lives calls upon us to summon forth our own capacities of nurturing, caring, forgiveness and generosity. The warrior is emerging, preparing to walk a new path in her life.

Waking up from numbness, superficiality or suppression is a demanding, often painful process. Surviving loss, coping with demands of making a transition, naming our demons, has been so arduous and taxing that we mistake this beginning of the journey as its end. We may be tempted to curl into a foetal ball, shutting out the world—the process of letting go has been so demanding that we want to retire, never mind facing the challenge of beginning anew. Conversely, we may feel filled with impulsiveness or restlessness. We have been confined too long within the limits of identities or circumstances that were unfulfilling or demeaning to us and we are impatient to move on. There is the temptation to hurl ourselves into a cycle of busyness and productivity—begin a new career, initiate new ventures. The work of finding the 'real and authentic me' attracts us in a compelling way.

The warrior woman knows that the winter of the spirit is a necessary consequence of autumn just as it is a forerunner of spring. It is a time of resting and renewing, of replenishing and healing. She learns how to curb impatience without sinking into lethargy, to resist withdrawal yet rest within an alert sensitivity.

After a painful separation from a spiritual group of which she had been a long term member, Petra felt filled with conflicting feelings. There were moments she ached for the loss of the direction and companionship that resulted from the separation. Moments when she wanted nothing more than to watch endless movies and read romances and moments when she pored through countless publications to find a new path to embark on. There is an inevitable winter of the spirit that follows change and transition. It may appear to be a time of gloom, a dreary pause in our lives, but looking beneath the surface we understand that winter is a time of germination and regeneration.

In the seasons of the spirit we must not mistake the winters of darkness for the absence of growth or deepening. In the dying away of the old we need to make the times and spaces for calming and composing ourselves; learning how to rest in a creative stillness that offers time for reflection and solitude. The winters of the spirit are often a testimony to the courage of the changes and renunciations we have faced. The wise warrior is not endlessly engaged in acting, doing and producing; this is the path of the counterfeit warrior who measures progress and success only by productivity and the numbers of trophies that can be displayed. The wise warrior knows not only the path of change and action but equally the path of attending inwardly, ensuring that action is rooted in receptivity and wisdom.

Reflection is a necessary companion to any cycle of change and letting go; it is the vehicle of completion and learning. There are many times when we are so delighted to see the end of identities, circumstances or demons that have brought limitation and pain that we have no desire to dwell any longer upon them; we wish for their banishment. There may be much that we need to learn from these demons so that we do not simply embrace them again in another form. What is the nature of the shadow that led us to passively accept the power or authority of another? What fuels the obsession that led us to be a captive of circumstances or people in a way that demeans us? What demon do we carry that led us to accept an identity that so inadequately expressed what was possible for us?

Reflection is not a process of analysis, dissecting the past and morbidly dwelling upon the varieties of pain we have endured. It is a calm contemplation; not pursuing answers but asking the questions that are important. What do we need to let go of or nurture to be free in our lives? What do we truly value and honour and how do we discover it? Intuition is not automatic, it requires careful nurturing. Taking time to be still, to reflect, provides us with the possibility of completion—to be at peace in the present requires us to be at peace with the past. It is exceedingly difficult to move on in our lives if we continue to battle with a past we can neither forgive or complete.

The spring of the spirit is a season of energy, inspiration and creativity. Letting go, completion, the dying away of the old initiate a new cycle in our lives. The warrior is not content to exist in a limbo of meaninglessness, aimlessness or a vacuum. The spring of the spirit is the season for manifesting the wisdom, vision and truths that are the harvest of the autumn and winter that have preceded it. For many women it is a time for returning to school or career, for climbing the mountain they've always admired from a distance, for taking the class they've postponed or finding the solitude they've yearned for. A sense of excitement, adventure and readiness begins to emerge as we contemplate a renewed sense of vision and possibility in our lives. These feelings carry their own shadows—doubt is primary among them. We carry our memories of the past with its shadows that have led us to become entangled in limitation or a surrender of freedom. Our confidence is fragile—we may feel apprehensive about taking risks or endangering ourselves in new ventures, directions and explorations.

The wise warrior does not hurl herself into the season of spring like a deranged gardener, randomly throwing seed or mindlessly rampaging through the landscape. Readiness needs to be balanced with patience, excitement needs to be tempered with mindfulness, adventurousness matched with composure. Wisdom is needed to discern the difference between impulsiveness and creativity and receptivity to ensure that our journey is guided by wisdom and sensitivity. The season of spring is a season of choice, creativity and the exploration of possibility. There are essential questions we need to ask of ourselves. Do we live in a spirit of freedom? Are our lives an organic expression of what we most deeply value and understand to be meaningful? Transition and change mean that the glue which has previously held together the puzzle of our lives has come unstuck and the primary question that arises is, 'Where do we go from here? Where and how do we begin to discover the authenticity and freedom precious to us?'

The season of spring is the season of choice, a time to be an aware participant in the creation of our own journeys, our lives and our world. The envisioning of our lives in new ways demands immense courage and wisdom. Choice delivers to us not only possibility but also responsibility. There is no one standing behind us to praise, censure or save us no matter how much we may long for such certainties. The gift we have inherited from the warrior women who have been trailblazers in their own journeys is the liberty to make choices—to consent or decline, to agree or disagree, to say yes or no. We can choose to mother or not, to marry or not, to dedicate ourselves to a spiritual life or create a professional life. Countless grandmothers look upon their granddaughters with awe, seeing them travel paths never offered to them or that would have been overwhelming if they had been offered. These liberties come as a remarkable revelation to any woman who has in her life experienced powerlessness or subjugation, but it would be an error to equate them with freedom. Choice is but an invitation to freedom, but not freedom itself; it is the beginning of a journey, but not an arrival.

The creativity of spring is a rediscovery of our lost or forgotten voice, a reclamation of our own uniqueness and authenticity. The warrior knows with certainty that authenticity and freedom in our lives is born of learning how to speak with her own voice; how to walk her chosen path with her own feet;

how to listen without the distraction of inherited voices, and how to see through her own eyes. To shake off the confines of old conditioning and outgrown identities introduces us to a landscape of possibilities; the choices available to us appear like an infinite menu.

Patricia was a nun who left her order to live as a laywoman. She described her bewilderment in making the transition. 'There were so many people I could be and so many voices telling me who I should be. I felt like a newborn in the body of a woman. One person told me I should get into a relationship to make up for all the time I'd spent alone. I was showered with brochures on courses and programmes. Another tried to persuade me to join a group of ex-nuns to work against sexism in the church. I felt myself to be imprisoned in a restaurant with a demanding waitress exhorting me to make a decision, to order everything on the menu.'

There is a great skill in hastening slowly and wisely in the spring of the spirit. Many women bow beneath the pressure of being told they must 'find themselves', 'be true to themselves', fulfil their potential and be authentic. Anxiety and feelings of inadequacy easily tempt us to propel ourselves into the pursuit of goals, achievements and the donning of an acceptable identity. This is not so much a path of creativity as a path of anxiety. Shouting at a bud does not make a flower blossom more quickly. In the season of envisioning and creating, the warrior is determined to bring about transformation yet is totally attuned to the quality of the process. She knows that if she wishes for peace she must travel her path in a peaceful way; a world of compassion begins with compassion for herself; a life of freedom begins with the freedom from compulsion—she will never separate her goals from the quality of her path.

The warrior woman carefully tills the ground for the unfoldment of creativity, gathering together her capacities to be focussed and clear, determined and receptive. Like explorers in a new land she is vigilant, alert and courageous. She knows where she has come from but there is little certainty about the destination she will finally arrive at. There are few maps to guide her but she is willing to live without guarantees; she is open to uncertainty. She is guided by a profound inner wisdom and faith that are dedicated to freedom.

Unless we devastate our embryonic journeys, vision and spirit through doubt, fear or denial, our path will unfold before us. Spring glides into the summer of the spirit and there is a growing oneness felt between our inner lives and the ways in which we manifest them in the world. The intuition and vision that previously had felt hidden or fragile to us grow in certainty and are both visible and accessible. We find the forms in our lives that communicate all that we value most deeply and we discover a greater authority in our choices, wisdom and expression. Summer is a celebration of the spirit—not only of the potential that lies within each of us to live as fully awake, compassionate and wise women, but also of the spirit of the warrior that enables us to realise our vision of freedom.

The seasons of the spirit are not linear or hierarchical, there is no predictable progression or graduation. They invite us to learn and grow. In her darkest or her most glorious moment, the wise warrior succumbs neither to despair nor to complacency. The warrior emerges from a culture of spiritual famine, she emerges from the grip of her own demons and shadows. The spark of passion which burns within the heart of every warrior can never be entirely dampened by the forces of stereotypes or expectations, nor enslaved by the chains of conditioning. Each one of us needs to fan our own spark of passion and reclaim our own inner warrior. To heal our world, to realise the freedom and integrity that are possible for us, we are asked to call forth the warrior spirit. She will guide us through our seasons of change, through the mazes constructed by our shadows, to our essence which is free. She is armed with an unwavering vision—a life of compassion, openheartedness and freedom.

There is an inevitable tension in bringing about any significant form of change in our lives. Tension is a catalyst, a trig-
ger for renewal of vision, for letting go, for walking new paths.
Change involves taking risks, clarifying our priorities, values
and directions—at times it means forsaking the comfort and
security of the familiar. There are many times we flinch from
the tension that is born of awareness and enquiry; there is a
great attraction in continuing to inhabit the rooms that are
familiar to us. We may resist disturbing the predictable
rhythms of our lives and fear attracting unwelcome feedback
from those who expect predictability from us—we are unsure
whether the fruits of tension will be worth the price we will be
asked to pay. The warrior of the spirit is one who welcomes the
signals of tension, alert to the messages they bring and responsive to the story they tell. Tension is the nature of that charged
moment that lies between the known and the unknown; it is
the forerunner of transformation.

The stories of transformation and awakening so central to
mythology and spirituality inevitably highlight the tension
and struggles intrinsic to bringing about change. The quest for
awakening is taking place amidst forces that seek to suppress it
to maintain the status quo. In mythology, evil stepmothers,
monsters and wicked kings symbolise the power of our inner
demons whose mission is to obstruct the awakening that is
sought. The tension involved in reaching for transformation is
an ancient struggle—it features in our spiritual journeys; it
exists equally between environmentalists and those who maintain an exploitative relationship with the earth. Peacemakers
struggle with forces of power and control and freedom seekers
are faced with those who seek oppression and subjugation. The
tension is unavoidable, it holds the potential to be creative. In
the face of struggle we may yearn for models and stories where
transformation arrives as a magical benediction, requiring no
expenditure of effort, struggle or determination. It is a yearning to be cautious of, tempting us only into the realms of fan-

tasy or, more lethally, the search for some authority outside of ourselves before whom we can lay down the burden of our search. There is no shortage of authorities who will gladly accept our burden in return for allegiance, devotion and servitude; a great relief may be discovered in this exchange, but not great freedom.

From the moment the warrior begins to awaken and nudge the walls of her confinement, a movement is initiated which is difficult to reverse. For a woman who has even momentarily discovered the wisdom of inner authority, the return to subservience is an impossible reverse. The woman who has learned to live with dignity and respect will not be tempted by any approval that will be rewarded for obedience. Awakening begins a psychological, emotional, spiritual movement away from what is known and familiar to us; from all that we find stifling, unfulfilling or limiting. It is a step towards a way of being, seeing and living that is not known to us. In an ideal world—a fantasy journey—this transition would take place with ease and tranquillity; in the real journey of the warrior this transition is accompanied by challenge. As we begin this movement we are faced with the discovery that we have conflicting loyalties and frequently polarised allegiances.

There speaks within us the voice that inspires us to explore horizons and reach for possibilities; its shadow voice equally remonstrates with us to retire, to make the best of what we have and relish the comfort of the familiar. We listen to the voice of the warrior that speaks to us of trust, autonomy and courage; it is matched by its shadow that reminds us of our fears, doubts and dependencies. The warrior guides us to reach for freedom, to open our hearts and minds to the possibility of change; its shadow explodes with caution, memories of failure, reminders of inadequacy. Our yearning for awakening may be matched by the investment we have in dependency and approval; the readiness to embrace challenge is contrasted by the stake we have in maintaining sanctioned images, roles and relationships.

The inevitable tension that is born of these conflicting loyalties cannot be ignored. The shadow voices that resist change and fear do not call for negation or transcendence, but care and understanding; suppressed demons do not agreeably retire but will incessantly drag at our heels. The demons that shadow us are deeply rooted, powerful in their influence and pervasive in their effect. In the past we have had a great variety of strategies and compromises that have allowed us to co-exist with their power. Fantasy and hope, postponement and appeasement are all strategies we have evolved to subdue our shadows. Many of them offer temporary relief from tension and conflict but not the awakening we sense is possible for us.

The voice of the warrior must be heeded to move through the tension of transformation or we will enter a famine of the spirit. The warrior will enable us to cut the ties of the past. Renunciation is at times organic and choiceless. In the face of mounting dissatisfaction or pain we understand that there is no choice but to seek change, to shed disguises that no longer fit us and walk new paths. We might go to a nunnery, start out on unplanned travels, quit our jobs—anything that allows us make a new beginning in our lives.

Paula belonged to a spiritual community that offered great support but allowed no questioning of the teacher in charge. Again and again she saw power misused and people abused but it was endlessly overlooked with the explanation that it was a 'teaching' in surrender and humility. She, too, for years, was unwilling to confront the hypocrisy she saw; it would make her an outcast. Eventually she had to confront her own hypocrisy—her willingness to collude in the cover-up even as she seethed with questions. She was ostracised and did lose the sense of belonging she had treasured; she also felt a deepening of her own integrity and authenticity.

Letting go of our demons is not always so dramatic, nor is it always born of intense suffering. We may simply acknowledge the ineffectiveness of the strategies we have previously employed and, unsatisfied with simply redecorating a room which no longer provides us with a home, we determine to move house. A clarification of priorities is made within the realm of our conflicting loyalties and that process itself reveals to us where the need for renunciation lies.

The process of transformation that is initiated by the warrior does not necessarily result in the death of our demons, but in a willingness to listen to the teaching they offer. They show us the way forward; what we need to let go of and what we need to nurture. Embraced with compassion and patience, they are not enemies to be overcome or obstacles to be transcended but allies in our journey of awakening. Embraced with openness and sensitivity, the demons of our fears and doubts become the parents of fearlessness and trust. Met with wisdom and steadfastness, the demons of distractedness and confusion are divested of authority. The challenges we have previously called opponents become, in the path of the genuine warrior, teachers.

There is clearly an element of risk in the journey of every warrior. She is travelling a rocky road where she will at times stumble, grope in the dusk and temporarily lose her way. Her path is not littered with guarantees and certainties, yet once her journey has begun there is no turning back: like the process of giving birth—once the contractions have begun it's too late to change your mind. Risk and uncertainty need to be a welcomed part of this journey; we have all travelled the well-trodden paths sanctioned by our cultures and religions that tell us of a woman's place and potential. The signposts have been followed and we have had the solace of a multitude of travelling companions but the destinations have failed to delight us. In the journey of the warrior we will be alone but not lonely; we will live with uncertainty but the warrior's faith will guide us. We will be detoured at times, but will have the humility to learn from our mistakes and the courage to take the next step.

Like Tushana, there will be a moment in each of our journeys where we find the courage to surrender our strategies and walk into the mouths of our demons: not blindly but guided by wisdom; not impulsively but with great balance; not bent upon destruction but upon learning. Our demons will not devour us but will offer themselves as a doorway to awakening. The shadows that have confined us will dissolve before the power of our courage. Forsaking limitation, intent on freedom, the warrior's journey has begun.

TWO

THE ROAR OF COURAGE
ENDOKY'S TASK

Endoky's earliest memories were of following in the footsteps of her grandmother and mother as they went each day to reap the harvest from the forest that was their home. The food that nourished their tribe, the plants for healing and the herbs for making protection spells were gleaned from the undergrowth. Her grandmother was the sorceress, healer, guide and teacher of the pygmy clan, revered for her power to shield them from harm and guide their spirits.

Under ner guidance Endoky learnt the magic of the forest; how to walk beneath the canopy of the great trees without a sound and how to call the forest creatures to her, using their own cries. Watching carefully she learnt to find the plants that healed, those that would feed the tribe and the ones that would harm. She learnt to walk with confidence in the forest, guided by the wind and light; to be still and read the signals of danger and how to blend in with the undergrowth until she was invisible. She was a forest creature—at one with its wildness; without fear. In the evenings she would sit by the fire beside her mother and grandmother as they wove the spells that would nourish the spirit of a sick child or ripen the womb of a woman without child. She learnt the chants that would ease the spirit of one of the dying elders and the rituals that celebrated the coming of age of the young. Her grandmother would tell her the stories of all the wise women in her family who had gone before her—each one of them a sorceress. She told Endoky that each sorceress would have one special task to perform in her life and she must listen to the forest to learn what her task would be.

On her grandmother's death, clans from distant clearing gathered to celebrate and honour her passing—in the firelight stories were recited to honour her power and in the early dawn her body was taken to rejoin the great forest. In the evening Endoky joined her clan to pay homage to her mother, the new sorceress. In the months that followed, the harmony of the tribe was disturbed by passing groups of travellers bringing with them stories of an invading people who had cast them out of their settlements, bringing sickness and felling the trees before them. The travellers would mumble their stories in frightened voices before hurrying on; several would stay seeking sanctuary and guidance from Endoky's mother. In a meeting of the clan's elders, she pronounced that as sorceress, she would travel to the forest's edge to discover the truth of the stories, taking Endoky with her. After travelling for many days the trees began to thin and the air became thick with smoke. Hiding in the trees at the forest's edge they saw a people they had never before met, borne on great noise-making machines. Before them the trees fell without pause and behind them lay a ruined land.

As they turned away in fear, Endoky saw that their terror was shared by the forest creatures who joined them in their flight. Deafened by the noise that echoed through the forest they were oblivious to the sound of the frantic leopard that leapt from the trees to land upon her mother. Endoky crouched near to the leopard mauling her mother and called to it in the voice of its mate. The bloodlust of the leopard gave way to confusion and laying back its ear it roared and fled into the undergrowth. Taking her mother into her arms, Endoky knew she could not survive her wounds. Fashioning a litter of vines and branches, she laid her mother upon it and began the long journey home, dragging the litter behind her.

As night fell and Endoky rested beside the litter, her mother spoke to her of the darkness that was falling upon her. 'Our people will need a sorceress of great courage,' she told Endoky. 'You will need to remember all I have taught you and give life to the magic of the sorceress who lives in your heart. Your name as sorceress will be Joachime—"the leopard's roar". Make your name the home of your spirit and be a sorceress of courage.' Endoky felt her spirit grow heavy at her mother's words and her thoughts were filled with fear and confusion. How could she protect and guide her people to stand against the great power she had seen at the edge of the forest? How could she wear the cloak of the sorceress when she had yet to reach the age of ripeness with so many lessons still unlearnt? She knew too, in her heart, that without a sorceress her tribe would die just as the forest was dying behind her.

Picking up the litter she turned towards her home and as the sun was high in the sky reached the clearing where her tribe was gathered. Seeing the marks of death upon the face of their sorceress, they began to wail and cry. Endoky stood firmly amidst them and drawing in her breath she released it in the great roar of the leopard. 'The spirit of the sorceress has passed to me,' she said in her boldest voice. 'I will be Joachime, blessed with the courage of the leopard.' Even as she spoke the words, Endoky felt herself quiver with fear and doubt.

That night her mother passed over and it was Joachime who chanted the songs of honour and placed her mother's body upon its bier of ferns. Gathering her clan to her, Joachime spoke to them of the death of the forest the devil people would bring and the courage each one of them would need to find. Joachime felt the writhings of fear in her heart even as she spoke, yet knew that to surrender to her fear would be to surrender her life and the life of her tribe. In the weeks that followed the sounds and the smoke that signalled the forest's dying came ever closer to the clearing of Joachime's tribe. Scenting danger the forest animals had begun to flee deeper into the forest and daily the tribe felt a lessening of their spirit. No longer could they read the sounds of the forest nor be guided by its light or wind. With her own spirit lost in darkness, Joachime could offer no guidance to her community but to flee in the trail of the animals that had already escaped. 'Leave behind you everything but that which is growing,' she told her clan. 'Gather together the growing, living seedlings and plants, that we may make a new home elsewhere.'

There began a time of wandering as the tribe moved from one clearing, beginning their planting, only to be uprooted once more as the tendrils of smoke crept through the trees. The children and old people tired and sickened and with no time to seek the healing plants or sing the healing songs, they began to die. The young people, strangers to hatred, began to seek out the plants of poison and fashion spears of attack. In the cycle of wandering they planted no more and became beggars in the forest; taking what they could forage but giving no life in return.

Joachime saw the sickening of the spirit of her tribe, the fear that shadowed them and determined that they would wander no more. Gathering the clan she spoke of the need to perform the cleansing ritual—the ceremony to cast out evil. Believing she meant to cast a spell of evil upon the intruders, the tribe grew excited; at last their sorceress was to guide them. Joachime cast the seeing stones and crouched in the firelight to read their message. 'We have lost the way of life,' she explained. 'The forest can no longer be our home because we have no home in ourselves; we will run forever because fear has become our guide and can lead us only to hide and beg. We no longer live in honour because we have taken death into our hearts.' Joachime sent the elders of the tribe into the forest with the instruction to return only when they had cleansed themselves of anger and sickness. After the passing of two moons they returned with their eyes clear and their faces shining. They spoke of the struggles they had gone through to shed the strangeness they took with them into the forest in order to reclaim the kinship they had once known. They told too of their yearning to return to the old ways, before the devil people had come. Joachime could only answer, 'The old ways have gone, perhaps never to return. What cannot be taken from us is our kinship with life and the forest. We must walk the path of life and show it to the devil people. If we give up our kinship we will forever wander like ghosts.'

The following day Joachime worked with the clan to gather together the plants of healing and the seedlings of new life from the forest. Trailing behind her, the tribe followed Joachime on the journey back to the edge of the forest. It was not long before they smelt again the smoke of the fires that burnt the remains of the great forest and heard again the noise of the death machines. With her people huddled behind her, Joachime stepped out of the trees onto the cleared ground. At first this tiny, pygmy woman remained unnoticed, hardly visible amidst the tree stumps. Then, taking a deep breath, she released it in the great roar of the leopard; behind her her clan echoed the call until the clearing rang with the bellows of many leopards.

One by one the machines grew quiet as the men got down and approached the group of tiny people almost lost beneath the seedlings and plants they carried. Joachime stepped towards them and placed at their feet the offerings of berries and fruit she carried, then taking the seedlings from her bag she began to dig small holes in the barren ground and plant them one by one. The men watched, both stunned and amused at the sight of this tiny woman crouched before them, planting the beginnings of a new forest. The days passed and soon Joachime and her clan became a familiar sight as they appeared each morning with a new bundle of seedlings, ready to begin a new day of planting. Joachime and her tribe began to follow in the wake of the loggers as they continued with their cutting, burning and the building of their road. Where trees were felled, saplings were planted; life was sown in the trail of death. In the evenings once more the tribe would gather around their fires, singing the songs of joy and celebrating their kinship with the forest and each other.

As the years passed, Joachime gave birth to her own daughter. A new sorceress began her training by listening and following in the footsteps of her mother. The young girl grew and learned for herself the magic of the new forest. Joachime passed on to her the same lesson she had learnt from her own mother; to listen to the forest to find the path she would be called upon to follow.

Awareness, compassion and courage are the three pillars of the warrior's journey. Awareness gives birth to wisdom and is the light that guides the warrior woman, teaching her what it is she needs to let go of and what it is she needs to nurture in her quest for awakening and freedom. Wisdom is born of listening inwardly, learning from our lives and stories; what brings sorrow and alienation and what brings joy and liberation. Wisdom does not always come in the guise of great revelations but is rooted in the unswerving commitment and openness we bring to learning from this very moment. What are we committed to right now in our lives? The choices we make, the areas to which we direct our time and energy, the aspirations we reach for—all of this reveals to us the nature of our commitment. Have we chosen these commitments or do we feel they have been chosen for us through expectations and forces outside of ourselves, or through the power of our own anxieties and fears? Are we deeply dedicated to integrity, dignity and wakefulness or do we find ourselves distracted by addictions to pleasure, security and the pursuit of approval? Do we live in the spirit of freedom or have we learnt the habits of limitation?

Awareness, the first pillar, illuminates our lives, reaches into the corners of our psyches and the shadows carried in our hearts. Awareness and the wisdom that is its offspring clarifies our journey and our path, encouraging us to focus and prioritise rather than flounder in indecisiveness and distractedness. Clarity of direction, born of reflection and inner listening, is intrinsic to beginning the warrior's journey. Without this clarity that is rooted in the truth of our lives we are too easily tempted to manufacture endless ideals and fantasies which are projected into the future, elusive and unattainable because of their separation from the present. Lacking this clarity and wisdom that illuminates, our lives are too often a chronicle of a blind and desperate searching for the keys to freedom and peace in places where they cannot be found. We dream of wholeness, of joy, of inner richness and seek to realise our dreams through ambitions, goals, roles and identities that bring us praise and acclaim. The disappointments and frustrations we experience are not always recognised as signals which invite us to look again at where we will actually find the realisation of our yearnings. Instead they are interpreted as signals of personal failure or inadequacy. Clarity returns us to this moment, dispels fantasy and reminds us that we cannot bypass who we are in this moment, in our quest for awakening. There are few shortcuts in the warrior's journey and few journeys that can begin on a foundation of denial or avoidance.

As young girls we fantasise about the delights of independence; finding it faulty we fantasise about the perfect mate. Still restless, we might dream of the perfect family or climbing the ladder of success. We might, in the search for peace and freedom we have yet to find, even begin to dream of retirement. We are caught within the grasp of a dullness of spirit that endlessly postpones awakening. Awareness is concerned with awakening to where and who we are right now in our lives.

Awareness brings the dedication so intrinsic to the warrior's journey. Like an artist that holds a vision in her mind of a moment she wants to capture on canvas, its reality will never be fulfilled if she lays down her brushes the first moment her picture does not match her vision. The warrior woman is asked to forge her own journey, create her own path, for she is unique and her path must be rooted in understanding her own story. In learning the lessons her own life offers, her path becomes clear. Frustration, conflict and struggle tell her of the need for a greater depth of understanding. Joy, peace and vitality tell her she is travelling a path that is enriching her spirit. A woman who has lived a life of passivity will need great determination to foster energy, effort and focus. A woman who has lived within an inner climate of bitterness and self-judgment will need great determination to foster the compassion and generosity of heart that will heal her. Dedication is the key the fearful woman holds to unlock her terrors of loneliness, that equally teaches her how to be together with others with trust. The awakening warrior may need to learn the lessons of decisiveness or the lessons of humility. We do not need to look any further than our lives in this moment, to learn the lessons of transformation they are offering to us and to understand the ways in which our own paths must begin. Dedication is a quality the warrior woman embraces wholeheartedly to realise her vision.

Dedication is the force that allows us to meet discontent in a creative way, rather than following the paths of avoidance that compel us to dwell upon the past or the future to seeking the richness and vitality we sense to be missing, or losing ourselves in distractedness in the present. Regret, fantasy and distractedness are the themes of the wounded warrior who plans, laments, dreams and mourns or sinks into numbness. Lost in these feelings, we may even overlook the state of expectancy they generate and the powerlessness they foster.

Judy used the analogy of standing in a queue to describe the expectancy with which she greeted her life. 'I was always sure that things were going to get better. When I was in school I was always convinced the next year would be better, when I was in a terrible relationship I was sure that one day I would meet the right partner, just as I was sure that at some point I would find the right direction. I always felt to be just one step away or one corner removed from everything I wanted. It just seemed like such a long step.'

Women have inherited a historical tradition that attempts to quell the quest of the warrior through distraction. Articulating their restlessness they are encouraged to take up a hobby, go shopping, have a baby, do something to fill up their time; prescriptions of avoidance that are avenues of numbness. Fantasy becomes a substitute for change, yet our fantasies are tied to a fairy tale brand of mythology that teaches us that freedom, richness and dignity are commodities that can be provided for us by someone or something else, outside of ourselves. Our whole life can be consumed in the search for the ideal relationship, the ideal job, the ideal lifestyle that is going to liberate us and offer us everything we have always sought. These are not the dreams of the warrior, of the wise woman. The warrior woman cultivates the dedication that allows her to step out of this cycle of numbness—is willing to bring her wholehearted attention to this moment. With wisdom she acknowledges that she is a conscious participant in the creation of this moment and her life. She holds within her hands and her heart a vision of possibilities and the inner resources to realise them. All that she needs for transformation lies within her—she is aware, committed, inspired and clear. The warrior's journey asks no more of us than this wholeheartedness.

Compassion is the second pillar of the warrior's journey. Compassion gives life to wisdom, gentleness to determination and draws forth from within us the strengths of generosity, forgiveness and acceptance. In the Buddhist tradition, wisdom and compassion are likened to the two wings of a bird—they balance and empower each other. It is not difficult to be wise and perceptive—able to analyse problems and proportion judgment and blame. In this perceptiveness there may emerge a wealth of answers and solutions to our difficulties and the sorrows of the world, yet this whole arsenal of prescriptions may not alter one single situation of conflict nor touch the heart of one single person. Perceptiveness, without compassion, suffers a famine of love and rather than connecting us more deeply with the heart of another person or with our own being, may instead serve to distance and disconnect us. The clear mind may be adept at finding fault and proportioning blame but these are not the ingredients of healing or transformation.

A young woman was accepted on probation in a sophisticated spiritual community. From the moment she arrived it seemed she was unable and unwilling to follow the lead of the long-established members; at meals she would dive into her food before grace was said and belched during the silence. She hummed during prayers and played with the cats during work. After suffering her lack of conformity for weeks the members finally presented an ultimatum to their leader, stating that either she would leave or they would. Their elder listened and responded, 'I am impressed with all of your wisdom; you know so well the difference between right and wrong. You, it seems, have no need to be here, but who would teach this new student if she was asked to leave? It is better that you go.'

Compassion nurtures the forgiveness that allows us to integrate the resentment and bitterness that chains us to the past with a power far greater than the events of the past has ever been able to exert. The rejections and wounds of the past which may have stripped us of dignity and wounded our sense of vision continue to mar our journey in the present until there is forgiveness. Compassion frees us of these chains; not condoning the abuse or the abusers who may have wounded us, but caring for ourselves with sufficient depth to no longer deliver power to them. Compassion is not blind but a clear understanding that letting go of resentment, hatred and bitterness is the most profound expression of dignity we can offer to ourselves. Fault and blame are the territory of the fearful, who do not have the courage to be generous, to let go and to see anew. Compassion is the territory of the courageous; the territory of the warrior who knows through her wisdom that no true satisfaction can be found in blame nor any true freedom discovered as long as she is bound to what has already gone by.

Compassion is intrinsic to the warrior tradition. We all carry within us the critical voice of the judge. Like a sniper it sits on our shoulder waiting to pass judgment upon anything that is deemed an imperfection. The judge demands an impossible perfection; will relentlessly discover further room for improvement and the undiscovered flaw. Like an unwelcome guest it takes up its home within our consciousness, eager to produce its endless judgments about right and wrong, good and bad, acceptable and unacceptable. It is a voice that rarely rests, delighting in comparison and evaluation, in rejection and denial. Enormous power is given to this voice, making us afraid to make changes, take risks, to see anew, to follow new paths, for fear of the punishment that will be meted out by the judge if we fail. Fearful of being wrong and of failure, we seek rightness and safety in adopting the postures, positions, appearances and roles that promise approval and sanctuary from blame. The power of the judge paralyses action and suffocates vision by threatening to assault us with a barrage of criticism and blame that will perhaps confirm our latent anxieties about our own inadequacy, imperfection and unacceptability. The voice of the judge is harsh and unforgiving; fuelled by fear. The judgments that hinder us are rarely new, they are the ghostly residues of every moment of blame and censure that has wounded us in our lives. The words of other judges are replayed again and again, given new authority by our belief in them. Through these words we have constructed beliefs about ourselves and these beliefs become our shadows.

Judgments inevitably create images—of ourselves and others. Images are frozen, become accepted truths and suffocate any true sense of vision or possibility. Every woman can look in the mirror and recite the images she carries—'I'm unattractive, I'm old, I'm bossy, I'm anxious.' Compassion is needed to disempower the judge, to break up the frozen images which deny change. Compassion is a generosity of heart that allows for imperfection and failure and in its light imperfection is not the beginning of denial or rejection but an invitation to humility and learning; failure is not a conclusion but a call to begin again.

There is not one woman who, in reflecting upon her life, will not find instances of hatred, jealousy or fear. There are moments when we have ignored the opportunities for freedom and compassion and times we have simply refused the chances to let go of limiting forces and circumstances out of fear: moments when we have been untrue to what we value. Like Endoky, every woman remembers a moment when she has fled with terror in the face of power. The warrior woman does not linger with regret and judgment over these moments, dwelling in thoughts of 'what could have been' or 'if only'.

A young woman in the armed forces found herself pregnant and was told she must choose between pregnancy or her career. Fearful of losing all she had worked for, she opted for the abortion and for years lived with the regret of not having the courage to challenge the authority of her commanding officer and explore the options that were possible. The warrior knows that moments of suffering and confusion warrant not judgment, but compassion.

Suffering and confusion exile us from the authenticity of our own being—compassion and wisdom are the beginning of the return to that authenticity. Wisdom is no longer accepting any judgment or image to be a conclusion about ourselves; compassion is the dedication to the true and authentic in ourselves and in others. Compassion does not require great expertise, just the simple willingness to bring generosity of heart to the harshness of the judging mind, and openness of mind to question the images we bear.

The warrior understands deeply that in her journey she cannot afford to separate her quest from the realisations she aspires to. To begin her journey in hatred, bitterness or denial will mean that her journey will be shadowed by the very power of those feelings. If she values compassion, she must learn the wisdom of undertaking her journey in the spirit of compassion. If she values the end of suffering and separation, she must equally be willing to renounce the seeds of suffering and separation that lie in judgment, denial and anger. There can be no exceptions to this compassion—every exception reveals to her where she is holding on to wounds from the past which are superimposing themselves upon the present. A woman of fire who treasures freedom is willing to renounce everything that undermines that freedom—images, judgments and resentments that bind us to the very habits of limitation we seek to be free from. Compassion, as much as wisdom, sets us free. The profound love of being awake, the utter dedication to the end of limitation, the deep passion for freedom are all expressions of compassion.

The third pillar of the warrior's journey is the quality of courage. It requires enormous courage to extend compassion in the face of the destructive; the shadows within ourselves and others. A well-known Vietnamese monk, in his work with refugees from his country, spoke of the courage needed for his people to see behind the masks of the pirates, rapists and murderers who had harried them in their journey to freedom. Profound courage is needed to make visible in our lives the wisdom we intellectually possess; we may be challenging the habits of a lifetime. We may need to challenge the expectations of others rather than submit; to let go of our own cravings for approval and safety rather than succumbing to them. We hold within ourselves a deep well of wisdom—to live in harmony with that wisdom and to express it in every area of our lives is the challenge of every warrior. It takes courage to probe our judgments, conclusions and images rather than assume their

48

veracity. Waking up from numbness, dullness or sleep in our lives can be a painful process; great courage is needed to be willing to open to that pain rather than pursuing avoidance or distractedness. Honesty is founded upon courage—to see clearly into ourselves rather than hiding in our pretences or disguises requires a true boldness of spirit.

There are few guarantees, assurances or certainties in the warrior's journey. We are attuned to the freedom, authenticity and end of division our hearts yearn for, yet lack any true certainty about how they will be discovered or where they lie. Travelling an ideal, romantic path we would first discover the truth of our being, freedom and connectedness and then we would let go of our anxieties, fears and doubts; it is a path existing only in our fantasies. On the warrior's path we are asked to find the courage to embrace our doubts and anxieties and to go forth into the unknown without the comfort of guarantees. It requires great courage to be willing to take this risk; to experiment, to open to the unknown, to question, to let go of safety.

Courage is about openness—being willing to question our preconceptions about how things are rather than accepting them blindly. The warrior is concerned with the discovery of what is true, authentic and every preconception is a diversion from this quest. To be receptive and open to different possibilities rather than sheltering in the comfort of our assumptions requires a profound courage that enables us to explore the possibilities that are offered to us. The same courage enables us to accept the consequences of our exploration rather than become locked into blame or regret. To be willing to experience the insubstantiality of our images, the death of the identities we have previously relied upon for security requires an audacious spirit.

Courage is the power that enables us to open to our shadows. Endless energy and effort are expended in our lives in constructing identities that promise a certain sanctuary, protecting and asserting our images and our defences. Accumulated pain is camouflaged in roles, habits and addiction. We become adept at presenting to the world and ourselves a persona that will not attract criticism or rejection and equally adept at suppressing or denying aspects of our own being that we fear or dislike. Through distraction, conformity and avoidance we attempt to divorce ourselves from our own shadows, fearing their power and consequences if they were visible to ourselves or to others. Every warrior's journey begins with themselves; with the willingness not only to celebrate the power of transformation they hold, but also with the willingness to embrace their shadows. Courage emboldens us to explore—to no longer accept inner fragmentation as a norm; to bring the healing and the light of wisdom and compassion to the shadows that fragment us.

We are inclined to separate our lives into the segments of past, present and future. We see them as separate from each other, the past holding our memories and residues of experiences already finished; the present an unfolding actuality and the future an unknown. In reality these segments of experience cannot be separated—our present is formed by our experiences of the past and the future is no more than the next moment, a simple extension of our past and present experience. The images we hold of ourselves in this moment, the ways in which we live and relate and the choices we make have much to do with the experiences and impressions we have been exposed to in the past, whether they have been painful or affirming. The choices and values we treasure in this moment become the personal history of the next moment we experience. Without being extraordinarily awake in our lives we become chained to this continuity, unable to make new choices or create fresh visions in our lives because of the underlying, even unconscious power that the past has to blind us. We are shadowed by the past in every moment that we are disconnected from the illuminating power of awareness.

The gift of awareness, of wakefulness, is that it brings light to shadows, removing the blinkers of the past, empowering us to see anew, to make choices that are rooted in wisdom rather than conditioning and to live in the spirit of freedom rather than being confined to the limitations which are the residue of the past. Awareness returns us to the present, the only place that the shadows of the past reveal themselves and can be understood, healed and let go of. The wounds of the past are healed in the present through the direct and immediate experience of no longer needing to be chained to them.

Karen is a rape survivor. The damage of her experience lay not only in her wounds or the theft of her dignity but in the ongoing fear that made it impossible for her to venture out alone, to speak to strangers or to be away from home at night. One evening her daughter became ill; all the friends she called to take her to the hospital didn't answer their phones, her doctor was unavailable to make a house call. As she saw her daughter's fever rising she knew that she could no longer postpone getting treatment or convince herself that the fever would pass. Gathering her child to her, she ventured into her underground car park, to her car. With every step she waited for someone to spring from the shadows to confront her and every sound signalled danger. Arriving at the hospital, having her child tended to, she knew that she had passed through a powerful barrier in her life. Through the imperative she had answered, the dark had lost its power.

In the light of one moment of deep trust, self images of fear appear to be less than substantial. In one gesture of true courage, previously held images of doubt become open to question. It becomes increasingly difficult to identify totally with self images of confusion and powerlessness in the light of making clear decisions and acting upon them. There are limits to the healing that is born of intellectual analysis or of tracing the causes of suffering and limitation. Transformation needs to be rooted in direct and immediate experience that reveals to us the transparency of the shadows that have haunted us. Through this healing and understanding there is offered to us the possibility of making new beginnings, choices and directions that are not coloured by past conditioning.

The past is carried in the shadows which dampen our spirit; it has life only as long as those shadows remain hidden to us. The enduring thread that links together the past, the present and the future is our own sense of inner vision. Who we are, who we believe ourselves to be may be terminally shaped by the influencing power of the shadows that mould us. Shadows are the forbidden parts of our being, forbidden by our culture or by ourselves because they are deemed to be dangerous, unacceptable or fearful. Our shadows are the feelings, thoughts and yearnings that we feel bound to deny or suppress because we believe that their exposure will invite rejection, harm or censure—countless women learn the importance of hiding their rage, power and boldness. Shadows are found in the aspirations and choices we feel compelled to surrender through fearing the consequences that their expression would bring—equal numbers of women learn to deny ambition, creativity and adventurousness. Our conscious minds reject those aspects of ourselves that signal danger to us and in that rejection we harm ourselves in far more lethal ways—we adopt a counterfeit life as our own and are exiled from realising the possibilities of freedom that are available to us.

The thoughts, feelings and yearnings that we reject are not necessarily negative in nature. Shadows do not imply that we carry around with us bottomless depths of anger, jealousy or destructiveness. The shadows that follow us can also be suppressed love and generosity; depths of openness or compassion may be equally denied the light of exposure out of fear. The child who has experienced her love being consistently plundered or her generosity repeatedly exploited soon learns the dangers of loving and giving. Her very survival may become dependent upon protecting herself and distancing herself from others. The child who has her trust and openness violated or her compassion abused learns to hide these qualities behind the defences of suspicion and wariness. The 'tomboy' young girl may find her vitality stamped out by the demands for conformity she receives from her peers or family and learns to prefer sameness over uniqueness. The bright child who earns enmity from her peers for her brilliance understandably learns to hide her gift, if its exposure results in her ostracism. The shadows we carry are not inherently negative but negative only in their effect, in that their power is suppressive and self-abandoning.

Our shadows may be seen in the fears and doubts that cripple us in our lives; the compulsion to prove ourselves, the inclination towards dependency or passivity all tell us a story about the shadows we carry within us. The judgments or hatred we direct towards ourselves, the envy we feel of others, the frustrations and bitterness that nag us; reveal an essentially wounded sense of vision that is impaired by shadows. Feelings of being endlessly wrong or never good enough; sacrifices of creativity or perpetual postponement of decisions—all of these invite us to explore the shadows that haunt us just as the constant bowing to authority or the addiction to approval send us urgent signals to look at the forces that are governing our being and our life. Shadows manifest in the present as a wounded sense of vision that is a consequence of past experience and of pain.

Shadows have very real beginnings in our lives. If honestly exposing our emotions or yearnings has led to shame or ridicule, it appears very much more attractive to sacrifice our feelings and yearnings than to sacrifice approval and praise. Figures of authority run through our lives—from God, to parents, to social standards and peer group pressures. We are trained to listen, to be obedient and to be good. If what we hear is a devaluation of ourselves, we are very likely to obediently continue this devaluation inwardly. Young girls are told that it is their poverty of faith that leads them to question the beliefs of their elders, their lack of appreciation that makes them rebel against the unjust strictures of their parents and their lack of worth that leads them to be rejected by their boyfriends. Rejection, disapproval and judgment make powerfully painful impressions upon our spirit and it is the rare and blessed child who is not exposed to those impressions. They are impressions that wound us; they become authority figures for us, determining what we will expose to the world and what we will hide. Denial becomes a habit; the trusting, open, creative child is hidden beneath layers of defence and the degree to which we identify with this wounded sense of vision is the degree to which it becomes our reality, our truth.

The woman who is in the hold of a wounded sense of vision will adopt a persona in the world that works. The definition of the persona that works is that it protects her from further pain or fear; it is sanctioned and brings applause or at least the absence of disapproval. She becomes an angel of goodness and light; optimistic, pleasing and agreeable. The consequence of pain is to dedicate ourselves to the avoidance of its repetition. In this pursuit the warrior, who throughout our lives seeks for authenticity, is suppressed, and becomes a captive—captive of her own fears, memories and shadows. It becomes easier to conceal our yearnings and the rebelliousness of our spirit and be the person others want us to be. Wearing of a mask, hiding in disguises, living a pretence can become a norm in our lives. Our yearnings appear only in our dreams or in private, tortured moments of regret when we think with longing of the paths we never followed or the choices we never attempted.

So much precious energy can be expended in perfecting the disguises and masks we feel compelled to present to the world. Captive of our own fears, we learn to dance like a puppet on the strings of others people's needs and expectations. The agreeable partner who airs her frustrations only in the safety of her

sister sufferers so that she can re-enter her turbulent relationship temporarily relieved of tension; the obliging employee
who smiles and nods while knowing that she could do her
employer's job with greater competence; the loving mother
who seeks comfort in the adventure stories of someone else;
the perfect spiritual devotee who conceals her doubts and questions beneath a guise of surrender—all of these disguises
require enormous energy for their maintenance. The masks
and disguises that are adopted are the visible expression on
unacknowledged shadows. Part of the agreement we enter into
when consenting to any disguise is to conceal the frustration
and resentment we feel about them; to acknowledge frustration would necessitate us reclaiming the warrior within us. If
living in the spirit of the warrior in the past has resulted in
pain, we are reluctant to take that step.

In suppressing or denying any aspect of our being we cannot live an authentic life; psychologically, emotionally and
spiritually we attempt to amputate parts of our being. The
lessons of every amputee are relearned by us—the missing
limbs continue to itch, irritate and remind us of what has gone.
We will be endlessly shadowed by any yearning, feeling or
aspiration dreams we have attempted to deny. Disguises and
masks become a way of being in control of our lives and experiences; a way of controlling the possibilities of pain. Control
is an inevitable reflex of fear and suppression. Punished for
rebelliousness in the past we become adept at agreeability; criticised for brilliance we will learn to underachieve. Concealing
what we consider to be the causes of pain—whether they are
our emotions or personalities or creativity—we attempt to
control the feedback we are going to receive from the world. To
do this we must equally learn how to control ourselves by distancing ourselves from, or suppressing, all that we are fearful
of expressing.

There are times in our lives when this pursuit of control
may have been a necessary facet of our survival. Honesty

attracts danger—in some Arab cultures women are stoned for revealing their ankles; in Asia wives are burned for rebellious-ness. In western culture, girls are censured for boldness and excommunicated for celebrating their deepest spiritual beliefs. We may equally become so habitual in control and suppression that we neglect to inquire whether its continuation is con-ducive to our present survival or freedom. Safety and approval may be hard won rewards; we may be afraid of risking vulner-ability again or doubt whether we possess the energy needed to untangle the complexity of our carefully-constructed dis-guises. As long as we continue dedicating ourselves to control, in our outer or inner lives, we continue to fuel the fears that our shadows represent. Control is a denial of openness and openness is the primary vehicle through which the warrior learns.

Controlling our shadows may be more dangerous to us than opening to them. Just because we feel compelled or decide to reject our shadows does not mean that our shadows will obe-diently consent to this rejection. The nature of a shadow is to cling and follow, to turn with us in every direction we choose. The shadows we deny look for ways to break out and find expression. The loving but frustrated mother finds herself rag-ing at or abusing her children; the agreeable partner walks out on her relationship, sacrificing the love as she struggles to free herself of the difficulties. The compliant employee drowns her resentment in the mindless addictions to gambling, pleasure, sex or gratification; the perfect spiritual devotee suddenly turns into the greatest consumer or critic of all time.

The frustrated warrior, bowed beneath the weight of her shadows, becomes a counterfeit warrior—filled with reaction, rage and intent on destruction. She chooses domination as an antidote to frustration, oppressive power as an antidote to sup-pression and anger as an antidote to fear.

Sheryl grew up in a family where she was ignored, criticised and humiliated. Through the force of her own will she gained good grades in school, a place in university and eventually a prestigious position in charge of a team of lawyers. She made their lives hell—demanding their constant obedience, unswerving loyalty and unwavering attendance. The counterfeit warrior enters into wars and battles with the circumstances, people or situations she has previously felt to be captive of, desperately trying to free herself of their power. Adopting the strategies of her captors as her own rejection and denial remain the central themes of her life.

The price of accepting captivity has been the rejection of our own yearnings and intuition, the price we pay for renouncing that captivity with control and reaction is to continue to live beneath the shadow of our captors. The warrior is unable to move forward, to make authentic changes, but is left floundering in a spiral of frustration and anger.

In their denial our shadows grow in stature and become tyrannical in nature. The power of the outbursts of our shadows, in depression or anger, may frighten us so much that our desire to disown them grows even stronger. We struggle for more control, attempt to regain our disguises through endless apology—'I don't know what came over me'—we take a tranquillizer or attempt to make amends. Domination of our own outbursts may be seen as the only possible solution to the chaos that appears to be the result of our shadows becoming visible. We need to learn to listen very carefully to the messages that frustration and anger are offering to us. What are the ways of understanding our shadows without falling into the familiar trap of domination? What qualities do we need to bring to our listening that enable us to learn from our shadows rather than becoming a victim of them? True courage has little to do with domination, its expression is found in integrity and impeccability. True compassion has little to do with submerging ourselves in pity or regret. It has a great deal to do with the withdrawal of prejudice and images.

The signals of having surrendered the warrior are unmistakable. Depression and denial are closely linked. Lethargy of spirit, the absence of vitality in our lives are symptoms of loss—the loss of creativity and authenticity. Numbness, the seeming inability to feel or receive the world around us or the world within us speaks to us of disconnection born of fear. Anxiety, exaggerated concern over decisions and doing things right, self-consciousness, tell us of our exile from inner authority. Fear of being alone, feeling compelled to endlessly fill our minds up with input and entertainment or our bodies with sensation are expressions of grief resulting from an inner sacrifice that diminishes us. A major part of beginning to awaken in our lives is learning to read the messages of our lives as carefully as a person without sight will read by touch the face of a person they love.

As we awaken to the shadows we carry and appreciate their effects in our lives we may open the door to a rage we direct at ourselves or at others. We may be tempted to trace our shadows through our past and blame ourselves for mistakes we have made or opportunities we ignored. We may be tempted to cast people who have wounded us into the role of an enemy who we hold in the greatest bitterness. Through blame we are tied into an eternal partnership with our shadows and dance to the tunes of 'if only' or 'should'. We get lost in a time warp— our preoccupation with the past serving only to camouflage the possibilities of transformation that the present moment is offering to us.

An elderly woman, married to an authoritarian husband, would endlessly wail to her daughter-in-law about how her life would have been better if she had never married. She would recount all the things he had never let her do—learn to drive, work, learn to manage money, be independent, take the painting class she'd always wanted to do. Her daughter-in-law would point out to her that it was not actually too late for her to do any of those things—she was healthy, active and supported. At that point her mother-in-law would become selectively deaf; her bitterness was a comforting home.

Forgiveness, patience and compassion are the vehicles for the renunciation of enemies and opponents. No longer consumed by thoughts of their defeat, we are freed to focus clearly upon the present and what is possible for us now. We are free to open to our shadows with profound compassion and understanding. We need not to be hurried in this opening but approach it with care and consistency. Like Joachime who approached the people she feared with offerings of life, we too must know how to offer the gifts of compassion, forgiveness and openness to our own shadows and fears, for they are the gifts of healing.

Some years ago in New England, when the large state psychiatric hospitals were ordered to close by the government, care workers found themselves having to connect with long-term patients on the 'back wards' to determine their future. On one ward was discovered a middle-aged woman called Jean, who had initially been admitted to the hospital for social order offences in her late teens. Diagnosed as schizophrenic and initially unresponsive to treatment, her drug levels were increasingly boosted. Unwanted by her family she remained in the hospital, drugged into manageability. Over the years Jean became increasingly passive and introverted to the point where she ceased to speak and rarely moved from her bed. Various meetings were held to discuss the limited options available for this woman—it was assumed that she would need long-term hospitalisation for the remainder of her life. One young woman on the team, moved by Jean's story, asked to be allowed to take on her case. For days she would sit on the end of the patient's bed just speaking to her of the things she had seen on her way to work that morning. Sometimes the fixed expression would almost imperceptibly soften and in response to some humorous story her eyes would begin to light up. She began to be able to coax Jean to get out of bed and to look out of the window. Each day she would walk a few steps with her towards the door of the ward Jean had never left of her own volition. Sometimes she would speak to Jean of going outside, words that at times would send her fleeing back to her bed to cower under the blankets. The day finally arrived when, holding on to her friend's hand, Jean walked to the open door of the ward, stood in the doorway and looked across the hallway to the doors that opened to the garden outside. She walked to that doorway many times until the moment she was willing to take the single step that took her out of the ward. That single step was her turning point. In the days that followed her journeys lengthened—she would lie on the grass watching the insects with inexhaustible fascination or stand for hours with her body pressed against a tree. Jean began to speak with the people she encountered and to speak to them of the world of darkness that had been her home. She spoke again and again of the wonder and the terror of taking that single step that took her out of the ward.

The courage and the determination of the warrior are manifested in taking the single step which expresses our willingness to leave behind us anything which limits our freedom. Patience, gentleness and compassion allow us to lay down the burdens of blame and resentment. It doesn't take grandiose gestures to be a warrior—we don't have to enter a nunnery or mount any barricades. The single steps that bring light to shadows and return us to a sense of authenticity in our being are born of the simple willingness to open to our shadows rather than accepting their truth. What would happen if we simply stopped listening so hungrily for prescriptions from external authorities about how to live our lives and listened inwardly? What would happen if we risked stepping beyond our fears of disapproval and expressed ourselves in genuine ways? What would happen if we made visible our feelings and aspirations and spoke the truths we perceive? Are we able to take the step of following our yearnings and manifesting our creativity? Can we let go of our defences and self-consciousness in our relationships? The courage of the warrior is made visible through her willingness to step out of the world of imagination and to challenge her shadows in the moments that they make themselves visible in her words, actions and choices.

There is a great boldness in this challenge—a boldness which is not integral to the conditioning of most women, it is bred out of us at an early age. Young boys are called cute and admired for their boldness whereas the experience of many girls is that boldness is rebuked and called 'pushiness'. Boys wrestle with their fathers; girls are directed to the kitchen to help their mothers. Young girls, confronted with a bully in the playground, are encouraged to seek a protector to stand up for them. Teenage girls learn that their independence is a threat to the emerging macho-aggressive behaviour of their male counterparts. Women are led to believe that they are essentially fragile, helpless, weak and dependant. Their boldness is replaced with learning how to listen to and care for the needs of others, to support and summon aid—essentially to be 'nice'.

The story of the young woman, skilled in self-defence and martial arts, who, when confronted with a mugger, found that she was primarily concerned with not hurting him, is the story we can endlessly replay in our own inner landscapes. We live in fear of our shadows revealing themselves and the consequences to ourselves and others should this happen.

The warrior needs to be bold to question the power of her childhood conditioning. The boldness of the warrior is not the boldness of domination but the willingness to test her own boundaries. How fragile and helpless are we? Do we need protectors and what would happen to macho-aggressive behaviour if it had no supporters? Testing our edges means looking at what we retreat and flee from; to look under the bed to discover whether there are any monsters hiding there rather than cowering under the blankets. We need to articulate our terrors to ourselves; pull them from the camouflage they are hidden in and embrace them. Nothing is exempt from this exploration—

not our images, beliefs, habits or disguises. Courage is in the boldness of spirit that no longer consents to the unacceptable—to anything that brings authenticity or alienation. Courage empowers us to go into uncharted territory.

Courage does not mean the absence of fear; fear is the inevitable companion of making any passage from the known to the unknown. Courage is the light that illuminates that passage rather than accepting fear as an instruction to retreat. No longer relying upon the controls of our strategies, disguises or will does not imply that our world is going to fall apart and we will be out of control, with our demons devastating our lives. We may well discover that the willingness to let go of the control we have learned to avoid pain is the key that opens the door to new visions of ourselves and our lives. The fears that grip us are invariably the fears of what 'might' happen to us if we were to open to our shadows. They are fears of the future, but the acceptance of that great 'might' is the acceptance of remaining within the confines of our shadows. The warrior's courage is the willingness to go through the 'might' into what 'is'. It is the difference between living a myth and connecting with what is real and possible.

No matter how camouflaged the warrior is within us, each one of us intuitively knows the ways in which we depart from the path of authenticity and truthfulness in our lives—when we please rather than challenge; submit rather than be steadfast; yield rather than persevere. The path of the warrior is to make her intuition visible in her life, to embody her wisdom in her words, actions and choices. The warrior is no longer willing to rely upon the evidence of the past to be her guiding truth in the present; because she has been vulnerable to power and rejection in the past does not imply she is perpetually sentenced to being overwhelmed. The experience of consenting to domination in the past does not imply she must abide forever in submission; because she has previously experienced powerlessness does not means she will endlessly dissolve in the face of authority.

The wisdom of the warrior intuits that the power of her shadows is flimsy, reinforced by her acceptance of and obedience to them. They describe only a wounded inner vision and are given life by her subscription to them. Courage does not have to do with the transcendence or domination of shadows nor with attaining goals or achievements. Courage is in bringing authenticity to our lives, nurturing the faith that we do not need to endlessly replay or work out the past but that there can be an immediacy of liberation from the past in the present.

Opening to our shadows and possibilities is a profound act of faith. To risk the journey of self-discovery through questioning our masks and disguises requires us to trust that it is this very vulnerability and openness that will allow the possibility of new growth. Faith is deepened as we see the shadows dissolve before the light of our compassion and courage. Faith and openness are the beginning of healing; every glimpse of freedom and every gesture of courage inspires new faith. The wisdom of the warrior knows that as she heals her own wounds, denials and division she is learning the lessons that empower her to heal her world. As she transforms the fears of her own spirit she is learning how to transform the consciousness of our planet from domination, ignorance and self-serving goals to a consciousness that knows the urgent need for compassion, wisdom and balance.

By planting the saplings of life in the trail of death, Joachime invited a renewal of consciousness in those who acted in heedlessness. In our refusal to participate in relationships or structures of oppression we invite a renewal of enquiry from all those involved in the structures. The women of our churches invite their colleagues to question what it means to live a spiritual life; the teenage girl who refuses to hide her spirit in giggles and helplessness invites her counterparts to re-examine the need and appropriateness of power and domination.

Spiritual legend stresses the need to strip ourselves of

knowing, of clinging to the familiar, of the confines of safety—
to be naked and open in order for a new spiritual and personal
reality to emerge. Vulnerability allows the possibility of new
growth; trust and faith are the fertile environments which
nurture that growth. Courage sustains opening and growth in
moments of doubt and uncertainty. Vision encourages us to
risk the journey of discovery and the exploration of freedom.
The warrior who sets out on a voyage of discovery, passing
through trials and challenges in quest of awakening, is the
most frequently-encountered theme in mythology and religion. In beginning our own journey we are travelling in the
footsteps of the ancients. We are never alone in this journey,
yet the uniqueness of our own story and our own being means
that our journey can never be replicated by another, no matter
how wise or loving they are. The enduring inspiration that
sustains us in this quest is our love of freedom, and the
courage and faith to discover its realisation amidst the immediacy of our lives.

THREE

THE POWER OF VISION
THE LOST CONDOR

Two children exploring in the forest found the nest of a great condor; nestled within it was one single egg. The children watched the nest throughout the day from the shelter of the nearby trees, but when the mother failed to visit the nest they assumed the egg had been abandoned. Wanting to save the baby bird, they took the egg home with them and placed it in the clutch of their farmyard goose. The young condor hatched with the rest of the goslings and grew up among them, adopted by their mother.

Throughout her life the young condor learned how to be a goose from her adoptive parents and siblings. She fought over the kitchen scraps, she hissed and waddled about the farmyard. She thrashed her wings and scrapped with the farm dogs and learnt to stay within the fences of the farmyard with the other geese, fearing the intrusion of the dogs. At night she huddled next to her siblings for warmth.

The young condor grew into maturity and old age with the rest of the geese, becoming ever more subdued with the passing of the seasons. One day, while out on her regular search for scraps, a great shadow passed over her and she looked up into the sky, fearing yet one more danger to hide from. Soaring above her she saw the most magnificent bird hovering in the air. Scarcely beating its wings the majestic bird glided in the wind currents, studying the ground beneath it.

The old condor craned her neck to peer at this awesome

creature more clearly. 'Who is that?' she whispered to her neighbour.

'That is a condor', replied her equally frail neighbour. 'She is the empress of the skies. No other bird can ever match her brilliance and power. No one can ever harm her. She belongs to the heavens. We belong to the farmyard—we are just geese.'

The old condor forgot her admiration as her attention was caught by a tempting scrap of food nearby. As she went to sleep that night a fleeting thought passed through her mind, wondering what it would be like to soar in the heavens. The next morning she had forgotten all about the bird she had so admired the day before, as she went about her relentless routine of scrapping and feeding. She lived and died a goose for that was what she believed she was.

Undoubtedly we would prefer a happier ending to this story. If the old condor were to awaken to her true nature and fly free, forsaking her mistaken identity as a goose, it would satisfy our desire for fairytale endings. Putting aside our fantasies and preferences, we understand the teaching of this story. Unawakened to our true nature we too find ourselves imprisoned by our beliefs. Like the deluded condor we resign ourselves to living within the fences of our own farmyards, believing that is where we belong. The old condor haunting the farmyard always had the power to fly. In her years of masquerading as a goose, she had simply forgotten the truth of her own being.

Through the power of belief the absurd becomes acceptable; the abnormal becomes normal and the false appears true. The beliefs we hold shape and condition the world we live in and our experience of it. They exert a profound power and influence over the quality of our lives and the internal and external realities we experience. The repetition of any opinion, creed, judgment or view lends it a veracity which is mistaken for the authority of truth. As truths they are absorbed into the unconscious, becoming inner authorities that dictate our social, political and spiritual structures and direct our individual lives. Misguided and blind assumptions dictate the boundaries of entire communities of people and define the possibilities of our own lives. Beliefs are both collective and individual. The degree of unconsciousness and fear that is held within them is the degree to which we zealously express and uphold them.

For centuries it was believed the world was flat and the horizons of people's worlds were limited by their fear of falling off the edge. The world ceased to be flat the moment the first courageous explorer discovered there was no edge. Throughout history, entire cultures of people have been decimated by the power of the beliefs held by conquering cultures. Religious beliefs in purity and superiority claimed by subscribing to a particular ideology continue to breed prejudice and hatred. Beliefs in social class hierarchies have justified centuries of injustice and oppression, while political allegiances and beliefs give legitimacy to war. Humankind's belief in its rightful dominion over nature has led to the despoilation our children inherit. Beliefs in hierarchies based upon race, colour or gender continue to spread waves of hatred in our world.

History is not only a record of events but also a chronicle of the power of beliefs. It records in graphic detail the destruction, oppression and hatred that are the inevitable consequence of beliefs that are rooted in fear and ignorance. Behind every chronicle of genocide, exploitation, oppression and injustice lurks the shadow of a collective belief system. The holocaust, the decimation of native populations, the destruction of Vietnam, the rape camps set up in warring countries, were and are justified in the pursuit of freedom, truth and morality. It would be an immense challenge to discover any belief system, collective or individual, that was free from fear and aggression. The conviction in the truth of beliefs separates the world into winners and losers, oppressors and victims, right and wrong.

The power of beliefs has shaped the lives of countless generations of women through the centuries. In their enactment, those beliefs create stereotypes and serve to 'normalise the abnormal'. Considered to be unintelligent, women were deprived of the right to direct their lives; deemed to be over-wrought they were given lobotomies; deemed to be overly sex-ual they were circumcised; sterilisation was the answer to their immorality and, believed to be lacking in political acumen they were made powerless. The crippling of a Chinese woman's feet to ensure her conformity to cultural expectation is essentially no different than the cosmetic surgery that moulds the bodies of contemporary western women into a socially acceptable shape. The Victorian stereotypes that defined femininity as malleability, frailty and senselessness find their extension in collective contemporary beliefs which continue to define fem-ininity in terms of beauty, emotionality and weakness. The Victorian woman felt unable to venture forth without her smelling salts to sustain her; many contemporary women feel unable to venture forth until they have found evidence of their acceptability in their mirrors or the arrows on their bathroom scales. The fear of sexuality that led Victorian women to shroud their bodies in concealing clothes differs only in degree from the fear that leads a woman to seek a surgeon to cure the 'diseases' of small- or large-breastedness.

Beliefs are passed on from generation to generation; condi-tioned by the experience of our elders, assuming greater cred-ibility with each recounting. Beliefs are inherited by us through the opinions and expectations of the authorities that influence us. The list is endless of the beliefs that women have inherited or had imposed upon them; the consequences bear a marked similarity. Beliefs are chains; forged of heavy metal or the finest silver—they are woven of fear and insecurity and imprison the spirit. Stereotypes and belief systems deprive women not only of uniqueness but also of inner authority. In this transaction powerlessness is ensured; pain, fear and self-doubt follow in its footsteps. History is also a record of the courage and wisdom manifested by women in their challenging and overturning of beliefs, assumptions and stereotypes that have attempted to confine and negate them. They set aside their smelling salts; chained themselves to railings; smiled at their mirrors; confronted their spiritual mentors and made choices that could not be denied.

As a teenager I had a friend brought up in an intensely conservative Mormon family. Her every action was overseen by her parents; she was unable to join the adolescent ventures most of us enjoyed. Predictably she rebelled; unfortunately she found herself pregnant. Turning to her parents for help, she was told that she could only redeem herself by standing before the full congregation of her church, confessing her immorality and begging their forgiveness. Desperate as she was she refused, unable to understand how humiliation would redeem her or how her parents could reject her when she was in such pain. Over many days of argument she stayed steadfast in her refusal. Eventually it was her parents who came to see that the response her pain demanded was not condemnation, but love.

The challenge of the warrior woman is to question, challenge and overturn any belief system that confines our freedom; whether it is inherited, chosen or created on the basis of our own past experience. Clinging to any belief system or creed is to be imprisoned by it, no matter how much authority or sanctity is ascribed to the belief. Beliefs carry conclusions, assumptions and conviction, but not freedom. The challenge of moving from shadows to light in our lives invites us to wisely explore the beliefs that shape and inform our own lives and realities in the present. The awakening warrior has the wisdom not to search for a finer dogma to replace a discarded one but is in quest for quality of freedom that has no dependence upon blind belief or dogma. In this quest she needs both vision and determination.

Our own lives are the visible expression, the living testimony of the belief systems we hold to be true. The victim anticipates tragedy and misfortune—what would happen if she were to awaken to the power she has to consciously affect the circumstances of her life? The aggressor believes that the only appropriate response to the unpredictability of life is control and domination. What happens to the aggressor if she connects with her own capacities for sensitivity, receptivity and compassion? The doubter paralysed by confusion and fear is radically altered by a single moment of conscious decisiveness. A single experience of faith, translated into action, becomes a catalyst for transformation. The willingness to challenge the conventions and belief systems of our lives is what distinguishes the visionary from the dreamer. Lacking this inspiration we may well emulate the disguised condor—dreaming dreams of freedom; divorced from her essence she could only admire from a distance this magnificent 'otherness', which was in truth none other than herself in a different form.

Every great journey, every profound spiritual teaching, every radical social transformation begins with a stirring of inner vision. Our own sense of vision is sparked by the stories of great seers and guides who have taught a path of peace and freedom in the midst of great hatred and violence. Our hearts are touched by the examples of women and men who have changed the world around them through the courage and integrity of their vision. Gotama Siddhartha, Teresa of Avila, Martin Luther King, Emmeline Pankhurst, the Dalai Lama and Mother Theresa: their vision has changed our lives. Vision is not the territory of only great and famous people, whose deeds and sacrifices are recorded in history books. We are also inspired by the example of ordinary, simple, but profoundly dedicated women and men who refuse to condone injustice, oppression or prejudice; people who repeatedly illustrate through their lives their love of dignity and integrity.

Like ourselves, the past and present visionaries we admire are born not with innate qualities of saintliness and vocation, but with simple, profound capacities to listen, to see, to learn and to love; the capacities to be aware and deepen in understanding. Out of these very gifts that lie within our hearts vision is born. They have looked at their world, their communities and lives and seen where sorrow and freedom lie.

Vision is not necessarily a profoundly mystical insight from the heavens, a magical benediction or startling revelation. Vision cannot be measured by grand and dramatic gestures but by the truth and impeccability with which we live our lives. Vision and the quest for transformation are inspired by many sources. Our own vision may be sparked by the examples of courage and transformation embodied in the lives of people we respect. My own path was stirred by arriving in a village of impoverished Tibetan refugees and being embraced by such profound depths of compassion, generosity and warmth that I was forced to question what is the real source of genuine happiness and freedom. To meet a homeless person who shares the harvest of her day's foraging with her less fortunate neighbour, challenges us to question the true meaning of caring and generosity. To spend an evening with a single mother and her children in a tenement room as she bends her tired body and mind to encourage her children in their hopes and dreams is to be deeply touched by the power of love and vision. Meeting the visible faces of vision we understand its power to overturn, transform and liberate.

Vision equally emerges from those moments of stillness and sensitivity in our experience when we are reminded in a powerful way of what truly matters in our lives. There is no substitute for living as an awake, compassionate, wise woman and no one can substitute for us in our quest to realise this. Moments of stillness that enable us to put aside our struggling and striving, our defending and manipulating, our busyness and our numbness, allow us to receive in a direct and immediate way the messages and the teachings of this moment. Vision banishes hopelessness and resignation, encourages us to challenge complacency, passivity and despair; the stirring of vision energises us to question and explore. It is a creative energy that is the beginning of the warrior's journey. Vision awakens our hearts, opening us to a sense and exploration of what is possible, rather than inhabiting a world that is defined by conclusions and a belief in the impossible. In those moments of stillness there can be a revival of the aspirations and yearnings of our hearts for wisdom, completeness and freedom. Aspirations, yearning, exploration and vision are the first casualties of habit, doubt and pain.

In the immediacy of opening in a wholehearted way to the messages of our lives and our world there can emerge a simple, but heartfelt refusal to accept the unacceptable in our lives or in our world. No longer willing to accept sorrow, exploitation or conflict as a norm in our lives or in our worlds we are inspired to question their source and explore the paths of joy, wisdom and freedom. Transformation begins with the exploration of possibilities. How do we know that something is truly unacceptable and not something that we subjectively just feel aversion for? No one likes pain, fear, loss or tension; our dislike does not mean it is unacceptable. Few people delight in making radical transitions, challenging unresponsive power structures or risking uncertainty; aversion does not deny the wisdom of entering these territories. Aversion caused through fear of offending or being challenged, or through the dislike of the unpleasant will not lead to transformation but only to the endless attempts to manipulate or redecorate our personal worlds to suit our desires. The relentless attempts to replace the unpleasant sensation or experience with the pleasant sensation or experience, which so consume our world, is not the path of the warrior who treasures liberation and integrity but the path of the manipulator.

Tova's life as a dancer was abruptly interrupted by a back injury. Forced to spend most of her days inactive, she found herself going to remarkable lengths to avoid confronting the changes her life demanded of her. She drowned pain with pills, then intensified it with bitterness and regret. Looming questions of 'What now?' were avoided with fantasy; anxiety suffocated by endless postponement. Her greatest obstacle was not her back but her aversion.

The unacceptable is not just what disturbs or challenges us, but is the theft of the freedom and dignity of any living being. The unacceptable is the imposition of limitation or suffering upon any living being by any person, structure or belief system. The unacceptable is the stockpiling of food while millions starve; the acceptance of gang rape as a justifiable spoil of war; it is revealed to us in the faces of those who meet the threats of racism, sexism and fear as predictable companions in their days. To live our lives as if we have no affect upon the world around us is to live with blindness and is unacceptable. The belief in limitation as truth and division as reality, are beliefs that are unacceptable because they are the breeding ground of prejudice, apathy and sorrow. The unacceptable is the sacrifice of our own freedom, potential and dignity on the altar of fear or ignorance. The refusal to 'accept the unacceptable' is the mother of vision.

The questioning that is the foundation of vision leads us not to shun our inner or outer worlds but draws us closer to them. If we no longer accept suffering or limitation as being the natural consequences of living we are inspired to explore the means to their end. Vision holds the elements of possibility and transformation, it inspires movement. Vision is a creative energy that moves, even propels us to attempt the seemingly impossible; to reach for change; to risk failure; to overturn the easier and safer conventions and belief systems that have governed our lives. Vision inspires movement towards ways of being and seeing that are not necessarily even clearly formulated in our minds. It is an energy that leads us to step beyond the boundaries of what we already know—our personal experience and the habits and beliefs of our individual lives.

This quality of vision is not dependent upon circumstances,

the absence of obstacles, or upon having the ideal circumstances for initiating change. It is the difficult, the imperfect, the unacceptable, the sorrowful, which is the fertile compost from which vision emerges.

An English doctor working in South America was arrested for treating the gunshot wound of a guerrilla fighter. For weeks she was tortured, abused and humiliated in pursuit of information she did not possess. On her release she spoke of that time as the true beginning of her spiritual life. In the darkness of her cell and the pain of her torture she first discovered the meaning of faith, compassion and courage. The migrant worker who refuses to succumb to the sexual demands of her overseer in return for favours draws upon the courage of her vision.

Vision is not dependent upon the sorrowful and the difficult. Our lives do not have to be filled with pain and conflict in order for us to nourish vision and transformation. Vision is born equally of joy and empathy. It is born of love: love of freedom, integrity and wisdom. It is sparked by the innocence of a child and the desire to protect that innocence; it is born of gratitude for the well-being we experience in our lives and the wish to share that well-being. Vision is born of our appreciation for the freedoms we have discovered and our yearning to see freedom grow wherever it is denied. Love inspires openness of heart and vastness of vision; indifference and resignation are the climates which deny it. Cynicism, hopelessness and helplessness are the shadows of the wounded warrior.

The combination of vision and determination create the foundations for the warrior's journey. Determination is the bridge between vision and its realisation. It is a powerful quality of heart and mind that spans the inner world of thoughts, feelings and vision and the outer world of choice, action, expression and fulfilment. Every seeker, every visionary and every warrior knows the need for perseverance, tenacity and steadfastness. Determination is the visible expression of our commitment to our path and our dedication to our vision. Between the moment that any aspiration for change or any glimmer of vision emerges and the moment that it begins to be realised there lies a space. In this space we encounter the shadows of doubt, belief systems and images that bind us to the past and to fear. We are standing on an abyss, certain we must leap, uncertain we can reach the other side. To move through this space without being paralysed by uncertainty or overwhelmed by resignation requires the strength and spiritual stamina of determination.

The strength of determination that characterises the warrior does not imply that we must transform ourselves into an arrogant, spiritually-musclebound fighter. Determination is not the perfection of willpower but a profound dedication to the realisation of possibilities. Determination is not an act of aggression but an act of communication. It is a means of communicating to ourselves and the world around us the clarity of our intention. The passion we feel for our vision and the loyalty we feel for what is true in ourselves and worthy in our world are aspects of determination. Determination is the willingness to begin again in the face of frustration; to evoke passion in the face of complacency. To be steadfast in the face of adversity and truthful when faced with the false requires the tenacity that is also needed to fulfil vision. Determination saves us from the temptations of predetermined identities and sanctioned roles. It offers us integrity and dignity.

The shadow to determination is doubt and paralysis. The temptation to throw our hands in the air in despair, seek for experts or flounder in indecision may be scenarios all too familiar to us. To understand doubt we need equally to understand the belief systems we hold about ourselves that fuel it.

The encounter with doubt and its accompanying paralysis is a frequently-repeated theme in spiritual mythology and legend. When the Buddha sat under the Bodhi tree on the eve of his enlightenment, he was assailed by the forces of doubt that challenged his claim to be a seeker and the authenticity of his search. His answer was not to parade his spiritual credentials, nor to justify himself, but simply to touch the earth he sat upon. The universe itself, his life and dedication were all the authority he needed for awakening.

Transformation in our lives and in our world rarely takes place to the applause of a cheering audience. Transformation and the communication of vision take place most frequently in the face of powerful investment in maintaining the status quo, from within ourselves, our contemporaries and our culture. Inwardly, we are challenged by the investment we may have in preserving identities which are safe and applauded. Outwardly we face the investment our culture has in its own expectations and standards. Change is never a process which takes place in isolation. Any transformation in our lives, our way of seeing or expressing ourselves, our values or directions, has inevitable consequences upon the people and world around us. In the absence of a victim, the oppressor is obliged to undertake their own journey of enquiry. In the absence of consumers, the beauty industry that thrives on women's self-hatred is forced to re-examine the basic tenets of their position. Determination communicates the power of vision and understanding.

Vision is so easily short-circuited by the power of the shadows we carry. Taught the virtues of compliance, malleability and agreeability from an early age, determination is a stranger to the inner landscape of many women. Taught the virtues of settling for the scraps from the feast laid upon the tables of social, political and spiritual greatness, countless women find themselves exiled from the greatness of their own hearts and being. Other people, it seems, make great decisions that alter our world, whereas the greatness of heart involved in a single woman living with love and devotion is somehow reduced in stature by calling it 'duty'. Resignation becomes a familiar companion in the psyche of any woman who has surrendered determination, which is simultaneously a sacrifice of vision. Resignation, linked with passivity, is a subduing factor; it is an inevitable consequence of investing identity in limited belief systems and self-images rather than in possibilities and vision.

When Danielle was passed over for a promotion she had set her heart on, she began to drink; at first moderately and eventually excessively. Everything was put at risk; her relationships, her work, her financial independence. Challenged by one of her closest friends, she explained that when she drank she didn't hurt and went on to explain the inevitability of her addiction. Her parents had been both alcoholics and failures. The success she had previously enjoyed had just been a fluke; her most recent rejection was obviously a result of her employer mistrusting her ability to handle the responsibility of promotion—an assessment she felt to be essentially true.

A certain comfort can be found within the acceptance of limited belief systems and a restricted sense of vision. To take no risks in our lives relieves us of the possibility of failure; to attempt few changes assures predictability. To accept the values and expectations of others relieves us of the need to discover the wisdom and determination that will lend authenticity to our lives. But the consequence for the acceptance of limited vision is to stay within its boundaries. As hope, vision and aspiration dwindle they leave in their wake only a sea of regret and sorrow. It is a cold sea, lacking in direction, empty of passion and devoid of creativity.

Vision that is thwarted draws into our consciousness the shadows and memories of previous failures and frustration. Profoundly moved by the plight of our planet we may determine not only to radically alter our own lifestyles, but also to actively engage in work to alter the cultural indifference that we believe to be responsible for the devastation. We may vocally challenge the greed and self-centredness and take up the warrior's call for radical transformation. Instead of applause, our efforts may be met by criticism, negativity and accusations of obsession that begin to erode our own determination. The response we seek is not forthcoming. Our cries for change fall on deaf ears, and disabled by our own shadow of mistrust or ineffectiveness, our vision begins to shrink and crumble. We may attempt to justify the sacrifice of our vision through listing all the reasons that prevent its realisation. Yet the sacrifice of vision leaves a gaping hole that is never adequately explained away.

Once I met an old woman in America who had 'adopted' part of a highway. The commitment she made was to keep two miles of road clean. Every morning she arose and began her task, dragging behind her the sacks for collecting the trash that had accumulated. She told me, 'It's a good life. I watch all these cars speeding by, people bent over the steering wheels, frowning, talking on phones. Everybody's in a rush, they're all going somewhere. Me, I'm not going anywhere. I just walk my miles, picking up my garbage. Sometimes it rains, sometimes the sun's shining. Sometimes people wave at me, sometimes they laugh. It's all ok; I go home and I know that for this day my miles of earth are just a little cleaner.'

Inspired by the stories of great spiritual mystics we may set out on our own path, intent on awakening, only to find ourselves hampered by the power of our conditioning and shadows. Our vision begins to falter in the face of what is seemingly impossible and we are tempted to settle for what appears easier or more accessible. If we can't have transformation perhaps we can at least find more acceptance. If we cannot be truly free, we may at least be able to discover more peace. Again a catalogue of reasons is produced to explain the contraction of our vision.

'I can't' is adopted as a mantra. Perhaps we don't have the right personality for awakening; perhaps we need to resolve the issues and residues of the past before we can be free. We need to be profoundly alert to the compromises we make in our lives. Are they an expression of flexibility and sensitivity or do they illustrate resignation and a sacrifice of vision? Ultimately, no-one needs any special credentials to seek freedom and transformation. Vision, dedication, passion, whole-heartedness and trust are the qualities that enable us to make radical leaps in our consciousness and our lives. To forsake sorrow, separation and limitation we need to love freedom, integrity and wisdom above all else. Out of this dedication comes the compassion and determination that allows us to forsake the tentacles of the belief systems that confine our spirit.

The journey of the warrior from shadow to light involves not only outer change but a truly radical inner revolution. There is no room for rigidity nor the inertness of images and stereotypes, in the openness and vitality of the wakeful warrior. Central to a life of freedom is a banishment of all images, whether they are imposed or adopted. There is little that is constant or static within the vitality of our spirits apart from our conclusions and images. To make icons out of them is to be endlessly tied to what has already gone by, but is not to be open and receptive to what is or what can be. The warrior woman is ready to challenge the power of her own images and belief systems.

The concealed danger of personal belief systems and self-images is that they are most frequently rooted in experiences of fear and pain, creating beliefs in limitation rather than possibility. They describe our boundaries rather than our potentiality. From the moment that a personal belief system has been adopted and taken root, we enact it in our world. The world, in turn, appears to supply endless evidence which testifies to the truth of that belief or image. It is no coincidence that the woman who believes firmly in her unacceptability will encounter endless instances of rejection and disapproval. It is no accident of fate that the woman who believes herself to be powerless meets a stream of dominating people in her life. Identifying with a belief system is to offer it our consent and to stereotype ourselves. The mistaken self-images camouflage our potential as women to be awake and free.

Personal belief systems, experienced as self-images, serve to hobble us, hindering change. Stereotypes and belief systems may endeavour to confine and define women, but confinement within them requires consent. There is a mutual dependency at play in the continuation of any belief system or stereotype. The master and the victim have married each other. Domination and passivity are partners in the same dance. The awakening warrior is willing to challenge any assumption or conclusion imposed upon her; she is equally willing to question the ways in which she has cloaked herself in the armour of any self-image. Despite the weight of confinement dictated by self-images they also offer a certain comfort; relieving us from the burden of change and the exploration of true possibilities. To say with certainty 'I know who I am', or 'I know who you are', is a sacrifice of openness and a denial of the willingness to learn and respond to the inevitable changes in our lives. They are statements that are alien to the spiritual warrior, representing frozen, static images based upon the past.

An old man recounted to his granddaughter an experience he had recently had with his wife. 'Your grandma is mad at me,' he said. 'She told me she wanted to go back to school. I told her she was too old. She spends half her life in her rocker; she'd probably break a leg getting to classes. She surprised me; I offended her. I wanted her to stay the same, I always want things to stay the same. I'm like a collector who puts pins in a butterfly and fixes them on a board with a label underneath them. Your grandmother taught me something. If you really love someone you have to let them move and change; be glad they surprise you. You can also do this with yourself.'

To be awake in our lives we must be willing to open to the truth of each moment and ourselves, which is change and unfoldment. The wisdom of the warrior guides her to seek the possibilities for wisdom and freedom that lie within change and unfoldment. She is not interested solely in outer modification but profoundly committed to exploring the boundaries and horizons of her inner world. She understands the fear and inner alienation that makes the adoption of beliefs and images so tempting. She is not content with exchanging one prison for another, but with discovering the truth of her own being and living in the spirit of that freedom. How many of our boundaries are the offspring of unconscious or latent personal belief systems? What manner of inner beliefs incline us to accept limitation or consent to the beliefs and stereotypes of others? The beliefs and images that inform and mould our lives need to be visible to us; awareness is the necessary first step of transformation. The questioning of limitation is the first augury of awakening from numbness. It does not seek blame but freedom.

The questioning which is intrinsic to the warrior's journey may not be welcomed by others, or indeed even by herself at times. It requires immense courage to explore what is unknown to us and not confine ourselves to endless repetitions of what we know or believe that we know. The weight of our conditioning teaches us to strive for the grace of acceptance and discover contentment within the boundaries of our lives. Questioning may be deemed unattractive or shrewish; socially or spiritually unacceptable; a failure of our femininity. A woman who wants to create rather than reproduce may meet resistance from her partner; a woman who wants to reproduce may find the same resistance from her more ambitious friends. A woman who wants to forge new paths in her life may be told that her desire for change evidences her unwillingness to accept herself. Acceptance and transformation are polarised and women are directed again and again to find their home in compliance. It is a false polarisation. True acceptance is not acquiescence but combines both openness of heart and discriminating wisdom. True acceptance embraces forgiveness and the wisdom to discern the difference between what contributes to freedom and what undermines it. It is the beginning of change.

The roles and identities we have chosen, adopted or simply fallen into, tell us a great deal about the personal belief systems that we carry. Our fears and aspirations, our fantasies and unfulfilled longings tell the story of our beliefs. Our frustrations and feelings of disappointment are pointers to the images that inform our lives just as our life experiences reveal to us the inner creeds that are governing us. The repetition of these experiences reveals to us the ways in which our life is shaped by our currently-held beliefs, just as our current beliefs are shaped by the power of past experience. The feminine warrior doesn't necessarily need the guidance of experts to travel from shadows to light. Our greatest teachers are rarely far from us. They live in our stories and invite us to understand what we need to let go of and what we need to nurture.

There are many situations of pain and conflict in our lives which are simply echoes of the same frustrations we have experienced repeatedly in the past. Feelings of disillusionment or disempowerment are greeted with a sense of both déjà vu and despair. Repeated experiences of rejection or betrayal are met with equal measures of familiarity and bewilderment. The 'battered wife' vents her anger then bandages her wounds and resigns herself to a life where pain is an accepted norm. The humiliated employee rebels against yet one more instance of rebuff and abasement then hides her outrage beneath a facade of acceptance. Questions of 'Why does this always happen to me?' surface in our minds to be met with feelings of helplessness or resignation. Humiliation and powerlessness may be no strangers to us, but so familiar that their arrival is anticipated.

We may find ourselves responding passionately to the possibility of making real changes in our lives yet, at the moment of making a decision, opting for maintaining familiarity in our work, relationships and direction; even when we know clearly that change is vital to our well-being. What we are experiencing in these moments is the power of our inner belief systems and self-images. Resolutions and willpower will not bring about transformation; neither is despair or resignation a valid option. Wisdom, commitment, determination and compassion are the vehicles needed to bring about understanding and transformation.

Unconscious and repeated beliefs, whether they are political, social, spiritual or personal, become the institutions we find ourselves inhabiting, willingly or unwillingly. The institutions that imprison us may be formed by static stereotypes, role models and images that are offered to us by social and cultural expectations.

In Ireland, in the 1960s, a young nun was sent as a temporary worker to another convent and stepped into a world she had not known existed. Her job was to supervise the women working in the convent laundry, a gloomy and claustrophobic room. The women wore old clothes; mostly they were quiet and passive apart from one or two who hadn't been there long and were rebellious. A number of them were single mothers whose children had been taken from them. The convent graveyard held the bodies of 183 women. Some were unmarried mothers rejected by their families. Others were destitute and homeless because of alcoholism or mental illness. Many of the women she supervised stayed in the convent until they died. The most extraordinary aspect of it is they were told they were not allowed to leave. They were locked in at night. Legally, they could have walked out of the gate any time they wanted, but very few did. For many, there was no place to go. They lived and died in a virtual prison. Until the 1950s thousands of Irish women were condemned to a life of servitude and confinement with the knowledge, coercion and approval of family, church and state. Places were created to remove from society 'unmanageable' women, whose alleged crimes varied from being socially inadequate to giving birth out of marriage. Not only were they never told they could leave but the regimes emphasised their sin and guilt and disbarred them from ever speaking about their past. They were called the 'laundry girls', seen but never spoken about. The nuns who cared for them were equally imprisoned by their own beliefs that led them to collude in the theft of the freedom and dignity of thousands of women.

Institutions are equally created within our own psyches through grasping hold of judgments, descriptions and images of ourselves. The anorexic teenager confined within a starving body is as much a prisoner of her self-image as the Irish 'laundry girls'. We define ourselves by judgments and experiences of pain and these judgments and experiences determine our lives, directions and choices. They become our institutions. An experience of failure becomes a judgment of our own inadequacy. Fearful of the repetition of failure, we avoid risk in the present and in the future. An institution has been created and we become institutionalised within it.

Rejected by someone we care for, we assume the rejection is rooted in our own unloveableness. Convinced by this truth, we are fearful of connections and relationships in our lives lest our 'unworthiness' will be revealed once more. We have become institutionalised within our own judgments and images. Every time we create a reference point, rules for behaviour or images arising from a judgment, fear or experience, we begin to build the walls of the institutions that confine us.

Some of our institutions have a long history, some are created on a moment to moment level. Whether old or new, institutions are featured by their lifelessness, lack of vitality and freedom. Regardless of how ancient our institutions are, it is vital to remember that they are constructed and conditioned. They can end, their life depends upon our participation in them. No institution can exist without an inmate. There are times when our institutions, although limiting and painful, offer to us the comfort and safety of familiarity. We know the rules and may cherish the sanctuary from pain they appear to offer us. The price we pay for that sanctuary is frustration and limitation. It is frightening to leave them but intolerable to stay within them.

Conservationists speak of the difficulties they encounter when moving tigers from a familiar environment, because the animals are endangered by drought or by poachers. To move them to safety, the tiger must first be sedated, placed in a cage and then transported to its new home which offers protection and food. This is not the difficult part. The real difficulties arise when the door of the cage is opened to allow the tiger to step out into unfamiliar territory. The tiger will attack anyone who attempts to encourage it to leave its cage; will fight to protect the familiar territory that is demarcated by bars. It is desperately afraid of the unknown; afraid of the offered freedom. We face the same fears in our own journeys. The fear of letting go of the familiar without any guarantees. The courage of the warrior lies in the taking of that first step; the step of letting go.

The celebration of freedom lies within our capacity to make wise choices that are not conditioned by the power of beliefs. We need to call upon our own inner wisdom to discern whether the choices we make in our lives lead to an exploration of possibility or a subscription to limitation. A spiritual journey is an invitation to envision ourselves in radically different ways. A genuine spiritual journey is not an admonition to subscribe to a new set of beliefs or to clothe ourselves in a more spiritually-excellent stereotype. A genuine spiritual journey leads us to understand who we are when we cast aside the disguises of all beliefs and stereotypes. Part of the process of envisioning ourselves in a qualitatively different way is to ask of ourselves what it is that we need to leave behind us and what it is that we need to nurture in order to fulfil the potential that is possible for us. Awareness leads to questioning. Enquiry conducted in a spirit of compassion and forgiveness leads to a renewal of vision. Determination and courage bring its realisation.

In exploring the web of beliefs that entangle us, both inwardly and outwardly, we are easily tempted into the arenas of denial and fantasy. Aware of the inner fears and doubts we carry, we may be tempted to substitute self-blame for blame of others when looking at the boundaries and shadows that haunt us. There is a fine line between inner exploration and a narcissism in which awareness is appropriated by the 'ego' to become a more 'refined' and 'spiritual' judge which we use to chastise ourselves for our imperfections and failings. In this transaction we clothe ourselves in a new layer of 'unworthiness', assuming the fault and blame for our lack of freedom. The warrior becomes neurotic in this process, formulating new images of spiritual perfection, possessing her own belief systems defining what is spiritually and socially acceptable. She tells herself she must be assertive, fearless, powerful and courageous. If her commands are distanced from the embracing of her shadows with compassion and forgiveness, they will lead only to suppression and renewed experiences of failure and pain. The new stereotype of spiritual excellence created by the neurotic warrior is no more than a reaction to old or current belief systems which are deemed to be inadequate and imperfect. In this transaction our fantasies of who we 'should' be and the striving they breed become our new prison, offering little understanding of who we are.

The feminine warrior knows deeply the need to banish the judge and is willing to discard the temptations and promises of any belief system or image it creates. She has the compassion to forgive and embrace the doubts and fears which live within her and the courage to step beyond their dictates. She is no longer willing to heed the belief that sanctuary, safety and acceptability are intrinsic to any image, creed or belief. Her concern is not affirmation and approval from others, nor fulfilling the expectations of her own inner judge, but the discovery of inner vision, authority and freedom. The warrior woman is willing to be vulnerable; stripped of certainty and guarantees; knowing that the openness that vulnerability offers is the doorway to discovery and awakening.

We are drawn to a spiritual journey because it offers to us a vision of possibility and freedom. The heart of all spiritual teaching is one that affirms our essential freedom, our potential to go beyond the confines of conditioning and limitation. It is a teaching that invites us to learn from our own histories but not to dwell upon them. The teaching of freedom is a teaching that reminds us of the possibility of radical transformation— the possibility to begin anew in each moment of our lives.

Mystics and sages in all traditions deliver a singular message—that freedom is our true inheritance and the essence of our being. Beliefs in limitation, in images and the inner structures that define our boundaries are essentially false and can never offer any profound understanding of who we truly are. Inner freedom, which is the core of all spiritual teaching, is not a state we will gain or achieve, nor a destination we must reach through striving, overcoming or transcending. Rather we will come to trust in our essential freedom through shedding the fears that bind us and understanding the fallacy of the false identities and beliefs that shadow us. The transparency of our beliefs is seen, not through complicated and esoteric methods, but through stillness and awareness. Through extending an unshakeable patience and commitment to listening inwardly, we will come to know inner calmness and compassion that enable us to undertake this journey without struggle or prejudice. We are not required to conquer or overcome the tangled webs of our beliefs but to see them clearly in the light of wisdom and awareness.

Belief systems are no more than the manifestation of insecure faith, faith that has faltered before the force of fear. Insecure faith leads us to seek stability and security in static systems, structures and images, demanding guarantees of safety and identity. Profound, balanced faith in ourselves and in the possibility of transformation enables us to make the radical changes in our lives and the leaps in our consciousness from the known to the unknown. Faith in possibility; trust in our capacity to realise possibilities, are the essential pillars of courage. They enable us to set aside stifling and limiting structures in our lives and our own psyches. Inner faith possesses the wisdom to recognise that destinations and assurances suffocate life and vision. Vision thrives on the courage and willingness to explore, question and trust in our own capacities for freedom.

The greatest gift of the spiritual life is the offering of vision. This is not only the invitation to envision ourselves in qualitatively new ways, but also to appreciate the implications of inner transformation upon the world around us. Genuine wisdom and freedom are not possessions that can be hoarded in a miserly way. Spiritual history holds too may stories of 'liberated' saints who have divorced themselves from the pain of the world. The inevitable consequence of authentic wisdom and freedom is its embodiment in our lives, our actions, relationships and choices. It is a force that touches the world around us with compassion, forgiveness and love.

The spiritual message of fulfilment and liberation is frequently expressed in the language of 'otherness'. Like the masqueraded condor looking with longing at the freedom of the skies, our own journeys express a yearning for something 'other' than pain, conflict and limitation. The 'other' is the promise of liberation of joy, wisdom and awakening. 'Otherness' is not a destination to strive for or a magical benediction we passively await. These projections, by their nature, imply separation and separation is a denial of freedom. The 'other' we seek cannot be found anywhere apart from within who we are and where we are. The challenge of the warrior woman is to discover joy amidst hardship, compassion amidst brutality, wisdom amidst chaos and freedom within the joys and sorrows of our world. She is bold enough to challenge the sources of pain, courageous enough to transform, compassionate enough to forsake judgment. Honouring the power of her commitment, sensitivity, wisdom and determination she learns to celebrate the freedom that lies within her. Her compassion and wisdom will touch and transform her world.

FOUR

INVISIBILITY TO VISIBILITY

I begin this chapter with the timeless story of 'The Ugly Duckling' by Hans Christian Andersen, offering to us the archetype of the invisible and the outcast. It is a story which continues to touch our hearts, telling us of the pain of being exiled from our true nature and the joy of its discovery. The tale of the floundering duckling teaches us the wisdom of never surrendering our search to understand ourselves and encourages us to sustain our quest for truth even in the midst of profound adversity. The theme of this story is repeated endlessly in fairytales and spiritual mythology.

Princesses and mythical heroines are sentenced to aeons of sleep, imprisonment or death on the basis of their appearance or behaviour. The invisibility of exile becomes the home of our storybook heroes and heroines who are feared for their goodness, virtue or potential power. They come to inhabit a ghost-like existence, unable to affect the world around them; unable to assert the truth of their own being. In their phantom world they are tortured by forces more powerful than themselves and by their own inability to break out of their invisibility. In the story of the Ugly Duckling, invisibility is simply the consequence of mistaken identity. In other stories, invisibility is the punishment for lack of conformity. Mythology and fable equally repeat the theme that invisibility is the inevitable consequence of being dispossessed of inner authority and authenticity. Invariably our stories have a happy ending—invisibility is transformed into visibility; the sorrow of dispossession turns to the joy of discovering the truth. It is rarely an accidental transformation. The transformation in which truth and goodness triumph is unfailingly linked to the intervention of unshakeable wisdom which dissolves the cloak of invisibility.

THE UGLY DUCKLING

Spring had arrived in the countryside and new life burst forth in the trees and on the banks of the river. Beneath the reeds a duck sat on her nest, patiently waiting for her eggs to hatch. Soon the eggs began to crack, one by one, and the new ducklings broke free of their shells. The tiny birds began to find their feet, tumbling over each other, wide-eyed at the new world that surrounded them. Still, one egg, the largest of all, remained unhatched, and the mother duck began to feel impatient. She had so much to do, teaching her new brood to swim and fish for food. Sighing she settled down on her nest again, unwillingly to abandon the last of her young. Sure enough the next day, the egg began to crack and a large beak, followed by an even larger head, began to emerge from the shell. The new chick towered over her brothers and sisters and the mother duck drew back thinking, 'What a terribly ugly duckling is this. Surely this is no chick of mine?' Yet seeing its helplessness, her heart softened and she made room for it in the nest. The next morning the sun shone warmly on the waters of the pond and, quacking loudly, the mother duck called for her chicks to follow her into the water. One by one they tumbled into the pond and were soon swimming. Seeing the clumsy late arrival follow, the mother duck sighed in relief. 'She is not so ugly after all. Swimming she even shows a little grace. She is my own child, surely, and as she grows she's bound to get better.'

Seeing that her brood were tiring in the water, the mother

duck decided it was time to introduce them to the farmyard and looked forward to receiving the admiration of her friends. As the little line of ducks waddled into the yard the other ducks gathered round to greet the new arrivals. They quacked in admiration until their eyes fell upon the last and the largest of the line. Their beaks fell open in horror and they began to quack amongst themselves and finally turned to the new mother. 'What a big, peculiar-looking duckling you have brought. We don't want her in our farmyard. She brings shame to us all.' They began to circle around the ugly duckling, taunting her and pecking her with their sharp beaks. The mother duck ran to her chick's protection, beseeching the other ducks to leave her alone. 'It is true she is not beautiful, but she will grow to be better looking. She can swim quite well and has a kind heart.' The ugly duckling looked out from under her mother's feathers and her heart was heavy.

That day was the beginning of many days that only grew worse for the grey ugly duckling. She was chased and teased by everyone. The ducks snapped at her and even her brothers and sisters became cruel and joined in the taunting. 'You are so ugly', they would cry. 'We hope the cat gets you!' As the days went by even the duckling's mother began to turn her back and murmured that she too wished the little duckling had never been born. Unable to bear it any longer, the ugly duckling decided to run away. That night she flew over the fence, startling the wild birds so that they flew into the air crying with alarm. 'It's because I am so ugly that they are afraid', thought the bedraggled duckling. Exhausted, she lay down beside the water's edge where two young ganders found her. Keeping their distance they began to question the young duckling, asking her where her mother was. Lowering their heads, one whispered to the other, 'She's so ugly it's no wonder she has no mother.' The young duckling of course overheard them and once more she began to pick herself up so she could go and hide her shame and tears. Suddenly shots rang out and the two ganders fell dead among the reeds and the water around them turned red with their blood. The marshes rang with the sound of shots and dogs barking. Terrified, the young duckling ran beneath cover of the reeds seeking safety.

All that day the duckling ran, hungry and afraid, until towards nightfall she came to a poor, decrepit shack on the edge of the woods. Seeing that the door hung askew, the young duckling slipped inside. Here lived an old woman, her cross-eyed cat and her hen. The old woman cackled with delight when she spotted the young duckling. Maybe it will lay eggs, and if it doesn't it will make a fine meal for me, she thought. But here too the duckling found herself chased by the cat, derided by the hen and shouted at by the old woman as the days went by. 'You are good for nothing', the old woman shouted at her. 'You lay no eggs and you are ugly to look at.' Picking up her broom she chased the duckling from her house.

The duckling wandered on until she arrived at the edge of another pond. Paddling on the water, tears dropped from her eyes and her spirit drooped with loneliness. 'If only I wasn't so ugly; if only I could do something useful, somewhere I could find a home', she thought. Just then, bending her head, she saw reflected in the water a flock of the most beautiful creatures she had ever seen flying overhead. Looking up, she watched them fly away and had never felt more alone or more unwanted. Winter came with its cold wind and falling snow. The duckling paddled furiously in circles as ice began to form over the surface of the pond. One morning she awoke to find herself frozen within the ice and she knew she would die. Fortunately a kindly farmer found her and, breaking the ice with his rake, he picked her up and carried her to the warmth of his kitchen. His children reached for her but she was afraid and flew up into the rafters, knocking dust into the milk. When the farmer's wife tried to catch her, she ended up falling into the milk and then into the flour. Exasperated, the farmer's wife chased her from the house as the children shrieked with laughter.

The whole winter was spent this way, running and hiding. The duckling hardly noticed as spring began to arrive, so tired and hungry was she. The duckling raised her wings. They seemed so much stronger than before and lifted her swiftly into the air to soar down the river. Beneath her she saw three of the beautiful creatures she'd seen the autumn before and she felt herself drawn to them. Settling on the water, she bowed her head and paddled towards them. 'They will probably peck me to death, these noble creatures, when they see how ugly I am', thought the young bird. 'But better to be pecked to death by such splendid creatures, than to be teased and pecked by the other ducks or to spend another winter alone.' As soon as the swans saw her they glided towards her and began to stroke her with their beaks. She bent her neck with joy and beneath her saw the reflection of the same splendid birds who were touching her lovingly with their wingtips. She opened her eyes with wonder at the reflection beneath her and realised it was herself. She was no ugly duckling, but a beautiful snowy swan. Proudly she arched her neck and joined the others. Just then some children came to the river bank and cried out, 'Look, there is a new swan and she is the most beautiful of all.'

The ugly duckling was not invisible to the creatures she met in her travels, but was visible to them and herself only through her appearance, her ugliness. Her appearance exiled her from belonging; she was made homeless by her lack of conformity. When her appearance was accepted as being the truth of her being, she became invisible to herself and others in her essence. The rejection faced by the Ugly Duckling forced her to begin a quest; initially for survival, ultimately for revelation. Unlike the masqueraded condor who found a home in a safe disguise and in resignation, the Ugly Duckling was stripped of all sanctuary and compelled to find her home in herself before she could find a home in the world.

Conventionally, visibility is defined by the impressions we

make upon the world. The more powerful the impression we make the more visible we are. Visibility is equated with appearance and performance. These two factors become our credentials for being 'someone'. We act out the identities we have adopted through our actions, presentation and roles. Appearance and performance become the means of making ourselves visible to others and to ourselves. The identities we find ourselves inhabiting may not be ones we have freely chosen. Fear, doubt and confusion can be powerful factors in the formation of the identities we inhabit, turning them into prisons. From the moment that Cinderella picked up her broom she was confined to the identity of the servant and her appearance and performance only served to confirm the truth of that identity.

The theme of invisibility, central to so many of our fairy tales, is powerful because it reflects the pain of the lives of so many people. Like the banished heroines of our fairy tales, countless women live with the pain of being discounted through their conformity or non-conformity to conventional ideas of beauty. Their intelligence viewed as threatening, they are silenced; their commitment to healing condemned as heretical. The sentence of invisibility serves to erase their power and aspiration.

Historically, the invisible in our world have always been the oppressed, the powerless, the wounded and minorities. They live in the shadows of life, sometimes thrust there by the power of circumstances or the dominance of others, other times remaining in the shadows through their own apparent choicelessnes and powerlessness. Invisibility is the consequence of being imprisoned within an image or stereotype; it is the consequence of being imprisoned by fear. The language of the invisible in our world is the language of silence. Unheard, unseen, they remain unnoticed and unnoticeable. Taken for granted, they inhabit a desert of depreciation and neglect. Ignored and overlooked, their silent pleas for recognition and love fall upon deaf ears.

The pain of invisibility is not confined to particular minority groups; it is endured by anyone who is defined by appearance, performance or role. The elderly woman who is patronised or spoken at in loud tones is inhabiting the territory of the invisible. The disabled person in a wheelchair who tries to capture the attention of a person who consistently ignores them to refer to their helper experiences the pain of being defined by appearance and performance. The partner or wife who is acknowledged only through her relationship to her husband experiences the confines of invisibility. Countless mothers experience the frustration of not being seen to be a woman, a human being, whose capacity to mother describes only one thread in the tapestry of her being.

The pain of invisibility is shared both by those who live in the shadows of life and those who are highly conspicuous. Success is not necessarily incompatible with invisibility. Through our appearance or performance we may well occupy a high-profile, applauded position in our lives. The successful model, the woman executive, enjoys all the accolades of achievement but may equally despair over being equated with her body or her performance. We may rejoice over our capacity to perform our roles and assert our identities with confidence and impeccability but carry a private grief when our capacity to do this seems to imply that we are no longer visible apart from those roles and identities.

A woman artist living in New York told me of the struggles she endured in order to have her work exhibited. Taking some of her paintings to galleries in New York, she and her work would be initially greeted with enthusiasm and praise, with the gallery owners initially eager to mount an exhibition. Then she would be asked the question, 'Where do you live?' When she replied that she lived in Long Island with her family the doors would begin to close. 'To be a respected artist', she was told, 'you have to live in Manhattan and live the life of an artist. No-one will buy from a Long Island housewife.' Meeting this refusal a number of times she rented a loft in Manhattan and began again to make the same rounds of galleries. This time there were no barriers to having an exhibition sponsored.

There are times when we fade into invisibility through the power of the expectations that are attached to our roles or identities or through the expectations of others. The healer may be disbarred from revealing feelings of vulnerability; moments of uncertainty expressed by a spiritual guide are interpreted as moments of failure.

Invisibility may also be part of a bargain we make with our families, partners, cultures or with ourselves. Unquestioning emotional and physical care may be expected in return for financial care; obedience exchanged for reflected prestige. Uncritical devotion may be the price asked for spiritual identity. In all of these transactions invisibility is accepted.

To a person who is burdened with a wounded sense of vision, invisibility appears a desirable landscape to inhabit. Remaining unseen, unheard and unnoticed offers a sanctuary from disapproval, rejection or blame. Our silence is welcomed as we provide the space for others to assert themselves. Our agreeability wins us approval and makes us less visible. Compliance is praised and through it we attract little attention to ourselves. We maintain and promote invisibility through the actions we perform or leave undone, the words we speak or leave unspoken, in the small and large choices we make in our lives. Roles and jobs may be chosen because they offer to us an identity which will attract little visibility and the safety of clear expectation and definition. Visibility may spell danger to us— we equate it with being exposed and vulnerable and believe ourselves unable to cope with the feedback that that exposure may attract. We are not always alert to the dangers that invisibility itself is exerting.

The debilitating effect of invisibility, whether it is chosen, imposed or simply grows through the repetition of our roles, is that we become invisible to ourselves. We go through the motions of our performances, take care of our appearances, perform our roles and begin to see ourselves only through the eyes of those identities. Our sense of authority and authenticity comes to rely upon the roles or identities we inhabit and is thus increasingly fragile. Identities that are based upon performance and appearance offer only a shallow safety that is easily shattered by the changing circumstances of our lives. Our bodies age, our successes are superseded by others, our roles fade in significance—relying upon the substantiality of all of these leaves us bereft in their passing. If our sense of who we are is circumscribed by an identity formed through expectation or fear we become dispossessed of authenticity in our lives.

When invisibility is sought for the protection it offers we bow beneath the weight of our unspoken words, our sacrificed choices and our denied actions. Integrity is undermined by the fear of visibility and creativity is denied. The skills and gifts we long to develop and express remain stifled, for their expression would make us visible and vulnerable to the feedback that expression invites. The wisdom and compassion that rise within us in response to situations of pain and conflict we encounter in the world are hidden and restrained; to express them, to intervene, to express ourselves is a step we are fearful of taking, knowing that it is a step into visibility.

Anne, a highly qualified nurse, worked in a team in a busy hospital. One of the consultants who supervised them was highly competent, also deeply insensitive. Patients were cases, not people, and he assessed his staff only in terms of productivity. Doing his rounds he would ignore the patients' pleas for reassurance and care, busily dictating his notes. He thought nothing of humiliating the junior staff. Anne found everything within her rebelling against his callousness, yet also knew that her promotion and stature depended upon his recommendation. Fearing that she would be next in line to receive his criticism and anger, she learned to hide her objections. Seething inwardly, she would follow in his wake with her face impassive. On his departure she would attempt to offer his patients the reassurance he neglected, yet even as she did so she knew that she was neglecting to challenge the real issue of the contempt he felt so free to express.

One day, as he turned his back on a patient, leaving her in tears, Anne reached out to touch his arm. Disregarding his impatience, Anne explained to him: 'It is only a few words of kindness this woman is asking of you. She wants to know that you see her.' The doctor shrugged off her hand and continued on his rounds. At the end of the shift, when passing through the ward, Anne was startled to see him once more beside the patient's bed. Somehow he had been touched.

Inhabiting the shadows of invisibility, alert to the dangers of visibility, we forget how to listen to ourselves and what we are able to hear carries far less authority than the expectations we feel bound to comply with. To live as a reflex of the expectations of others is to become a beggar for approval and affirmation. The silence we adopt to remain unnoticed serves to deafen us. It becomes increasingly difficult to listen inwardly when we feel called to be constantly alert, intently listening for the signals from others that spell danger for us—signals of disapproval or failure. Integrity and dignity are sacrificed in this transaction and we are burdened by the pain of being exiled from the authenticity of our own being. Performance and appearance may teach us the lessons of how to assume an identity, but they teach us little about being.

For centuries women have discovered that invisibility and silence are rewarded with praise. Obedience is called humility, subservience called meekness and timidity called modesty. The rebellious, assertive, challenging or independent woman is rarely offered a home in any conventional political, social or spiritual structure. History tells us that these very qualities are the domain of the warrior who has the power and vision to bring transformation, yet it is a domain which excludes the warrior woman. Exhibiting these qualities she is called unfeminine and punished with rejection and dismissal. She finds herself accused of being too proud, lacking in faith and wisdom; her rebelliousness and boldness are defined as problems she must overcome. Faced with the alternatives of acceptance or rejection, she is forced to choose between invisibility and visibility. It is a choice between fear and courage.

There is a curious paradox that operates in our relationship to invisibility. Through not attracting attention, remaining unseen, we invite little challenge and are protected by the cloak of invisibility; equally we are imprisoned by the very invisibility we adopt to protect us. It is an ongoing experience of safe frustration, protective custody. Like a Muslim woman wrapped in the folds of a chador, who can move safely through the world anonymous and invisible, we too can don the cloak of invisibility by wrapping ourselves in silence and conformity. Protection is offered but the sun is never felt on the face of a shrouded woman. The wind never touches her cheek and it is exceedingly difficult to run or dance wrapped in a cloak.

The last decades have borne witness to the movement of many women from invisibility to visibility. The feminine warriors that guide us inwardly and outwardly invite us to emerge from the shadows of life and to cast off the cloak of invisibility. We learn to honour the forms and roles in our lives that embody our most deeply understood wisdom and not to be circumscribed by them. We learn that to live as a free and conscious woman we need to be connected with a sense of inner authority and being that is vaster than any conditioned identity. We are no longer willing to exchange acceptance and praise for authenticity, or to invest our identities in appearance and performance. The transition to visibility has challenged many of us deeply—asking us to question our assumptions about ourselves, the expectations we have adopted and the truth of the identities we embody. It has taught us the need to listen inwardly, to discover the source of genuine authority and to be visible to ourselves.

The process of women becoming increasingly visible in our world also carries with it it's own dangers and pressure. Invisibility is named negative, suppressive, a failure of potential—to be discarded without delay. This naming carries its own pressure and burden of expectation. Current literature and the media tell us it is no longer good enough to be 'just' a wife, a mother—nor is it good enough just to succeed and achieve. We may feel a certain obligation and command to fulfil our potential and endless images are dispensed that define what that potential is. New models of the whole woman are dictated—she is sexually liberated, articulate, creative, politically-engaged, socially conscious and nurturing. Attempting to conform to this new model can become a compulsion so urgent that we are once more consumed by the need to realise expectation. In our heroic efforts to have it all, to be everything, we easily become invisible to ourselves once more as our attention is again focussed upon assuming an identity that is more 'real'.

Performance and appearance once more assume a sacredness, testifying to our 'wholeness', 'freedom' and visibility. Ensnared by the busyness which this search demands, it is possible that we have neither the time nor energy to wonder whether or not we have once more become entangled in the expectations of someone else. Rising in the morning to be immediately assailed by the endless thoughts of all that has to be performed and undertaken in that day; at night seeking the healing darkness of sleep; alert through the day to signs of failure or inadequacy—all of these are symptoms of addiction to performance and appearance. Authority has been given to the realisation of an identity which will satisfy expectation—either our own or others—what is absent is the patient and clear inner listening which is the source of genuine authority.

Francesca returned to her home after many years' travelling, faced with the prospect of creating a life for herself. Work, friends, a home and lifestyle all required building. The news-papers she read told her she must be ready to sell herself. Soon she found herself caught in a web of busyness—exercise class-es, social engagements, job interviews—all seemed situations that demanded that she prove her desirability. Everyone around her seemed so engaged—reading the right books, see-ing the latest movies, going through the latest therapy and building enviable lifestyles. She found herself working hard just to keep up, to create a presentation of herself that would win approval. Increasingly exhausted, she realised that she had no idea what she wanted, valued or aspired to. She was living somebody else's life. If we do not meet the power of other peo-ple's expectations with an equally powerful willingness to find our own paths, we abandon ourselves.

The call that inspires the spiritual warrior in her journey is the call to discover authenticity and freedom within herself and to embody that in her life. Answering this call does not demand that we divorce our partners, leave our children or renounce our jobs and aspirations. It does require us to ques-tion whether the forms and roles we have chosen communicate the values and wisdom we honour. Responding to the call for authenticity does not ask us to convert to new identities or roles that are sanctioned by a cultural or spiritual authority we admire or fear. To understand what is authentic within our-selves and within our lives we are asked to reflect with wisdom and compassion upon the identities we do inhabit. Do they embody authenticity or have they been adopted through the force of external authorities in our lives—the authorities of people, expectation or fear?

Authority is the primary force in the formation of identity. From the moment of our birth we are surrounded by authori-ties who appear to hold the power to deliver happiness or pain. Learning how to please and how to avoid punishment become second nature to us as long as we accept that our well-being, happiness and freedom lie in the hands of someone else.

Obedience to the authorities of expectation or fear will win us a harvest of affirmation but not freedom. Authenticity is directly related to our connection with inner authority. Exiled from inner authority through fear, rejection or ignorance we are endlessly tempted to rely upon identities, appearance and performance to provide us with the authority we feel to be lacking within ourselves.

The spiritual warrior treasures freedom deeply enough to willingly challenge the authorities that govern her inwardly and outwardly. It is a challenge of exploration, not reaction; of questioning, not denial. The spiritual journey that is dedicated to the discovery of authenticity mirrors much of the searching that has taken place elsewhere in our lives. In western culture we live beneath an immense pressure to be 'someone'—to make our mark in the world in a visible way, to achieve, to earn recognition and stature. These are defined as the marks of success, the trophies that the winners in life earn. To be 'no-one', to be invisible, is defined as failure—to be cast in the role of one of life's losers, unworthy of recognition. There are many rewards for the 'winners' and an equal number of penalties for the 'losers'. Achievement of the hallowed identity of being 'someone' is rewarded with visibility and the capacity to affect and change the world around us. The penalty for being 'no-one' is to be sentenced to the shadows of life; the purgatory of being able to feel, being affected by life's rhythms and changes, but being powerless to respond to or affect what is received. Success is graded through our lives—by our families, our peers, our churches, by the standards of our culture and by the standards of our own expectations. Commendations, credentials, trophies and awards bear witness to our power to succeed. Loneliness, rejection and feelings of unworthiness are the companions of the 'losers'. The path to being 'someone' is through the accepted and sanctioned identities dictated by the authorities that impact upon our lives.

Girls are introduced at an early age to the paths available to them in the journey to become 'someone'. Beauty and cuteness are rewarded; sexual attractiveness will assure approval. They will be encouraged to excel and to learn how to dismiss their excellence. They will learn to have power yet never to be threatening; to be independent while still knowing how to display an appealing vulnerability that invites protection. In carefully adhering to the unwritten rules that define femininity, contemporary women will be awarded the deeply cherished identity of being 'someone'.

Our lives are a map of the searches we undertake in our quest for identity. The variety of roles we have adopted or had thrust upon us, the choices we make and the changes we initiate record our search for an identity we feel in harmony with, that embodies authenticity. We search for the 'real' self that enables us to live with dignity and integrity. Certainty about our identity is equated with happiness and security and is seen to be the authority that will liberate us from the chains of external expectations. We are clearly familiar with the pain that is the consequence of being deprived of this inner authority. In its absence we live reflexively, reacting to the feedback, demands and expectations of others. The showering of praise and approval upon us from others allows us to accept ourselves whereas negativity or judgment leave us devastated, doubting in our own worth and value. Divorced from inner authority our lives become not an embodiment of freedom but of fear and avoidance as our sense of 'self' becomes entirely dependent upon how we are perceived by others or is graded solely in the light of the authority of internalised expectations.

No-one is born with an unshakeable or pre-formed sense of 'self' or identity. Rather like clay, our childhood identities are shaped and moulded by the power of the authorities that surround us and guide us. Love, acceptance, forgiveness and generosity make profound impressions upon us, influencing our sense of 'self' and shaping the ways in which we relate to the world around us. The child who is showered with love and care will invariably find itself walking a different path in life than the child who is abused and rejected. Inevitably we face the power of the expectations, standards and values of the authorities in our lives and these too profoundly influence our sense of identity and flavour the relationships we form with others.

Through the impact of the authorities in our lives we learn to see ourselves through the eyes of others and to become what other people would like us to be. These are not the lessons only derived in suppressive or abusive childhoods. Even the most loving of parents, the dearest of friends, bequeath to those dear to them the legacy of their own standards, values and expectations. We inherit self-definition, partially through its imposition upon us and partially because of our longing for it. The feedback we receive from the authorities in our lives, based on our response to their expectations and standards, creates an appetite within us. The hunger for approval, acceptance and love; the apprehensiveness over disapproval, rejection or contempt. The Ugly Duckling was not only a casualty of the rejection she received from others, but was equally a casualty of her own appetite for acceptance and affirmation. She could not be held to blame for this appetite—clearly it was an inevitable consequence of her misunderstanding of who she was.

Maturity in our lives is understanding that we do not need to live as an obedient and fearful subject of the tyrannical appetite for approval and affirmation. Experience and wisdom teach us the folly of constantly listening and looking only outwardly and upwardly for guidance and authorisation. A Zen master was once asked, 'What is the source of good judgment?' He answered, 'Experience.' 'And what is the source of experience?' he was further questioned. 'Bad judgment', was his reply. Our experience teaches us that to pin our sense of worth, value and identity to the changing expectations and desires of others is to endlessly wander in the world seeking for permission to be. As the Ugly Duckling wandered endlessly, craving to find a home which would offer her a sanctioned identity, we too remain perpetually homeless if our self-definition depends upon the permission of anything outside of ourselves. The gift of experience and inner listening teaches us to no longer link our choices, directions or aspirations upon what we perceive the rewards to be. We know deeply that approval and affirmation are poor substitutes for authenticity, that blame or disapproval can never be taken as any true measure of our worth or our being. Wisdom teaches us to look beyond the limits of performance and appearance for self-understanding and to find the courage to discard identities which offer only a shallow appearance of authenticity.

In the Tibetan tradition of Buddhism there is portrayed a realm of phantom-like beings whose existence is governed by the compulsion for repletion and gratification. Their hunger is endless and powerful, driving them to a ceaseless search for appeasement. In their wanderings they are faced with an infinite variety of feasts and delights offering the possibility of satisfaction. The difficulty the hungry ghosts face is being born with the tiniest of throats which prevent them from quenching their appetite. The possibilities of contentment are endlessly denied to them, so they wander on, casualties of their own hunger. This, too, is the experience we endure when exiled from inner authenticity. The world appears to offer us so many possibilities in the form of identities, roles and existences. We need only to glance through any contemporary women's magazine to be beguiled by the array of identities, appearances and roles that undertake to deliver happiness and accomplishment. Despite their promise of fulfilment and freedom, few are able to realise their pledge while we remain exiled from the authenticity of our own being.

Divorcing ourselves from the tyrants of approval and disapproval is one of the greatest challenges of our journeys, just as the capacity to listen inwardly is one of the greatest arts of the spiritual path. Weaning ourselves from dependency upon others for affirmation is the beginning of an inner exploration to discover the source of the hunger that propels us to adopt unauthentic identities. It is not a rejection of the authorities which impact our sense of being. It is born of the innate understanding that we can never be who we are as long as we are addicted to being who someone else wants us to be.

There are inevitable companions that accompany any authoritarian standard, value or expectation. Blame, judgment and rejection are the consequences we receive for non-conformity to the expectations and models that are sanctioned by our social structures. Praise, approval and acceptance are showered upon us when our performance and appearance satisfy those expectations and models. Blame and rejection leave us isolated, homeless and starved of inclusion. Through praise and acceptance we learn the warmth of belonging and sanctuary. Dispossessed of an authentic sense of being, the refuge of inclusion comes to be treasured above all else. In the desperation of our dispossession the authorities in our lives are endowed with an archetypal power to save us or to condemn us. They appear to possess ultimate dominion over the polarities of right and wrong, acceptable and unacceptable, good and bad.

Kamila is one of the numerous young Asian women, born and raised in the west, who are now confronting the power of cultural expectation. Preparing her application for college, her parents told her that a marriage had been arranged for her. Her initial refusal invited weeks of argument and coercion. Her family told her that if she refused she would be cast out of the family forever and bring unbearable shame to them. They would not support her in her course, nor would she ever be welcomed again in her community. Her older women relatives told endless tales of the terror of being outcast, unmarried and rejected. Her father and brothers refused to allow her out of the house. Eventually she agreed to the marriage on the condition that her husband would permit her to continue her studies. It was a short-lived commitment. Her husband forced her to quit her course and stay within the home; he felt shamed by her independence. Soon afterwards he began to beat her. The first time she ran to her parents, but when her husband turned up they returned her to him. Eventually she ran away and found refuge in a hostel. Even there she found herself unable to escape the power of her community's dictates. She believed herself to be a failure through her inability to accept the model provided for her. She cried endless tears over the shame she had brought upon her family. It took months of recovery for her to understand that their shame was not her shame, nor were their models and commandments sacred.

The territory of the authorities in our lives seems boundless, covering every aspect of appearance and performance. Models are dispensed which inform us of the acceptable shape we must mould our bodies into while seers of the fashion industry prescribe the ways in which we must present ourselves. Authorities provide us with models which govern performance—the values our lives should embody, the goals that are worth striving for and the modes of living that should be disdained. Our minds and hearts are not exempted from models dispensed by a variety of authorities. Endless books inform us of the right fantasies to entertain, the correct ways of loving, the correct sexual experience to seek and categorise feelings into acceptable and unacceptable.

The endlessness of the standards and the rewards promised for their achievement stimulate our own appetite for identity, approval and belonging. The lure of infinite rainbows creates a perpetual hunger to discover an identity in which we can rest. To be actively engaged in a search for definition offers an identity in itself which attracts approval. To be seen to be trying, improving ourselves, perfecting ourselves, to be busily engaged in the search for a 'real' self is sufficient to save us from disapproval. We may not yet qualify to be a winner but at least we will not be classed as a loser as long as we are involved in the pursuit of identity.

Self-improvement is a powerful addiction. We can be so engaged in its satisfaction that we forget to pause and ask ourselves whose rainbow we are pursuing and the real worth of the rewards that are offered. We mould our bodies into the right shape, don our power suits, get our promotions and entertain the right kinds of thoughts and feelings. As we hang our diplomas on the wall and receive the handshakes of our bosses, we may well find that our appetite for identity remains unsatisfied. Like going on a long and demanding journey only to discover that we are travelling on the wrong train, we too may discover that the rewards we receive for all our efforts look unhappily and suspiciously different to the ones we hoped for or were promised.

The perseverance that sustains the Ugly Duckling in her search for identity is a theme that is endlessly repeated in our fairy tales and in the spiritual stories that inspire us. We are encouraged never to surrender, never to succumb to resignation, despair or hopelessness, but to continue seeking, questioning and exploring. Tenacity alone sustains many of the heroines in mythology. Adversity, rejection, criticism and doubt are encountered, yet the warrior spirit in our heroines refuses to accept the vocabulary of the impossible, unreachable or of failure. Tenacity is found not only in our story books but in the hearts of women who are committed to their quest for wisdom, dignity and love. The nuns of the Sisters of Mercy caring for the dying in Calcutta will never see in their lifetimes an end to the stream of the sick and dying. They continue to seek the face of God in each person they touch. The lone woman struggling to raise her children alone in one of our inner cities amidst violence and danger, and who still finds the kindness to care for a sick neighbour speaks to us of the power of tenacity.

Transformation is one of the most oft-repeated words in the spiritual vocabulary. Transformation involves perseverance, action, effort and dedication. In the demise of the era of the fairy godmothers, transformation is clearly linked to our own commitment and energy. There is a vast difference between the 'doing' that is born of the disbelief in inner authenticity and the 'doing' that is born of inner listening and wisdom. 'Doing' that is born of a hunger for identity, approval and affirmation will focus solely upon enhancing appearance and performance. Like the Ugly Duckling, it is a relentless attempt to make a nest in someone else's home. There is an underlying thread of desperation to our 'doing' as it takes place beneath the assessment of someone else's standards or our own internalised expectations. Am I good enough? Have I changed enough? Have I pleased? These are the underlying questions and threats that lie behind our efforts. Effort born of wisdom and the willingness to learn is dedicated to the enhancement of freedom. Appearance and performance are non-issues; a qualitative deepening of happiness and freedom are the only measures we employ to assess the worth of our 'doing'. In the journey of the spiritual warrior there is no desperation in the perseverance she brings to her quest for freedom, but a profound grace and receptivity.

Whether the authorities that impact upon our lives are malevolent or benevolent is secondary to our relationship to them. Dispossessed of inner authority and authenticity we create child-like relationships to authorities—regardless of whether they are external or internalised. They appear to possess ultimate and sacred power to bestow banishment or acceptance; consequently we perceive that the only way to be sanctioned by them is through conformity. There is a vast gap which lies between us and the authorities we find ourselves looking up to for guidance. The archetypal 'gods' which overshadow our lives are invested a power, supremacy and 'rightness' which appears unobtainable to us. The 'gods' of parents, teachers, media models or spiritual commands appear to occupy a territory of superiority and flawlessness we can never match. In a child-like relationship to these authorities we settle for the windfalls of affirmation and approval rather than trusting that authority can be reclaimed inwardly. Appearance and performance, conformity and obedience become the tickets for gaining the praise and identity we seek. They equally provide us with an appearance of credibility and authority.

When Tessa was going through a particularly intense period of confusion in her life she found herself attracted to a spiritual group that offered very specific guidelines and doctrine. Arriving at meetings she was always welcomed warmly and enthusiastically and increasingly the group became her family, providing her with direction, love and guidance. She was able to have decisions made for her and her life, in many ways, became simpler. It was when she found herself asking for permission to take time to visit her family and having the permission refused that she realised the degree to which she had surrendered her freedom in exchange for the privilege of belonging.

The lineage of archetypal authorities continues in the spiritual life. We form relationships with teachers and guides, trusting in their experience and wisdom to shepherd and inspire us in our journeys. The beginnings of these relationships are marked by an unavoidable inequality. The hierarchy of teacher and student, guru and disciple is no stranger to us. It features in our families, our education, our work and in our spiritual quests. One of the participants in this relationship hands down advice, wisdom, paths and models while the other is the recipient. One of the participants appears to possess the knowledge and the authority while the other is desirous of learning and absorbing the wisdom that is offered. In itself this hierarchy is neither negative nor positive. Both humility and sincerity in our search ask us to have a willingness to learn, to receive guidance and to be honest in relation to what we understand and what we do not understand. The hierarchies we encounter in our life and our spiritual journeys possess the potential for deepening in wisdom or for endangering our own freedom. Which potential is fulfilled and realised depends upon the skillfulness and wisdom of both participants in the relationship.

The danger that shadows anyone in a position of authority is that they become overly fascinated with their own appearance and performance. Power carries an addictive potential. To be the recipient of admiration and adulation is immensely satisfying to anyone addicted to power, leading to a deep reluctance to relinquish the role of supremacy. The role can only be protected by maintaining the separation between parent and child, teacher and student, guru and disciple. Power, born of this grasping, is inevitably abused. Spiritual control, at times called devotion, bears remarkable similarity to the control exerted by abusive parents or teachers. Blame and isolation become the weapons that are used to ensure conformity and obedience. Praise and affirmation are the hooks that are used to ensure that the relationship continues. The authority becomes authoritarian; everyone involved colludes in the maintenance of the hierarchy as everyone benefits—no matter how distorted those benefits are. The child, student or disciple is sheltered by the authority, has a sense of belonging in the hierarchy and gains both identity and certainty. The blossoming of the countless sects which abound in the spiritual life are clear expressions of these relationships. They continue to feature a central authority figure and there are rarely, if ever, any graduates. To the student who is dispossessed of inner authority, graduation seems a small sacrifice to make in the face of the more immediate benefits of belonging and affirmation.

In this distorted hierarchy both the authority and the student become invisible through clinging to the identities they inhabit. The authority is made invisible as they become a model, an image, and through the appearance of perfection and infallibility that everyone has an investment in maintaining. The exposure of their humanness and their fallibility would lethally endanger the hierarchy—dissolving the separation between teacher and student, authority and acolyte. The student, disciple, child or devotee becomes invisible through their dependency upon the authority and the projection of supremacy upon them. Appearance and performance become all-important to the inwardly dispossessed and homeless for these are the only means available to secure their identity and sense of belonging. Countless people begin a spiritual journey inspired by the possibilities of freedom that are offered only to find themselves overcome by the habit of their addiction to praise and affirmation. The performance of 'show and tell' that featured in our lives as school children is repeated as we produce the experiences, words, responses and actions that will earn us the acceptance and praise that affirms our place and identity in the hierarchy.

Hierarchies may be inevitable when we enter into any territory of learning and exploration unfamiliar to us. Their inevitability does not imply rigidity or the perpetuation of separation. The credentials of any authority lie in their utter dedication to our graduation and their refusal to become hypnotised or enthralled with their own appearance and performance. A wise authority has no interest in conformity from their disciple nor any interest in praise or blame as means of maintaining the umbilical cord that supports the hierarchy. They are willing to learn, humble in their wisdom and willing to be taught. They celebrate and welcome the stumbling and the strides of their disciples, children or students. They have the wisdom not to mistake appearance and performance for truth. They have no fear of being displaced by the visibility of their children, students or devotees, but deeply understand that this visibility is an embodiment of the freedom they are committed to.

The warrior woman approaches the hierarchies she encounters with great care. Her journey to discover what is authentic and free within herself is a sacred quest. In exploring the identities she inhabits, in her quest to discover a home within herself that is free of boundaries, she must inevitably explore her own relationship with authority. She will encounter the child in herself who thrives on praise and affirmation, who longs to belong. She may meet the rebellious child, so distrustful of authority that she is unable to receive compassionate guidance from another. She may meet the child who crumbles before the face of authority, locked within her own terror of homelessness and isolation. That child, deeply rooted in her conditioning, will emerge as she meets the variety of authorities she encounters in her journey. The feminine warrior will be challenged to find the balance between listening outwardly and trusting inwardly; between a willingness and openness to learn and the integrity of her own search. She will choose her teachers wisely without ever forgetting that her greatest teacher lies within her own story and experience. Understanding the shallowness and fragility of identities that are based upon appearance and performance, she is willing to explore the experience of homelessness, knowing that it is the death of unauthentic identities that allows for renewal of vision.

A Zen teacher once said with a great smile, 'When my house burned down I gained an unobstructed view of the moonlit sky.' Our identities are like the wall we build around ourselves to find sanctuary in. Encouraged by our culture to ceaselessly pursue the goal of being 'someone', we may find ourselves stunned to suddenly encounter the variety of spiritual teachings which proclaim the wisdom of being 'no-one'. It is a statement that evokes our greatest fears of invisibility and homelessness. At the same time it finds an echo of response and joy in our hearts. We sense the liberation accessible to us in laying down the burden of constantly being a sparkling personality, a successful parent, partner, worker; of needing to make impressions upon the world that will bring merit and credentials. We sense the joy possible for us when our lives no longer revolve around proving ourselves or chasing approval. From the perspective of fear the possibility of being 'no-one' opens the door to endless terrors and darkness. From the perspective of trust and dedication to freedom it is a possibility that opens the door to the emergence of authenticity and freedom.

Anyone who has ever undertaken any sustained period of silence, meditation and exploration appreciates that a process is set in motion which strips away all of the images and identities which have previously defined us. It is a process which introduces us to a profound inner openness and vulnerability—we are naked and visible to ourselves. Our terrors, demons and imperfections are revealed; our capacities for courage, trust and perseverance are tested. The same process is experienced in the face of radical changes and shifts in our lives which disturb or upset our sense of order. Loss, rejection, disillusionment, failure are all experiences which open us to the same qualities of vulnerability and homelessness. They strip us of the roles, order and certainties which have previously sustained our identities. These are crucial moments in our lives—they beckon us to discover what is truly authentic; what cannot be lost or stripped away. The warrior woman, who is committed to freedom, learns to welcome these turning points, despite the terrors that are hinted at.

Turning points, chosen or unchosen, ask us to reach within ourselves and summon forth the qualities of integrity, wise effort and patience to explore their potential; they are open doorways. Being 'no-one' doesn't demand that we shave our heads, don robes and retreat to the nearest monastery. Nor does it invite us to sink into inertness, hoping to be struck by a grand revelation of authenticity. Understanding what it means to be 'no-one' is not a sentence of invisibility but an encouragement to see beneath the layers of identities which may well only camouflage our uniqueness, creativity and authenticity. The quest to understand what it means to be 'no-one' releases a vital and creative energy to explore what is true. In this exploration we are asked to learn the skill of balancing receptivity and action; to combine the qualities of the benevolent grandmother with the vitality of the creative warrior.

The path of the warrior woman is distinguished by her will-ingness to attend to the quality of every step she takes. If her journey is to be a sacred journey, one of dignity and compas-sion, she knows that it must be founded upon the bedrock of unassailable ethics and integrity. Her personal morality, hon-esty and sense of honour are what provide the wisdom to make choices that are not blurred by anxiety or conditioned by the desire to please. Integrity and ethics guide her between the extremes of devaluing herself into invisibility or basing her visibility only upon what she produces or performs. It would not be an overstatement to say that freedom cannot be divorced from integrity and ethics. Personal integrity informs the words we speak, the actions we perform, the quality of the relationships we form with others and ourselves.

The ethics which enrich our exploration of freedom are not concerned with absolutes of right and wrong, good and bad, acceptable or unacceptable. Codes of ethics based upon such absolutes may provide rules to govern our behaviour and appearance and provide us with an appearance and a perfor-mance which are sanctioned but may equally lack the authen-ticity that can only be provided through our own wisdom. Women have a long history of obeying commands for good-ness and selflessness. Discarding this history, it remains clear that women's sense of personal integrity is deeply interwoven with the ethic of care. Consciously and unconsciously we live beneath the umbrella of understanding the undeniable inter-connectedness and interdependence that bonds us with all life. Our bodies reflect nature's rhythms, our seasons are reflected in the world around us, our hearts carry the same potential for joy and fear as any other heart. The consequences of our actions, choices and words ripple in the world, just as we are touched by the ripples of every other life. The knowledge of this on a cellular level inevitably informs the ethics and integrity that shape our lives. In a survey done on the ethics of euthanasia, the majority of men questioned concerned themselves with the process and result of such a decision. The majority of women questioned responded with their own questions concerning how such a decision would affect all of the involved participants. Integrity is the embodiment of sensitivity, love and compassion, honours interconnectedness and is the foundation of the journey of the warrior woman.

Care also provides its own dilemma to many women. Ideals of selflessness have the power to suffocate the truth of our own needs and aspirations. Dedicating ourselves to the physical, emotional and psychological needs of others satisfies our ideals of selflessness yet may equally demand the sacrifice of personal integrity. Not hurting others, caring for others can become absolutes that lead directly to invisibility. Learning how to protect and care for themselves are lessons countless women are still in the process of understanding. In an investigation conducted to attempt to understand the rising cases of AIDS in heterosexual women, it was discovered that many women felt unable to protect themselves. One woman summarised the dilemma saying, 'If I was to produce a condom to a new-found partner he might assume I was a "whore" or had contrived the encounter. He might think I didn't trust him or become suspicious of me. It's easier to let it go.'

There is little time for the honouring of personal direction, wisdom or truth when our lives are busily consumed in satisfying the bottomless wells of other peoples needs. The ideal woman practises selflessness in every moment of her day, as she wipes her children's faces, pleases her employers or employees, flatters and supports her mate and then dwindles with exhaustion and frustration. Guilt strikes at the thought of caring for herself or craving time for her own aspirations. There is always another need which is more pressing and more significant. Entangled by her ideals of selflessness, the moments of solitude or creativity she is able to find amidst the relentless schedule of meeting others demands cannot be appreciated or explored wholeheartedly. They are seen to be moments that detract from the well-being of someone else— who is essentially more important. 'Selfish' is a word that carries the power to hobble the journey of countless women. In a partnership that is faced with the reality of caring for an aging relative, a sick child, a family crisis, it is invariably assumed that the woman will volunteer to sacrifice her time, work and creativity. The very imbalance of a life which finds its purpose only through caring for or pleasing others is a betrayal of personal integrity. It expresses not interconnectedness and interdependence but separation, hierarchy and invisibility.

Integrity cannot be found in a life in which the truth of our own needs and aspirations is constantly superseded by the needs of others or by the imperatives of our own addiction to pleasing others. Nor can integrity be found in a life which is dedicated to the enhancement and perfection of 'self' as a way of being visible to ourselves or in the world. The perfection of 'self' is a full time job—analysing the past, altering our bodies and personalities, obsessing about our imperfections and possibilities of perfection, formulating goals and pursuing ideals. It is also an endless task—the permutations of self are boundless in their possibilities.

A woman who had gone through many radical changes in her life in a very short period of time described the way in which she began her journey to discover her real 'self'. Having been stripped of her relationship, her role, and facing a future of boundless possibilities, she began to leaf through women's magazines hoping for a sense of direction. Presented to her were the countless images of the 'someone' it was possible for her to strive for. The earth mother, the executive, the mysterious model, the victim—endless possibilities offering a life complete with its own rules, appearance and goals. Saved by her own wisdom, she realised that none of these offered authenticity and that to pursue any one of them would entail the sacrifice of integrity.

A journey based upon integrity, which treasures freedom, is rooted in the ethic of care; it is equally free from hierarchies. 'Self' is not superseded by 'other' nor is 'other' superseded by 'self'. Understanding interconnectedness is to know that the quality of all life is essentially interwoven. Integrity embraces the willingness to be responsible for the consequences of our actions and choices. Self-sacrifice and self-negation may offer the appearance of selflessness—too often they are a sacrifice of integrity. Resentment, contempt and invisibility are their offspring. Integrity is directly related to our capacity to consciously honour interconnectedness, freedom and wisdom. Knowing what contributes to suffering, conflict and alienation; knowing what enhances understanding, freedom and wellbeing—these are the building blocks of integrity that allow us to live our lives with honour.

Integrity is embodied in the quality of effort, the quality of graceful 'doing' that guides our journey of transformation. The warrior woman explores the balance of receptivity and effort. In any effort to bring transformation we walk a finely-balanced tightrope. Ambition, striving and control are the expressions of effort that are alienated from grace and receptivity. Lethargy, resignation, complacency and the acceptance of limited horizons express an inner surrender to self-doubt. Effort is the natural expression of dedication—no-one can walk our path for us. Letting go of the limiting nurturing, the qualities that enhance freedom, without ever being preoccupied with superficial goals of improvement or modification—this is effort that is sacred.

Effort is needed to honour and to foster the wholesome, skilful qualities of being already present within us. Sensitivity, compassion, love, clarity and dedication are no strangers to any of us. They express the deepest longings of our hearts and we are intimate with their power to foster forgiveness and peace. Learning to celebrate and manifest our own power to heal, transform and live in a sacred way requires clearly-focussed effort. Learning how to honour herself, to cultivate appreciation and respect for the nobility of her heart and journey is intrinsic to the warrior's journey. It is the effort intended to counter the habit of devaluation that hobbles the spirit of the warrior.

There are many moments when, floundering in confusion, effort is needed to foster and cultivate the qualities of heart and mind that we intuit will bring healing and freedom. In moments of darkness we are tempted to follow familiar pathways of reaction. Blame, guilt, self-doubt and denial rear their heads to tell us of the impossibility of our quest. Yet every woman holds within her reservoirs of compassion, courage and perseverance. Wisdom tells her to pause when she stumbles. The compassion and courage she needs to illuminate the darkness and begin again are only the next moment away.

Wise effort is equally the heartfelt willingness to abandon the qualities of heart and mind, conditioned by repetition, that lead only to imbalance, confusion and the suffocation of our spirit. Our experience tells us clearly what brings sorrow to our lives. We know the ways in which our journeys and freedom are distorted through fear, self-judgment, doubt and through our appetite for acceptance. Learning the lessons of our experience is expressed through our unwillingness to keep repeating them. Renouncing the habits of limitation is a profound expression of trust in our potential and in our essential freedom. The courage of renunciation is an honouring of the warrior spirit.

Conscious effort is needed to consciously avoid the unskilful, the debilitating, the disempowering qualities of heart and mind and modes of being that undermine freedom and integrity. Avoidance can be a child of wisdom as well as a consequence of fear. The habit of investing in performance and appearance is powerful, the habit of disenfranchising ourselves from authenticity has a long and involved history. The habit of being tempted to seek identity through others, to pursue avenues that offer safety rather than freedom may be overly familiar to us. We know where the pathways of self-judgment, doubt and negation lead us. Determination to no longer travel pathways of sorrow requires effort that is rooted in wisdom. Dedication to authenticity is manifested in our willingness to abandon the habits of pain; it is an honouring of our freedom and the truth of our being.

Sacred effort is the art of finding the balance of action and grace. It is an alert vigilance, a creative responsive that is not bound by formulas but intimately rooted in our responsiveness to each moment. It is not directed to becoming 'someone', to constructing a new, more attractive identity, but to learning the art of being. The art of connectedness is the willingness to listen to and learn from the changing inner rhythms of our own being. In the open-hearted sensitivity we bring to being present with ourselves we are visible to ourselves.

The warrior woman embraces the authority of her own vision—trusting profoundly in the heritage of freedom and authenticity that lies within her. Honouring this authority, she is wholeheartedly willing to be 'no-one' yet totally dedicated to communicating and embodying the creativity and freedom she treasures. She can dance without ever being a dancer, paint without ever being a painter and love without ever being a lover. The warrior woman cannot be confined by definition. She is questing for what is true and authentic but not obsessed with goals or destinations. Her quest is rooted in her present, guided by patience and wisdom. Conclusions, definitions and descriptions fall away in her profound dedication to wisdom and freedom. She learns how to honour the forms in her life without ever needing to be defined by them. She learns how to grow through the pain in her life without being cowed by it. She learns how to travel her path with grace and compassion. The warrior woman is visible to herself and makes visible in her world the wisdom and compassion that guide her.

FIVE

MULTITUDE OF VOICES
THE JOURNEY HOME

When the farmer went out to milk his cows in the misty light of dawn he found a young girl wandering in the farmyard. Dismayed at the sight of her pinched, tear-streaked face he knelt before her. 'Who are you? Where do you come from? How did you get here? Where are your parents?' The questions burst from him but the only reply he received was more tears and an anguished croaking. The kindly man picked her up in his arms and carried her into the kitchen, calling for his wife. They bustled around her, wrapping her in a blanket, pulling her chair near the warmth of the stove and plying her with hot milk. Before long the tears stopped, but no matter how many questions they asked, the tiny girl could only answer with a hoarse croak. As the days went by the mystery of the lost girl proved impossible to solve. It seemed she had lost the power to speak, and no-one in the surrounding countryside had any news of a lost child.

Being gentle and warm-hearted people, the couple made a place in their home for the lost girl, loving her as they did their other children. She would follow in their footsteps as they did their chores, but nothing they could do could bring a smile to her face or entice her to speak. Not everyone the little girl met was filled with the same kindness. When she met the neighbouring children they would tease her for her solemn face and make fun of the harsh croaks that came from her lips. She would stand apart and watch them at play and run away whenever the teasing became too painful. Her adoptive mother would comfort her and promise her that one day she would be able to speak and be happy again. Instead things only seemed to get worse. Going to the village school, the teacher would become impatient with her refusal to answer and scold her. This would delight the other children who would tease her even more. At night she would lie, lonely and forlorn in her little bed, and a familiar dream would come to her. She remembered nothing of how she had come to the farmer's house, but each night as she lay in her bed she would dream of another time.

In her dream there was a wondrous castle, filled with light and music. She saw herself running and playing in the castle courtyard and her heart would fill with happiness. In her dream she was always singing—singing to the birds, the people around her and singing to herself. Lying in her bed, the dream would become more real to her than the walls around her and she would begin to sing. It was a song from another time, a song from her dreams and in singing it, her loneliness and unhappiness would vanish. The song was her secret.

As the years passed, the little girl grew, but remained silent and alone. She retreated more and more into the land of her dreams, waiting for the nights to come so she could sing her song and lose herself in her dreams of a happier time and place. Her adoptive parents despaired and the other children became even more cruel in their taunting as her differences set her even more apart from them. In the hours of her lonely nights, the young girl became more and more convinced that she had to go out and look for her dream. She knew that only if she found the castle in her dreams would she also find her voice and her happiness.

One morning, as the household slept, she slipped out of her bed and crept out of the house and the farmyard. Running across the field she reached the edge of the dark and gloomy forest just as the sun was beginning to rise. Stopping to look around, she saw three paths. One went back the way she had come and in the distance the lights in her old home seemed to call her back to its warmth. One path was level and well-worn, running along the edge of the forest to the village on the horizon and the last path led straight into the heart of the dark forest. The wind swayed the branches in the towering trees and small animals rustled in the undergrowth. The sounds seemed to shriek at her to go away and she trembled with fear. Yet she knew she had travelled the other paths and had never found her castle. She began to sing the song of her dreams and walked into the forest. The moment she entered it the light disappeared and she stumbled over fallen logs, scratching herself on the thorns of the brambles and tearing her hair on the branches she pushed through. Throughout the day she pushed on, even as her fear seemed to scream at her, 'Go back. Go back.' When she looked behind her she realised that she had lost the path and could not go back even if she wished. Night fell and the tears ran down her face as she huddled beneath a tree. 'Look what has happened to me for following a dream,' she thought; ' I am more lost and alone than ever.' Cold and exhausted she fell asleep, planning to find her way back to the farm in the morning. Too tired even to sing her song, her last waking thoughts were of her failure.

The calling of the birds woke her and she rose with a heavy heart, thinking of the day that lay before her. As she looked around her she realised that the forest was not so dark as the day before and in the distance a light seemed to beckon her. With new hope she plotted her path in her mind, determined to reach the light that day. As the day went on she realised she had been travelling in circles despite her plan and the light was just as distant as before. 'Stupid girl', she scolded herself. 'Why don't you just give up. You can't do anything right, not even follow a light.' Another day was over and again too tired even to sing a line of her song, she fell asleep with her own harsh words ringing in her ears.

Waking in the morning she felt a new surge of hope as she focussed on the light. 'All I have to do is keep my eyes on the light, let nothing distract me and I will find my way out of the forest', she told herself. Setting off without ever taking her eyes off the light, she stumbled through the undergrowth. So intently did she fasten her eyes to the light, she was unable to look where she was putting her feet. Many times she stumbled, scratching and cutting herself, and she never saw the gaping hole before her until she tumbled into it. Hours passed as she clawed her way to the surface, only to find the light she'd followed had once more been swallowed up by the gloom of the forest. All that lay before her was another night of despair.

As the sun rose a new thought came to her. 'If I cannot find my dream through all the ways I have tried, I must make my dream come to me.' Settling herself beneath the shelter of the tree, she began to sing to herself the song of her dreams. With her singing her heart shed the despair of the days before and began to lighten with happiness. Closing her eyes she lost herself in her song and her fears and her desperation fled. Opening her eyes she saw that the light she had been chasing was all around her; it took only a few steps to leave the gloomy forest behind her. On a hill before her she saw the castle she had seen a thousand times in her dreams. The people in the grounds saw her and with joyful cries came running to surround her. Her mother, her father, her brothers and sisters kissed and hugged her with delight crying, 'We have found you at last. So long you have been lost and in our hearts we have longed for you.' The young girl opened her mouth and from it came not the harsh croaking of her lost days but a sweet and musical voice. 'My dream has brought me home. It is I who have found you.' Opening the door to the castle, she went in and found it all just as it had been in her dream.

A sacred journey is one that is guided by intuition and vision. To travel a journey dedicated to freedom and understanding we must set aside our distractions and preoccupations and learn to listen inwardly. The world is filled with experts willing to offer us prescriptions and formulas, yet none of them can fully define and direct our path or deliver us wisdom. We may be blessed in our lives to receive compassionate and wise counsel from guides and teachers, yet their wisdom cannot substitute entirely for inner attunement and vision. An authentic spiritual path is rooted in the wisdom of our own stories and experiences, and guided by the simple but profound art of being able to listen inwardly. The warrior woman knows the need to find a sanctuary within herself of calm, sensitivity and stillness. There is no 'only' way to discover this inner sanctuary. Meditation, creativity, time spent in nature or simply learning how to pause amidst the myriad of engagements in our lives, are all ways of creating sanctuaries of stillness. The discovery of an inner refuge which offers calm, compassion and spaciousness is a precious gift. Within the sanctuary of inner serenity we learn how to listen to ourselves and how to draw upon the resources of wisdom and clarity that lie within us.

The ethos of our culture which values productivity and consumption, combined with the busyness of our own lives, leads us to devalue the significance of nurturing refuges of calm. The demands in our lives are relentless; endlessly we are called to answer one more imperative. Our sense doors are bombarded with intruding impressions as our minds are filled with the never-ending lists of the tasks that require attention. The busyness of our world and minds trespasses upon the rare moments of calm we carve out of hecticness. There is an extraordinary skill in learning how to balance action and nonaction, giving and receiving, engagement and aloneness. Developing this skill is one of the greatest gifts of compassion we can offer to ourselves. It is also a prerequisite to learning how to listen inwardly that we may be guided by a wisdom that is intuitive.

Every contemplative tradition invites us to be still and turn our attention inward. Ancient and contemporary teachings tell us that this inner attunement is the source of the wisdom that guides us to live in a sacred way. To discover peace in our lives we are asked to understand what it means to be at peace with ourselves. There is an unshakeable link between a life of compassion and dignity and our own capacity to be free of the forces of anger, greed and delusion that breed alienation and sorrow. We explore the most intimate relationship in our lives, our relationship with ourselves, not out of rejection or contempt for the world but as an act of respect. Our inner relationship is a microcosm of every other relationship. It is the wise woman, free of shadows and endowed with an open heart, who knows how to live with wisdom and integrity in her life.

The invitation to be still and listen inwardly has the appearance of great simplicity; in reality it is one of the greatest challenges ever undertaken. Attuning our attention to our changing inner rhythms and movements, the complexity of our inner world quickly becomes apparent to us. Love turns to hatred, elation to depression and courage is swallowed by fear. Our allegiances are mixed and our intentions ambivalent. We rarely find ourselves listening to one singular, integrated voice of inner wisdom that guides us with certainty and clarity in our journeys. More likely we find ourselves listening to a host of competing, often conflicting voices, within our own psyches. Like entering a maze that offers endless choices and possibilities, attuning ourselves to our inner world is to introduce ourselves to a multitude of voices that demand our attention. Within this multitude we listen eagerly and expectantly for the voice of authenticity and truth that will guide us on our paths. Instead we too often hear the babble of a crowd. We are left uncertain about who it is we are listening to, or deafened by the noise of the inner voices that demand our attention.

Every woman knows moments in her life when she is listening to an inner voice that longs for freedom and the end of limitation. She may experience an equal number of moments when that call is drowned by other voices that are dismissive and mistrustful of any such possibility. The voice of creativity and energy spurs us to explore, question and extend ourselves; our inspiration is overwhelmed by an equally strident voice that warns us of danger and the virtues of finding contentment within the boundaries of our lives. A voice within us gladly welcomes the opportunity to be still and listen inwardly; in the next moment we find ourselves involved in a familiar fantasy or hunger for distractedness. We listen to a voice that praises us for our efforts and the genuineness of our quest; it is suffocated in the next moment by the harsh voice of doubt and blame. We encounter the conflicting allegiances we have between grasping and letting go, between trust and fear, faith and doubt. Our loyalties are divided between the safety of the known and the mystery of the unknown, between the quest for authenticity and the familiarity of identity. Each of the voices that call our attention speaks to us with great conviction and logic, leading us to flounder in confusion.

A woman undertook a long, silent retreat determined to discover a renewal of direction. Instead of bliss she found confusion and described it saying, 'Before I came here I was a pretty normal person. My life felt a little flat but there was no great problem I came here to resolve. After two days of listening to myself I've begun to believe I am possessed of multiple personalities. I begin a meditation determined to be calm and find myself planning menus. Instead of renewal of vision I'm replaying every hurt I suffered in the playground. I go for a walk to look at the forest and return to find that my entire walk was so preoccupied with fantasy that I saw nothing. I came to be with myself and it seems I've brought with me every single person I've ever had an argument with and the dialogues are still continuing. I tell my mind to be still and it chatters. I tell myself how grateful I should be for the luxury of this time without demands and instead I'm planning all the activities I've postponed. The only thing that is clear to me is that it would be a mistake to draw any conclusions. The voices that move me are so contradictory that it is impossible to know what is authentic. All that I can do is be still and listen well, and trust that everything that is inauthentic will die away.'

Inner listening reveals a medley of inner voices, speaking with their own authority and shatters the facade of a singular, integrated identity. We discover that our consciousness plays hostess to an inner crowd of patterns and tendencies that combine together to give the appearance of identity; an appearance that changes constantly and unpredictably, dependent upon the power of whatever voice is most dominant in our consciousness. The playful child of one moment bears little resemblance to the anxious worrier of the next, the doubter looks very different from the visionary, and the warrior appears irrevocably divorced from the fearful figure that looks for shadows to hide in. This may be a frightening revelation: where is there certainty, integration or oneness amidst these changing faces? We need not be terrorised by this revelation; unravelling the layers of superficiality to discover what is true has spurred every spiritual warrior on the quest to discover authenticity.

In conventional psychological terms, the crumbling of identity may be viewed with alarm. From the perspective of a spiritual journey dedicated to profound understanding, it is welcomed with relief. It is a discovery that enables us to lay down the burden of preserving appearances and definitions that imprison us. Our definitions and images are bound to the past and in being tied to them we are sentenced to repeating the past over and over. No longer believing any definition or image to be the whole truth of ourselves allows the birth of a deeper intuition.

The encounter with the variety of voices that live within us and the division of loyalties we experience in relationship to them, inspires us to ask the questions that are crucial to the warrior's journey. Which of these inner voices enhances our journeys and enriches wisdom? How do we know which voices are authentic, genuine, speaking with wisdom, and which of the voices we are listening to are simply conditioned voices from the past, replaying old and familiar tunes over and over? What quality of listening will enable us to discern the true from the false, to guide us wisely in our quests rather than leading to greater confusion? These are essential questions to ask of ourselves—it is not only the content of what we listen to that informs our journeys and our lives, but equally the quality of attention we bring to listening.

A woman related the relief she felt when, after a lifetime of being told the virtues of being logical and rational, she was encouraged instead to listen to her feelings. For her they became the bastion of truth. If she felt resistance to doing something, she dropped it. If she felt aversion for someone, she assumed that avoidance was the rightful response. If she felt afraid of something, she accepted it as evidence that justified retreating from it. She said, 'I began to notice that feeling had become the new tyrant in my life, arbitrating right and wrong, good and bad. I believed I could trust my feelings but couldn't ignore that many of them were tying me into a world that was free of risk, but also very enclosed.'

The division of loyalties, with its resulting fragmentation, which we encounter in listening to ourselves, reflects the same fragmentation that has wrought alienation in our lives. Dominant voices prescribe for us, command us and lead us into the adoption of values, standards and expectations. Women are raised in an ethos where obedience is recommended and challenge rebuked; gentleness praised and assertiveness criticised. Powerful voices and figures in our lives encourage us to suppress or deny certain aspects of our being and to cherish others. Anger is deemed unfeminine as is ambitiousness, while meekness and even confusion continue to be considered appealingly feminine. We are conditioned by the power of external voices to pursue particular goals and yearnings and to reject others.

Freedom of choice is worshipped in our culture, yet when our choices are unconsciously determined or compelled by the force of a dominant influence or voice, whether inner or outer, our choices are singularly lacking in genuine freedom. There is no freedom in choices rooted in fear or confusion. We may believe we choose to live a life unencumbered by a committed relationship, yet if we do so out of a fear of intimacy, our choice reflects fear and not freedom. We may alternatively believe that a committed relationship is what we have always longed for. If our quest is based on a terror of aloneness rather than the potential that intimacy offers, we may not discern the degree to which we are driven by anxiety.

Deafened by the power of the voices we are exposed to, we end up fragmented and alienated from intuition. The invitation to listen inwardly offers us the opportunity to end this pattern of fragmentation; to bid farewell to the pattern of living in obedience to whichever voice commands us most fervently. To learn how to listen, without being driven by what we hear, provides us with the opportunity to develop a wise intuition, rather than being enslaved by the dominance of conditioning. Like the silent girl, we discover a guide in our intuition that is not deceived by the voices of conditioning.

Listening inwardly we perceive the ways in which our identities are shaped by whatever feeling, impression, thought, image or memory is most dominant in that moment. It is exceedingly difficult to discover within these constantly changing appearances consistency, reliability or refuge. The devotee is replaced by the cynic, the lover follows in the footsteps of the hater, the eager seeker seems only a dim memory when locked in the hold of doubt and mistrust. The images we have relied upon as a way of defining ourselves crumble and it proves impossible to find any sanctuary of stability or predictability within the changing faces and voices that pass through our consciousness.

To be at peace with ourselves we must first discover which 'self' we are meant to be at peace with. Should we honour the devotee or the cynic? Is it the seeker or the protector we should trust? Self-acceptance sounds a wonderful idea—first we must discover which self it is wise to accept. Inner harmony is an attractive ideal, but the spiritual warrior is disinterested in a pseudo-harmony which only superficially embraces the excitements and depressions of our inner voices. The understanding of genuine oneness and peace requires that we dive deeply beneath the appearances that tempt us into beliefs and definitions and discover who we are apart from conditioning. Inner peace and oneness is denied to us when we are repeatedly entangled and ensnared within the multitude of competing, struggling and warring inner voices. Instead we find confusion subscribing to one powerful voice after another. The willingness to listen inwardly, with a compassionate heart, discriminating wisdom and the eye of intuition is to discover an inner oneness that is not subject to fragmentation.

Evoking intuition requires us to be willing to renounce many of our preferences. The voices of our conditioning will endlessly tempt us to follow paths that promise reassurance, ease and comfort. Refraining from their commands we develop a finely-tuned quality of listening that allows us to hear not only the voices that clamour for attention, but also the ones that only whisper. Some of the voices that mould our inner and outer lives are unique to us. They carry our memories of fear and joy, pain and pleasure, and recycle our past in our present, giving it life and continuity. It is also true that many of the voices that plague or encourage us are not unique to us, but feature within the psyche and journeys of every woman who nurtures intuition.

The inspiration that embarks us on a journey of questioning, exploring and opening is the voice of intuition. There is a remarkable power and wisdom embodied within this voice. From it we draw the strength to embrace the shadows and darkness in our world and ourselves and the strength to meet the inevitable challenges and trials of our journeys. Intuition inspires us to continue in our quest for freedom when everything within us calls us to surrender. The voice of wisdom refuses to accept that life is synonymous with conflict and struggle or that separation can ever describe the reality of life. Intuitively we trust that we hold within us the capacity to live as a fully awake, wise and compassionate woman and the sanctity of this trust inspires us to reach for horizons and dedicate ourselves to liberation. Intuition is the mainstay of any spiritual journey—it emboldens us to meet the valleys of our experience with a willingness to learn. It carries the compassion to accommodate the fears, anxieties and frustrations we encounter. Intuition equally holds the clarity and vision that enables us to listen to the chatter of the voices from the past that speak of danger and impossibility, without being overpowered.

There is nothing magical about intuition; we all have within ourselves a body of wisdom that inspires us to see the truth in every encounter in our lives and in every moment in ourselves. Intuition is not the sole property of a spiritually-endowed select minority. Each one of us possesses a finely-tuned intuition—the warrior is learning to listen to it. Intuition is not irrationality, nor is it found in the impulsiveness of being swept before the tide of every powerful feeling or desire that moves us. The voice of intuition is like the wise grandmother that lives within our spirit—her purpose is to preserve, protect and foster our integrity and our freedom. She is the knowing, listening, seeing and discerning consciousness that is always accessible to us. She has the power to filter and wring the truth from the appearances and the voices we are endlessly exposed to in our lives. She knows when to trust and when there is wisdom in doubt, she sees the hidden agendas that lie beneath the world of appearances. She knows when to say yes and when to say no. She is not deceived by the chatter of the world or the babble and commands of her own conditioning. The wise grandmother has travelled the landscape of fear and learnt its lessons. She has listened to the dictates of many voices in her life and knows the time has come to listen to herself.

The spiritual warrior must learn the art of reclaiming her intuition. The reclamation is uncharted territory—we are all asked to find our own ways of learning how to listen to ourselves. If we are surrounded by voices that hold the power to compel and command us in an overwhelming way, we must find the courage to separate ourselves from them. If we are endlessly propelled and distracted by our own fears, anxieties and dependencies, we must have the courage to acquaint ourselves with a greater solitude, unencumbered by the props which consistently divert us from listening inwardly. Creating spaces to be alone and still enables us to listen to our changing inner rhythms, yearnings and fears. The consequences of being alienated from intuition are more than we can afford. If we cannot listen to ourselves we are always going to be listening to someone else. If we are not profoundly connected with the wisdom of our intuition we will be endlessly chained to obedience to voices other than our own.

The voice of intuition is dedicated to the protection of our spirit. To be alienated from it is to enter a spiral of self-destructiveness. Numerous relationships that end in the same pain of abandonment may be more than coincidence. Countless situations that end in the same consequence of surrendering to someone else's authority are asking us to wake up. Our lives become a record of regrets and remorse as a consequence of ignoring our own intuition. Disregarding the intuitive voice within us we suffer a chronic case of retrospective wisdom. Conflict reminds us of the way in which we have ignored the intuition that cautioned us to make different choices and follow different avenues than the ones we adopted. Suffering the ravages of a recent débacle in our lives brought about by bad judgment or disconnection from our own intuition we once more say to ourselves, 'I knew better. I should have listened to myself.' Wisdom tells us to learn from the past; compelled by fear or addiction to pleasure, our hearts close to the lessons we need to learn and the entanglements of the past are repeated again and again. The voices of conditioning that demand certainty and familiarity in our lives propel us into busyness, pursuit or avoidance even while the voice of our own intuition asks us to pause, to be still and to venture down different pathways.

The self-destructiveness that shadows the alienation from intuition takes many forms in our lives. Depression, fantasy, the abuse of our bodies through drugs or food or the adoption of unauthentic existences all tell the story of the consequences of being exiled from intuition. The habit of listening outwardly or listening only to the voices within ourselves that lead to fragmentation or denial are difficult to break. It takes a remarkable courage to salvage our own inner wisdom and to end spirals of self-punishment. If we accept that we hold within us a wise and intuitive inner voice it is valid to ask of ourselves, why we do not listen to her? Years of abuse, fear and oppression clearly can result in our own suppression of inner intuition. Years of addiction to gratification and the avoidance of fear serve to exile us from ourselves. But intuition doesn't die, it is latent and awaiting our attention. Its reclamation awaits our attendance, our willingness to be present within ourselves.

Sheryl began to overeat as a teenager when her parents were in the process of a divorce. The more criticism she received, the more she ate. The more she ate, the more she punished her parents and herself. Yet there was power in her addiction. No-one could control her, everyone was forced to be extraordinarily careful in their relationships with her lest they became responsible for a new eating binge. It was her younger sister who helped her to salvage herself from the spiral of destructiveness. She had loved Sheryl thin, she loved her fat. She was not afraid to ask Sheryl why she was choosing to eat herself into insensibility. She became a mirror for Sheryl, inviting her to understand the way in which she was becoming the victim of her desire to punish someone for the pain she felt.

There may be many moments when we choose not to listen to ourselves or be guided by our intuition. Waking up from numbness can be an extraordinarily painful experience. If our lives have been lived to please others, deriving meaning only through others, then certainty and safety are shattered by the intuition that asks us to discover some more sacred purpose in our lives. If suppression or denial of our own wisdom has brought the rewards of safety, complacency or predictability, inner listening may well result in the loss of those compensations. If inner listening requires us to make radical changes in our choices, lifestyles or identities it is no surprise that we shirk from it. These are the risks the warrior woman is willing to embrace. Better to be alive and at risk than numb and safe. Waking up from numbness is also extraordinarily joyful; nothing can substitute for a profound connection with the vitality of intuition.

In the spiritual life intuition manifests in the voice of the seeker. It is the voice that holds our deepest wisdom and vision. The seeker is the vessel of trust and wisdom that leads us out of defeatism and passivity to explore the land of our yearnings and vision. The seeker refuses to succumb to superficiality but seeks the greatest meaning and truth in herself and in her life. The seeker is not cowed by failure or disappointment, nor is she obsessed with goals and achievements. The seeker is not preoccupied with either past or future, she learns how to rest with wakefulness in the present. She is calmly vigilant, patiently alert, receptive and transformative, a healer and a renunciate. The seeker is empowered by trust and vision to sustain her search for the source of peace and integrity in the face of adversity and apparent impossibility. The whole of the spiritual life is dedicated to learning how to listen to and to honour this voice. Listening to this voice requires a deep commitment. At times it is only a tiny whisper amidst the clamour of the variety of other voices we carry. The genuineness of the seeker is evidenced through the changes she inspires. Her path is to dispel confusion, banish limitation and end sorrow. She is creative and vital, transforming of ourselves and affecting the world she lives in. The concern of the seeker is to be awake, creative and transformative. Learning to listen inwardly, the transparency of judgments, labels and appearances is revealed. The seeker is our guide, alert to the call of wisdom. Like the silent girl who had only a song to sustain her, the warrior woman is guided and sustained by the power of the intuition she learns to listen to. It speaks to her of freedom and possibility.

Intuition is latent and accessible, inviting us to listen. Our capacity to be guided by the wisdom of intuition is linked to the dedication we bring to listening. The seeker is suffocated by the power of conditioned voices that compel and command us, just as it is deafened by the fear that lends a coercive power to the external voices we encounter. At every turning in our lives someone or something awaits us with new prescriptions, goals and directions, carrying a commanding aura. We feel equally compelled by our own inner voices that are endlessly eager to judge, command or frighten us. We need to learn how to pause in the beginnings and turnings we initiate and ask where our guidance comes from. Who or what are we listening to? Wise intuition will guide us to freedom and discovery; the voices of fear or habit will lead us to self-banishment. Disconnection and limitation are externalised not solely through the dictates and commands of the conditioned voices that compel us, but equally through our obedience and consent to them.

A woman may be told it is sinful to protect her family and herself through contraception. To cloak herself in the mantle of sin requires that she consents to the belief of an external authority. A woman may be told that her request to hold authority in her spiritual path is indicative of the spiritual failing of pride. To accept the image of failure requires the surrender of her intuition and the acceptance of the dictates of another.

The impact that authoritarian voices make upon us is determined by our life stories and the conditioning we have been exposed to and carry. A woman carrying a history of rejection is deeply susceptible to the voice of the judge. If criticism and denial have featured in our lives, we are easily tempted by the voices that promise affirmation and praise. The experience of being repeatedly overpowered or discounted in the past gives prominence to the voice of the victim in the present. A history of failure leads us to subscribe to the voice of the achiever or the voice of the loser, dependent upon the ways in which we have understood failure. Our relationship to ourselves in this moment, the choices and directions we follow in our lives, evidence the power of the voices we are listening to. The joy or the sorrow we experience in this moment tells us the story of what is guiding us in our lives. The seeker is smothered by the chatter and the stridency of the conditioned voices we carry. Discriminating wisdom is learning how to listen well and to discern the difference between what benefits us and what undermines us in the messages and guidance we receive.

We may be tempted to assume that the achiever appears only in the tradition of patriarchal warriors who are driven by goals and the desire for achievement. Countless women driven by the need to prove their worth and adequacy equally find themselves compelled by the voice of the achiever. The language of the achiever is one of will power and striving; her vocabulary is concerned with 'should' and 'must'. The achiever has a plan and the realisation of that plan always lies in the future. In pursuit of that plan the achiever has little interest in the present—it is seen only as a currency which can be used to purchase the future and the goals that are desired. In focussing upon the future, the achiever paints a landscape of lofty ideals and dreams and lives in a state of constant evaluation, endlessly alert to the signposts of progress and success. Striving to fulfil the manifold expectations it carries, the achiever is obsessed with its own agendas.

A beautiful woman, raised in an environment of admiration, perceived her beauty as the way to win the ideal partner she envisaged. A woman brought up in a family where her brothers were the recipients of her parents' praise saw her intelligence as the currency that would win the stature she desired. A woman in a religious order, perceiving that unfailing kindness won the favouritism of her superiors, determined to make herself a paragon of selflessness.

Images of desirability are created that represent the expectations of the achiever who then sets out to find an experience that conforms to those images. The images that compel the achiever paint the portraits of the perfect lifestyle, the perfect relationship, the perfect appearance and the perfect experience. The achiever lives in a constant state of discontent as long as she is separated from the attainments she demands. The achiever is obsessed with attainment and success and defines her worth solely upon the basis of achieving desired goals. She relies upon achievement as evidence of credibility. Dismissing the present moment, dismissing the possibility of inner richness and completeness, the achiever is constantly reaching towards the next moment, the next goal, the next experience, believing them to capable of offering what this moment is lacking. The achiever thrives on promises and hope. She is never passive but strident and wilful, believing that transformation relies totally upon her striving.

Accompanying the achiever's obsession with signposts of success and progress is a profound fear of failure and regression. The achiever does not have the wisdom to recognise the inseparable nature of these polarities. Gail, who had achieved tenure in her university after years of struggle and competition, returned home every evening feeling she had just survived a battle. Her life was ruled by her anxiety over the impressions she made upon her students, the popularity she had with her colleagues and the feedback received from her department head. Asked if she enjoyed teaching, she answered that she could not afford to relax enough to enjoy it. Gain lives in the shadow of loss, success in the shadow of failure and praise in the shadow of blame. The achiever, unwilling to acknowledge these shadows, lives in fear of them.

An inevitable companion to the greed for acquisition and the trophies of success is anger. The obstacles to success that are encountered become enemies, and lost within the habit of her own wilfulness the achiever has only one response to perceived enemies—to overpower them through suppression or willpower. The achiever features in our professional lives, our relationships and our spiritual journeys. A woman determined to be the world's best mother or the world's greatest lover is governed by the same compulsions. The achiever finds successes but equally discovers that trophies do little to assuage the bleakness of inner alienation. Driven by the need to prove herself, the achiever travels many paths except the one of greatest importance, the journey to herself. The bleakness that lies in the heart of the achiever spurs her on to a more and more relentless pursuit of credibility.

The achiever is the voice of the inner dictator, the tyrant of our spirit. Appreciating its destructiveness we rarely welcome its appearance yet find ourselves chained in obedience to it. We fear that the consequence of renouncing striving and willpower will be to be sentenced to a bottomless pit of confusion, powerlessness and passivity. Intuitively we know that the next moment in our lives guarantees no more promise of happiness and well-being than the moment we are in, but trust is not one of the achiever's gifts. One of the basic characteristics of the achiever is the unwillingness to learn from her own experience that tells her that discontent and beliefs in unworthiness cannot be resolved through trophies of success or proof of credibility.

The voice of the achiever is deeply rooted within our conditioning and within our psyche. It speaks to us with the authority of countless voices from our past that have questioned our worthiness. It carries the expectations of a legion of other authorities that have impacted upon our lives. The achiever equally is bowed beneath the weight of her own fears of failure and unacceptability. The achiever was born in the classroom in her first introduction to comparison and evaluation. She matured in the schools and professions where the judgment and evaluation of others were interpreted as guidelines for acceptability. She gained strength through the experience of rejection that convinced her of the need to prove herself. She has learnt to equate credentials of success with worthiness and acceptability.

Discontent is the nature of alienation from ourselves, from intuition and from the present moment. Discontent is healed through diving into its source and exploring the nature of inner separation. The spiritual warrior is distinguished from the achiever through the impeccability she brings to her relationship to the present moment and through the wisdom that tells her that the future can never be separated from the present. The spiritual warrior is intent upon transformation and is impelled by vision but she turns not to the next moment but to the one she is in. She doesn't try to fix, overpower or transcend the discontent she may feel, but is willing to allow its ripples to flow through her. She has the patience, compassion and sensitivity to appreciate the learning it is offering.

The spiritual warrior knows that the qualities of acceptance, compassion and serenity are crucial to transformation. She is not intent on proving herself but on knowing how to honour

141

herself. Unwilling to live on promises, she has the courage to disobey the imperatives and commands the achiever imposes. The warrior woman listens to the restlessness of the achiever, appreciates the fear that lies beneath it and intuitively knows that beneath the layers of restlessness lie the serenity, openness and trust that offer an end to the tyrannical voice of our inner dictators. The spiritual warrior aspires for greatness— not for the shallow greatness evidenced by acquisitions or credentials, but for the greatness of heart and spirit born of unconditional openness and compassion. The achiever is strident and demanding, focussed upon the future and pinning her own sense of worth and value to the successes she achieves. The visionary is patient and accepting, focussed upon the present and deriving her own strength and integrity from the genuineness of her commitment to wisdom and transformation.

The achiever is propelled by the power of expectations she carries—her own and the ones she has absorbed and internalised from the authorities that have influenced her past. The authority of expectation imposed upon women—to be good, to be perfect, to succeed, to excel—continue to mould our present through either consenting to them or resisting them. Intense ambition or intense passivity can both be responses to the expectation to be perfect, depending upon whether we consent or resist. Either response gives power and credibility to the expectation. Apart from our consent or resistance the achiever mouths only empty words and commands. The spiritual warrior who knows deeply the power of compassion and acceptance does not seek to exile, suppress or transcend the strident voice of the achiever. She learns to bring to its presence the very qualities it is lacking. She listens, but does not feel compelled to obey; her own intuition has taught her the folly and futility of attempting to discover completeness and happiness through conforming to or resisting expectation. The warrior woman learns to hold the restlessness of the achiever in the spirit of compassion and kindness. Through our willingness to understand the compulsions and fears of the achiever, it serves as a vehicle which deepens intuition.

To partake of the invitation to listen inwardly does not imply that we must subscribe to everything we hear. It is like opening our door to discover a righteous fundamentalist on our doorstep. We can listen to their words with the respect and sensitivity every human being deserves, but this does not sentence us to sign up for a lifetime membership. There is a place and a need for discriminating wisdom in our listening—to be able to discern the difference between what contributes to our well-being and what undermines it; what is useful and what is not. Intuition is the source of discriminating wisdom—learning to listen to the wise instincts within us that guide us to say yes or no, to act or to restrain, and in the face of uncertainty to learn how to pause and wait for the guidance we need. If you have lost a treasure in a murky pond it is unlikely that you will find it through constantly stirring the waters and groping blindly among the weeds. We must learn the patience to allow the mud to settle so the guidance we seek will reveal itself.

Following in the wake of the achiever is the voice of the judge. It is the influence of the judge that determines many of the pursuits and choices of the achiever. The achiever pursues the goals, but it is the judge who selects which of the goals are deemed achievable, for the judge is terrified of failure and lives within the parameters of right and wrong. The achiever is equally terrified of the judge and will make choices that will offer protection from the wrath of the judge. So many journeys are never begun, aspirations never followed, words never spoken and longings never explored because of the prohibitions of the judge. The voice of the inner critic occupies a hallowed seat within our consciousness and carries a wealth of damnations and opinions that evaluate our every action, word, thought and feeling. It is filled with standards, values and decrees about right and wrong, good and bad, acceptable and unacceptable. It shouts at us with the voice of our religious authorities, our parents and social models, extending contempt and praise. The judge rarely rests: even in the sanctuary of sleep the judge appears in our dreams, berating us over the errors we have committed.

The voice of the judge is rarely impartial or objective—its interest is not so much in justice as in punishment. Flavoured with negativity, it focuses upon imperfection—rejecting, denying and condemning. Given free play within the landscape of our own psyches it extends outwardly, moulding every relationship and connection we encounter, creating distance and highlighting all that we cannot make room in our hearts for. Divisions are solidified as the judge dwells upon its prejudices, likes and dislikes and opinions that accept or reject. There is little happiness in the judge, only the mind storms, confusion and sorrow that follow in the footsteps of its presence.

The experience of beginning a spiritual path to deepen in compassion, only to encounter how deeply ingrained the judgmental mind is, is not unusual for anyone. Tamsin took a year's sabbatical to spend in a number of spiritual centres. 'I was dismayed at the catalogue of imperfections I discover. One person I criticised for the clothes they wore, another person smiled too much and someone else ate in a way that offended me. In fact I was always offended. I decided I was the most critical person who ever attempted the spiritual life.'

Even when the messages of the judge are not particularly negative it finds contentment only in the busyness of superimposing its descriptions, labels and definitions upon everything that is seen, heard, felt and perceived. We walk in the countryside seeking respite from a world of busyness and, like a commentator at a sports match, the judge accompanies us, filling every moment with an abundance of evaluations, words and descriptions. A day of silence and contemplation ends in exhaustion as the busyness of the judge leeches energy and spaciousness. Through all its words and labels the judge creates

a world of familiarity which is controllable. It is made controllable through emptying each moment of surprise, unpredictability and mystery. Control is the most highly-treasured
possession of the inner critic—it is not enchanted by mystery
but by safety. The results of our judgments are not a deepening in connection and understanding with ourselves or with
anything or anyone. The results are self-denial or negation of
others. We are understandably disheartened by the intrusions
and persistence of the judge, appreciating the ways our lives
are deprived of mystery and innocence through its incessant
pronouncements. The world, ourselves and other people are
compartmentalised into the frozen boxes of the known, stored
into the overcrowded warehouses of our psyches, only to be
retrieved in a future time to judge and control another experience, another person, another moment.

We are not powerless before the voice of the judge regardless of the length of its history. It possesses no inherent cer-
tificate of residency within our psyche. The judge thrives upon
and is nourished by our own tendencies towards inner devaluation, mistrust and self-negation. The ability to free ourselves
of the shadow of the judge is not found through the adoption
of naïve affirmations of our own worth. Learning to honour
ourselves is an immense challenge which must embrace the
whole of our lives. Countless women discover to their dismay
that they possess far greater expertise in self-negation and
denial than in the art of knowing how to honour themselves.
Exploring the landscape of our own being, our lives and spirit,
we see the inclination to highlight what remains undone
rather than celebrating what has been completed, to judge
rather than affirm, to deny more than give thanks. We may
find greater ease in focussing upon imperfection than in being
able to offer ourselves acknowledgment for the transformations we have nurtured in our lives. Learning how to embody
our intuition in our words, actions, choices and directions is to
begin to build true foundations for honour and dignity. In

ceasing to live a life which embodies only the voices of inner and outer conditioning the judge will find little fuel for its continuity. The judge cannot survive a life which is lived with profound sincerity, integrity and nobility.

There is a story of a group of young nuns who were debating the best way to gain entrance to heaven. One said the most direct way was to gain the humility of St Catherine. Another disagreed and said the most assured way of gaining entrance was to emulate the piety of St Mary. Yet another put forth the opinion that the gates of heaven would open if they were to follow the compassionate example of St Jude. Taking their debate to their Mother Superior, they laid before her their opinions on how to make the gates of heaven open. The Mother Superior said to them, 'These are indeed all wonderful ways to live and I cannot say which is better than the other.' Disappointed, the young nuns asked her, 'Will you then tell us which way you are following to paradise?' The elderly nun answered, 'I do not know of any way that will guarantee the gates of heaven will open for me. I only hope that the day I meet St Peter I will be able to look him in the eye and say that I have done my best to be myself.'

Judgment is a habit; its continuity depends upon dullness. Rather than recoiling from our judgments or accepting their veracity there is a great skillfulness in listening to them carefully. What do they tell us about ourselves, what do they actually tell us about anyone or anything? In the steadfastness of our attention and listening we remain connected not only with the superficial words of our judgments but equally with the recipient of our judgment—whether it is another person, ourselves or an experience or situation we have encountered. The sensitivity our attention brings means that none of these are reduced to a conclusion, assumption or truth. Through making room in our hearts for our judgments we make room in our hearts for whatever our judgments are projected upon and there is born the possibility of greater depth, understanding, forgiveness and compassion.

Inextricably entangled with the achiever is the voice of the victim. Sharing the same loss of intuition, the achiever sets out to conquer the world while the victim believes herself to be at the mercy of the same world. The voice of the victim carries the weight of doubt and fear and speaks to us of the truth of our own limitation and imperfection. Power and authority are seen to be always the territory and possession of someone else. Trust and vision are seen to be magical benedictions only endowed upon others. Life seems to happen to the victim— failure, sorrow, betrayal, loss and rejection become the mile- stones that measure her journey. The victim feels powerless to effect change and remains lost in paralysis—waiting for the next blow to fall. The roots of the victim may well lie in a life story where she has been victimised by forces more powerful than herself, where she has been stripped of authority, power and choice.

Compassion is the only valid response we can apply to the cruelty and powerlessness which brutalise the spirit and psy- che of those who cannot avail themselves of the power to transform. Yet we must always be wary that compassion does not lend credence and continuity to the voice of the victim in the present. Compassion is qualitatively different to just being sorry for ourselves or for others. Martyrdom may well be the consequence of being sorry for ourselves or for subscribing to powerlessness and offer us the possibility of drawing sympa- thy from others—but sympathy is a poor substitute for free- dom and dignity. Compassion is a response of the heart, strengthened by wisdom, and rests upon trusting that the end of suffering is a real and tangible possibility. Self-pity has too often accepted impossibility. Terrible and tragic things happen to us in our lives, great violations of our spirit occur—in their midst and in their endings we must learn how to bandage our wounds and begin again. The alternative is to surrender to the past, to hopelessness and to the perpetual role of the victim.

There is the story of a young woman, grieving over the death of her baby, who came to the Buddha seeking for help. 'You are so powerful and so wise,' she beseeched him. 'I beg you to use your power to restore my son to me.' Siddhartha answered her saying, 'I would ask you to go to each house in the village and bring to me a mustard seed from the home of any family who has not suffered loss and grief. When you are able to do this, I will help you.' The young woman knocked on door after door asking each family if they had managed to live without sorrow and loss. One after another they would speak to her of the grief that had marked their own lives. There was not one family who was exempt. Listening to them, the young woman felt humbled by their stories which mirrored her own. She understood the ways in which sorrow bonded her with others. She also saw that grief did not deny the possibilities of new life and joy.

We cannot return to the past to undo what has been done, to complete what has been uncompleted or to alter the circumstances of our lives. None of these are the paths to healing. To continue to bewail our fate or to hammer at the doors of the past in anger or sorrow is to deny to ourselves the opening of the doors of the present. We are all life's survivors and this is an actuality to be celebrated. It is time to cease dwelling on what has already gone by and to open to what is possible for us in this moment, this life, this journey. This is the path of the warrior.

At what point do we cease being victimised by others and begin to victimise ourselves? If we find ourselves reluctant to make effort in our lives because we disbelieve in the efficacy of our own effort; if we are always looking over our shoulders waiting to be directed or guided by someone or something outside of ourselves; if we feel uninspired to dive into the depths of our consciousness because we do not believe that there is anything of worth to discover—then we must question how identified we may be with the role and voice of the victim. If

GIVE THE GIFT OF Vegetarian TIMES

Greetings by mail • We're American hearts • Safeguarding your water

Vegetarian TIMES

Best-Ever Dinners!

Recipe contest winners
Satisfying sweet potatoes
Lov/fat fast soups

A gentle way to get fit

One year gifts (or your own subscription) are just $29.95 - that's 30% off the cover price!

Send one year of VEGETARIAN TIMES to:

Name

Address   Apt

City/State/Zip

Send one year of VEGETARIAN TIMES to:

Name

Address   Apt

City/State/Zip

FROM: F6O3AO

Name

Address   Apt

City/State/Zip

☐ Payment enclosed   ☐ Bill me
☐ Enter   ☐ Extend my subscription

Account # _____

(from address label)

Gift cards & envelopes will be mailed to you on receipt of order.

To Canada: $41.95. (GST included) Other foreign: $54.91.
Payment in US funds only.

NO POSTAGE
NECESSARY
IF MAILED
IN THE
UNITED STATES

BUSINESS REPLY MAIL

FIRST-CLASS MAIL   PERMIT NO. 106   FLAGLER BEACH FL

POSTAGE WILL BE PAID BY ADDRESSEE

Vegetarian
T I M E S

PO BOX 420164
PALM COAST FL 32142-9103

we find ourselves looking to be consoled rather than inspired; seeking sympathy rather than empathy, and dwelling upon the past rather than exploring possibilities in the present, we are called upon to question how much we are being guided by the voice of the victim. Conclusions, resignation and hopelessness are all the manifestations of the victim. Compassion may not be sufficient to uproot the habit of paralysis and passivity that shadow the victim. There is a deep need to hone the cutting edge of effort, agency and inner empowerment.

There is no doubt that the image of being a victim is born of a history of being wounded, disempowered or negated. The residues of pain born of those experiences hobble the victim's capacity to envision new possibilities. Dedicated to avoiding pain and the repetition of the trauma of the past consumes energy, vision and the possibility of transformation. The words 'I can't' signal her disbelief in possibility. 'I can't' change, relate differently, see freshly, let go, say no, open—the litany is endlessly recited by the victim, describing only impossibility. The recitation of this mantra hypnotises the victim into passivity and lifelessness. Envy creeps in—of all those who seem to possess what she cannot achieve; of those who are able to engage in the world in ways the victim feels exiled from. The warrior woman is willing to challenge these words, 'I can't' and plumb the depths of the power they seem to possess.

There are many things 'I can't' do—'I can't' be someone else, guarantee the future, alter the past, walk through fire unscathed or reverse the aging process. There are far more possibilities and avenues in our lives that fall into the realms of 'I don't know' or 'I am open to learning'. For a woman of the spirit, the time to hang up her skates, put away her bicycle and retire into the world of conclusions never arrives. We hold within ourselves energy, the capacity to be aware, the power to learn, the capacity for effort and life. We need no more than these for transformation. The only factor that drives us into retirement of the spirit is the subscription to our conclusions and these are the only things that are worthy of retiring. No-one but ourselves can explore our edges, nudge our boundaries or challenge our conclusions. No-one can substitute for us in the process of transformation.

There comes a time when we must cease to look over our shoulders for authorisation to explore what is possible for us. There is a time to forsake what is easiest, most comfortable and familiar. This does not require grandiose and dramatic gestures—we are not asked to scale a mountain, donate our possessions to charity or hole ourselves up in a cave. We need simply to look at where our boundaries contain us in the most powerful ways and take one step beyond them. If you find it difficult to give—commit yourself to one moment of generosity. If you find it difficult to take risks—take a single journey without a compass, hot water bottle and parachute. If you find it difficult to say no—find just one instance where it is possible for you. Take a day without make-up, a day without checking the bathroom scales, surrender your car keys and go on retreat, spend a day alone, paint a picture and ask for no-one's approval. In one moment of pure commitment it is not only our boundaries that are challenged but the very position and image of the victim. That one moment is the most difficult but from it is born the courage and faith to sustain many more moments. The spiritual warrior is on an adventure. She does not know what lies on the other side of the fence but is willing to live without the guarantees. She is open to learning, open to stumbling and open to beginning again.

The controller is a presence, a voice within our psyche that makes a frequent and powerful appearance in our journeys. The controller, like a campaign manager, is the holder of strategies and plans. The controller carries an overflowing portfolio of prescriptions, formulas and required responses with which to meet and control the variety of life and inner experiences that unfold in each moment. If the unpredictable is encountered, the controller will find a way of making it familiar, labelling it and finding a comparison from the past. If chaos is met the controller learns to subdue it, if confusion is met the way to escape into numbness is readily available. Despair is countered with busyness, elation countered with caution and fear subdued through distraction. Action, busyness, planning and ordering are the territories of the controller. It lives in a state of defensiveness, on guard against the intrusion of anything that threatens the control which is so highly treasured. Manipulation and modification are the only avenues the controller is willing to engage in—they are avenues dedicated to the preservation of a state of being undisturbed and unchallenged.

There are moments in our lives and in our journeys when strategies can be an expression of wisdom. We need to know how to protect ourselves—not everyone in the world treasures our well-being and freedom. There are moments in our journeys when fear looms and we need the wisdom to step back and restore the equanimity and balance that allow us to meet fear without being overwhelmed. We also need to be aware of when we use the strategies of retreat and protection as a means of denying or rejecting people, circumstances or ourselves because we have labelled them unacceptable. Many times people do not conform to our expectations, nor does life accord with our images. There are many moments when we do not conform to deeply-held images of social, emotional or spiritual excellence. We want to be generous and find ourselves lost in greed; we want to be compassionate and find ourselves immersed in judgment; we want to be loving and reject the feelings of hatred or anger that emerge from our hearts.

Different possibilities are offered to us in those moments when our lives, our relationships and our inner experience refuse to fit in with the plans and images we hold. We can judge or use coercion to make another person or ourself fit in with our moulds and models. We can attempt to subdue them through the force of our will and control them with our strategies. Or we can listen; learn the art of being present and embrace them with the power of our own awareness. Not being in control does not imply being out of control. We can learn to trust in the power of our own awareness and wisdom. We treasure the breakthroughs we make in our lives and in our spiritual paths but the most profound breakthrough we can ever make is breaking through our resistance to being with what is actual and present in this moment. To attempt to change anything in our world or to bring transformation within ourselves on the basis of aversion or denial will succeed only in cosmetic modifications. To see what is before us, what is within us—whether it is painful or pleasant, joyful or sorrowful—with an open heart and a clear mind is the first step of any profound transformation.

The alternative to openness and clarity is struggle and disconnection. We despair over violence and cruelty in the world, we anguish over feelings of envy, greed or hatred that appear in our own psyches. There are only two avenues available to us in the face of the challenging and disturbing—to move away from what we see with avoidance, judgment or contempt; or to move towards that which disturbs us with the willingness to understand and embrace it in a heart and mind of compassion and wisdom.

A therapist who had worked for many years with incest survivors was taken aback when a new client arrived, who had a history of abusing children. At first she felt rage, knowing the hurt so many of her clients had lived with so many years. She was tempted to throw him out of her office or confront him with the consequences of his actions. As she began to voice her objections she saw in his face that she was not the first to turn him down. She knew that she had to match his vulnerability with the courage of her own compassion. The compassion of the warrior is found in the willingness to step beyond our initial reactions of aversion and denial. Denial can bring a facade of control but equally disconnects us from our world, our minds and our hearts.

Surrender, openness and compassion do not imply a sacrifice of power, integrity or freedom but only a sacrifice of resistance and separateness. Compassion is liberating, dissolving distance and disconnection. None of our plans and strategies, no matter how carefully considered and constructed they are, can offer us the intimacy and oneness with all things that the letting go of resistance offers to us.

Intuition sings to us a song of home. It guides us and protects us. Like the young girl who found sanctuary with her song of another time, our intuition offers us a sanctuary which sustains us in our moments of darkness and in the valleys of our journeys. Intuition reminds us of the wisdom of opening, of listening, of pausing, of nurturing and of letting go. It reminds us of where our true home lies—not through defining ourselves by the voices of the past which impose themselves upon the present—but in the freedom of being able to listen, attributing truth to any conclusion or image. Inner listening is the power that reveals to us that we are never lost. The very variety of voices that pass through our consciousness reveals their own transparency. They arise and pass, appear and disappear—carrying their own stories and offering to us their own teaching. Impermanent in nature, transparent and conditioned, they invite us to understand that we cannot be defined or restricted by them. To refrain from dwelling or lingering upon any of the voices that appear is to see their insubstantiality. The warrior of the spirit loves what is true and discards what is false. She finds her home in the power of her awareness and vision.

SIX

IMAGES OF PERFECTION
THE QUEEN WHO MISSED THE POINT

A baby girl was born to the delighted king and queen who had long awaited a child to warm their hearts and succeed them to the throne. She was a perfect princess—beautiful, charming and even in her childhood days, regal. The king and queen doted upon her, surrounding her with magnificent clothes, endless toys and a long line of people who existed only to answer the princess's every desire. From the moment she could speak the princess knew her destiny; to be the most exquisite queen ever to rule the country. The troubles and trials of other children never touched the life of the little girl—protected and cossetted she knew no other life than that of a princess, awaiting her crown. She was sheltered from hearing any news of troubles that might disturb her; being available to receive the praise and accolades that were showered upon her was a full-time job.

In time the princess grew up and one after the other her parents died. For many weeks, her time was filled with ceremonies and rituals—the grand funerals of her parents and the even grander ceremony to celebrate her investiture. Party followed party, the new queen danced her way through the days proudly wearing her crown. The days turned into weeks, the weeks to months and the months to years and still the now, not so new queen, continued to celebrate. Her ministers tried to remind her that there was more to being a queen than wearing a crown but she was much too busy having a good time to listen to such dreary advice. When her feet got tired from dancing she found new pleasures to enjoy—cutting ribbons to open new buildings, receiving gifts from visiting dignitaries and standing on the balcony of her palace to wave at the gathered crowds who surrounded the palace walls. Again her ministers timidly tried to tell her that the crowds were actually not gathered to praise her but to complain about the sorry state the nation was falling into, but she dismissed them with a regal wave of her hand. 'Nonsense', she would say. 'Is it not enough that I am such a perfect queen for them to admire?' Imperiously gathering her train behind her she would return to her chambers to dress for the next event where she would bestow her presence. She had little time for listening to complaints when it took so much time to be a perfect queen.

Many years passed and the queen enjoyed them all. One day, looking in the mirror, it struck her that her image was looking a little tarnished. Her face was lined with wrinkles, her hair thin and grey and the wonderful clothes of her younger years hung on her body. Even her crown felt too heavy to wear and her neck complained at its weight. 'I am old', she realised. In a panic she called her ministers to her and rebuked them for failing to remind her that one of the jobs of a perfect queen was to have a perfect princess. 'It is too late now for me to have a perfect princess to follow my fine example. We must find the worthiest young girl in the country to follow me.' She commanded them to go forth and bring to her the worthiest, most perfect girl they could find. 'But what about the nation'? her ministers beseeched her. 'There is much hardship and struggle. Will you not save it?' Again the queen waved away their words. 'Find the perfect queen and all will be well.'

Over the months that followed one girl after another was brought for the queen's inspection. One was endowed with great beauty but was terribly clumsy and was dismissed. One could sing like a nightingale but was thin as a rake and was sent away as unworthy. One was a meticulous housekeeper and couldn't restrain herself from polishing the throne even as the queen inspected her, but couldn't string two intelligible words together. She too was sent away. One young girl was terrible regal but equally unattractive while yet another could speak in an imperious voice and wave well but couldn't dance.

All were sent away after much pondering on the part of the queen. Again she called her ministers to her to encourage them to renew their search for the perfect princess. Instead of obeying they shuffled before her with their heads hung low. 'What are you waiting for?' she whispered, for by this time she was too frail to speak in a commanding voice. 'Your majesty', they said, 'it is too late. In all the long months of our search for the perfect princess, famine has devastated the land. Armies from our neighbouring kingdom have invaded and pillaged and laid waste to the countryside. The people have sickened and been killed and all those who survived have fled. We regret to tell you that there is no longer a country that needs a queen, perfect or not.' Holding her crown close to her bosom the queen could only ask, 'But how could this happen? I was such a perfect queen.'

Unlike the princess in this story, most women do not go through their lives assured of their perfection. Images of feminine perfection are placed upon pedestals, worshipped as goddesses and their attainment endowed with sanctity. Throughout our lives we receive the message that perfection exists and that for our existence to be worthy and significant we must dedicate ourselves to its attainment. The earliest lessons we learn in our lives are ones that highlight our imperfections, inadequacies, failings and weaknesses. They are accompanied by another powerful teaching—our unworthiness can be transformed into worthiness, our unacceptability into acceptability and inadequacy into capability. Absorbing this teaching, our lives become dedicated to the earning of our own personal halos, for they are the ticket and the means to entering the hallowed ground of the perfect.

Endless images of perfection are imposed upon us. The images projected from the pages of magazines, advertising and billboards thrust upon us the portrait of the perfect face and body of the ideal woman. She is young, flawless and free of apparent imperfection. Rarely do we open any publication and meet the image of an aging woman who smiles with benevolence upon her wrinkles, her softening body and her greying hair, inviting us to share in the grace of aging. Our television presentations and films collude in the promotion of perfection—the perfect woman succeeds in all she does. She conquers dirt and disorder, she is the queen of the laundry room, she succeeds in the boardroom and goes forth to charm all in her social life. This paragon of virtue raises perfect children, plans perfect menus and in her spare time finds the opportunity to improve her mind. There is little in our entertainment programmes that speaks to the realities of countless women who struggle to juggle a demanding working life with the challenges of raising children and caring for themselves. The image of perfection, capability and order we have thrust upon us bears little resemblance to the reality of a woman who learns to survive on a few hours' sleep, who may well live under a constant shadow of financial hardship, for whom the notion of spare time is a long-forgotten luxury. The perfect woman doesn't wear on her face the lines of pain etched through meeting disappointment, sorrow and loss in her life.

As children, our elders read to us the stories of other children who excel in sweetness and obedience, who overcome dragons and evil stepmothers by the power of their virtue and goodness. Lack of conformity, more often called badness, is rarely rewarded. Goodness is the ticket to present and indeed future happiness. The perfect children of our stories do not fight with their siblings, do not rebel against their parents and are of course asexual. The perfect children of our stories are often abused, but it seems that goodness is prescribed as the antidote for transcending abuse and ensuring that the abusers are punished. These models of perfection are far removed from the realities of a child who struggles to find a home within herself and within her world that accepts her fears and rage, her rebelliousness and insecurity, her failures and successes.

The spiritually-perfect woman is defined for us by our religious mythology. Her saintliness is distinguished by her meekness, humility, self-sacrifice and most particularly by her silence. There are few stories of women who are promoted to sainthood by virtue of their refusal to consent to the status quo, by their dedication to truth or through their own efforts and integrity. Saintliness seems far removed from the actuality of countless women's lives that are spent endeavouring to live with dignity, compassion and wisdom in the midst of circumstances that are at times demeaning, often demanding, and that require saintly proportions of patience, fortitude and courage. The saintly woman of our religious fables seems to have miraculously transcended the struggles contemporary women face in the spiritual life to make themselves visible in patriarchal religions that resent their presence. The message delivered is one that teaches that saintliness is attained essentially through benevolent silence and not through authority or visibility.

Too many of our stories transport us from the realities of our own lives and into the realm of fantasy where the essential teaching is one of the desirability of pursuing perfection. We inherit images of perfection from our culture, the media, our parents, our religions and our peers. We construct images of perfection on the basis of our own fears of disapproval, 'not making it' and rejection. We create images of perfection out of our own pressing desire to join the ranks of the winners and the perfect. Young girls continue to be force-fed a diet rich with models of glamour and sexual attractiveness and proceed to diet themselves into illness. All of this is the food for fantasy and the breeding ground for stereotypes and models.

The gloss of the models of perfection we are exposed to entices us and deceives us. The model of the perfect woman, the perfect child and the perfect saint attracts in that it epitomises the end of all pain. She appears to have it all—acclaim, certainty, confidence, admiration, relationships, prestige. We can envision her floating through life wrapped in a cocoon of beauty and applause just as she floats through the advertisements thrust upon us. She has no past and she appears to face no future that could ever threaten her perfection. She has the world at her feet. We receive her image into our minds and hearts and see reflected in that image the promise of the end of pain in our own lives as long as we are able to emulate the image we admire and have prescribed for us.

Lost in the enticement of these models of perfection, we do not appreciate their deceptiveness. The gloss of the images conceals the shadows of pain that lie hidden beneath its window-dressing. We do not see the terror of aging that lurks beneath the perfect smile, nor is the lurking insecurity over identity apparent to us. We do not see the anxiety that arises with the appearance of the first flaw or the relentless tyrant of comparison that hounds her days. We do not see the fear of loss or the pain of being possessed by a model of perfection. Every day the perfect woman must face her reflection and ask the age old question—'Mirror, mirror on the wall, who is the fairest of them all?'

In the model of the perfect mother we do not see our own face reflected—the anxieties over failing our children, being unable to provide the time and attention that their changing needs require. The perfect mother in the perfect kitchen reaches with composure and ease the end of the countless tasks and work that are the reality of a mother's life—this end is one that never seems to arrive for us. The perfect mother of our advertising glories in her supremacy over disorder. Frustration and rebelliousness over the relentlessness of the needs that fill her days do not feature in the portfolio of the perfect mother, nor does she suffer the feelings of inadequacy that mar the spirit of countless mothers.

The new model of the superwoman who succeeds in the office, enjoys a perfect relationship and raises delightful children has become yet another tyrant in our lives. She convinces us that we can do all of these, that we are possessed of capabilities of heroic proportions that enable us to have everything we want, without sacrifice and without struggle. The model shows us arrival but not the path. A model of independence is provided for us but the secret of an independence that doesn't demand the sacrifice of interconnectedness and humility is not revealed. She seems unable to advise us on how to compete in a corporate world without sacrificing our femininity or how to embody ourselves creatively without becoming caught in the trap of having to prove ourselves. The superwoman image offers us a model of perfection to attain but there seems an unbridgeable abyss between the ideal and our own actuality.

The model of the saintly woman entrances us. She appears to abide in a profound serenity. Demure, modest, smiling and serving, her purity impresses us deeply. Enticed by her image, it seems almost sacrilegious to question this model of saintliness. In our hearts we secretly wonder whether Mary didn't feel great anger and grief when her son died on the cross. When the young Siddhartha set forth on his quest for Buddhahood leaving behind him a young wife and child, did she not experience the pain of abandonment or question the responsibility of his departure? The stories and models we inherit primarily overlook these significant points, an omission which clearly presents yet another model—the insignificance, perhaps even the irrelevance of these feelings. We are repeatedly told of the virtues of forgiveness, compassion and acceptance. The realities of our lives also include moments of great grief, anger, the pain of abandonment and sorrow. The absence of attention that is given to them in our stories and models implies that they do not hold any intrinsic spiritual value. To be saintly, it seems we too must learn to ignore the presence of these very real feelings and sorrows and strive for the halos of forgiveness, self-sacrifice and meekness. Impressed and deceived by our models, we do not always appreciate that this is a prescription for fragmentation.

The fascination inspired in us by the models of perfection we are exposed to is easily understood. They provide the food through which we can nurture our own fantasies that provide an alternative to pain, loneliness and fears of inadequacy. Losing ourselves in our movies, our stories of heroines and daydreams, we are able to depart from the reality of our own lives. Fantasy provides pleasure, forgetfulness and solace. Reality provides challenge, sorrow as well as joy and the demand to take responsibility for the quality of our own lives. The preference for fantasy illustrates the terror that reality holds for us.

There is a story of a young woman who survived a shipwreck to find herself stranded alone on an island. When she awoke each morning she would think of her partner and children who were awaiting her arrival and knew the grief and anxiety they would be undergoing when her ship failed to arrive. Seeing other ships on the horizon, she knew that all she had to do was light a fire to attract their attention and she would be rescued. Yet she had discovered on this island the most wonderful of all springs. When she took a drink of this magical water she was filled with happiness, contentment and the most wonderful of dreams. The whole day would pass as she wandered in her reveries and she would forget all about her family and all ideas of being rescued. The next day she would make the same resolve to attract help but her eyes would fall again on the bubbling spring and the delights it offered. Many week passed in this fashion and she enjoyed them all, lost in euphoria and bliss. By chance one day a passing boat stopped at the island and, on discovering her, set about returning her to her family. When she arrived home, her weeping children and partner gathered around her joyously, having been convinced that she was no longer alive. She told them of the magical spring and the wonderful dreams and happiness she had enjoyed. Her children asked her if she had also dreamt that they too were so content. She told them that her dreams of their happiness had made her dreams even more delightful. Looking at her with tear-filled eyes her children said, 'But this was not true. These many weeks we have longed for you, we have cried and grieved. Your dreams took you away from us.' Our dreams and models equally rest upon the denial of pain and of reality.

Models of perfection provide us with a goal to strive for that promises rich rewards. We are not asked to be who we are—we are asked to emulate someone else. We are at times reluctant to face the deceptiveness of our models of perfection and our fascination with them for this could well deprive our lives of meaning and direction. We could be asked to make radical changes in our lives; to forsake the journeys that were directed to achieving perfection; to forsake fantasy and to embrace the challenges of our own realities. Pursuing models of perfection provides us with a map with clearly-defined signposts; there is no such map for embarking on a journey of discovering meaning, value and purpose in the midst of our own realities. The renunciation of chasing perfection appears to sentence us to imperfection. Imperfection is not a state that is glorified in any story or mythology—it is presented only as the state to flee from and a problem to be overcome.

The demon of perfection may not be a conscious presence in our lives. We may be convinced that we have no ambitions for sainthood and are willing to accept the imperfections of our bodies, minds and personalities. We may find difficulty in associating ourselves with the compulsion to succeed, improve and perfect ourselves. Before we dismiss this demon too quickly we should ask ourselves what force it is that leads us to endlessly compare ourselves to others and judge ourselves on the basis of those comparisons? How completely are we able to banish the faces and bodies on the billboards that stare at us, without a trace of inner disquiet? What is it that leads us to dismiss or suppress feelings of envy, jealousy or resentment with aversion or contempt? Who are we modelling ourselves after as we attempt to mould ourselves into a particular image through altering, modifying or manipulating our bodies, minds and personalities? On what basis do we judge, reject or dismiss others? Is it wisdom or the worship of false gods?

The conditioning and ethos of our culture tell us that anything less than perfection is unacceptable. Imperfection is always someone's fault, a sign of personal failure and inadequacy; a sign of deficiency in others. It is a fault, we are assured, that can be cured through repentance, working harder, striving more ardently, through changing our dress, diet or lifestyle or through overcoming with resoluteness the imperfections we have isolated. It is not difficult for us to pinpoint the deficiencies that bar us from attaining the hallowed state of perfection. The models of perfection we are exposed to essentially teach us about our own areas of unacceptability and imperfection. We need only to look at their images to be convinced of what we need to fix, cure and solve within ourselves in order to be sufficiently worthy to join their ranks—whether it is our bodies, minds, personalities or aspirations. The underlying purpose of any model of perfection promoted by advertising, industry or social more is to convince us of its desirability so that we will be inclined, if not driven, to pursue it. Not surprisingly the products, techniques, guides and merchandise are readily available to aid us in our improvement.

The models of perfection that are thrust upon women change with time and circumstance but it seems their message, which promotes the twin forces of striving and denial, is eternal. The laws that govern the standards of unacceptability and acceptability only go through cosmetic changes. The perfect woman has appeared in the figure of the simpering, swooning de-sexed Victorian. She has been portrayed as the loyal, inexhaustible supporter standing behind her man. She has appeared as the flirtatious, sexually-desirable plaything; the competent earth-mother dedicated to nurturing and creating; she is the new star in the business world startling all with her resolve and ambition; she is the Madonna, venerated and removed from all earthly passions and feeling. So bombarded are we with her image that it takes great courage to enquire into who endows these models with such unassailable sanctity and authority.

Perfection implies rightness, truth and goodness. Perfection evidences faultlessness, excellence, flawlessness and of course success. The models of perfection thrust upon us have earned the right to wear a halo through their attainment of these qualities. Our stories provide us with the endless examples of this goodness, telling us what it means to be a good child, good mother, good partner, good worker and good disciple. Goodness is about self-sacrifice and self-denial. It is found through perpetually giving higher priority to the needs of others over our own and calling this selflessness. Goodness is about being 'nice', interpreted to mean not disturbing or upsetting others, not challenging and offering selfless service and care. At times, goodness is presented as being endlessly available, unassuming, agreeable and generous. Goodness certainly demands boundless patience, forgiveness and tolerance. It is no surprise that generations of women have been haunted by the spectre of failure and inadequacy in the face of such goodness.

Forgiveness, born of wisdom and compassion, has the power to end hatred and division. Forgiveness and selflessness born of the fear of attracting anger or denunciation will only perpetuate it. For countless women, self-sacrifice and renunciation are as familiar to them as their own heartbeat. To mother a child, support a friend, serve a parent, requires boundless tolerance and selflessness. Their generosity of heart teaches them the joy of letting go as they care for others. Selflessness, born of love, is qualitatively different to self-negation, which is flavoured by fear. For a woman to dedicate her life to caring for a growing child or an aging parent can be a profound act of selflessness. It can also provide her with purpose, and identity, and relieve her of assuming the responsibility for the authenticity of her own life. Intention creates our worlds—we need to be extraordinarily awake to the motivations that lie beneath selflessness.

Tolerance allows us to accept and embrace a world of differences, but true tolerance is not blind and refuses to condone injustice or exploitation. To be accepting does not mean that all things are acceptable. A woman who allows herself to be discounted or harassed because she feels sympathy for her persecutor may not be practising tolerance but collusion. If we are erased in the process of supporting others we would need to question the wisdom of our care. Success is the natural outflow of manifesting our capabilities and vision in work, mothering or creativity. Success motivated by the need to prove ourselves or disprove the age-old accusation levelled against women about passivity, non-productivity or inadequacy is a talisman to display, but does little to enrich our lives or our spirits in a meaningful way.

Goodness may bring applause; it rarely liberates. The rewards for goodness are well publicised. Its practice and cultivation sets us firmly upon the road to perfection. Its achievement will bring great bounty in the form of salvation, recognition, love, gratitude and hopefully saintliness. Embarked upon the pursuit of goodness, we are somehow persuaded to overlook the penalties involved if we fail to cultivate the path in a sufficiently tenacious way. The penalties for imperfection are real and faced daily by generations of women. The experience of being devalued and dismissed; the pain of being ignored and overlooked, the negative feedback we receive from other people, are all consequences we face for imperfection. The more lethal penalties suffered for imperfection take place within our own hearts and spirits—devaluing ourselves, belittling ourselves as we elevate others, self-hatred and self-negation wound our spirit as we ceaselessly attempt to jump the abyss that lies between our ideals and our actualities. The pain experienced does not necessarily lead us to question the models and images which shadow our lives—more frequently it encourages us to blame and beat ourselves more harshly. We assume and absorb the pain—the teaching we garner from it is an ever-deepening conviction that imperfection is our fault. Like the abused child, or the child of divorced parents, we assume the responsibility for imperfection. We are spurred to greater efforts to improve ourselves, strive more heroically and judge ourselves yet more harshly.

The desire for goodness has an inevitable companion—the fear of not being good enough. The pursuit of halos is shadowed by the fear of being unworthy to wear the halos that are pursued. Unlike the models of excellence and perfection imposed upon us, the halos we pursue seem invariably to lie just beyond our reach. Enslaved by the models of perfection and our own fantasies, we are sentenced to live in a state of perpetually reaching for the rightness and goodness we believe can be gained, yet which remains elusive. We succeed, but another goal immediately is sought for; we cultivate all the good qualities within our personalities, becoming a paragon of 'niceness', only to discover yet one more objectionable thought or feeling that is in need of alteration. We punish our bodies, heroically moulding them into the 'right' shape, but they are never good enough. Spiritually we practise devotion and goodness, seeking the inner madonna, yet excellence continues to lie beyond the horizons.

The pursuit of goodness and the fear of not being good enough deprive us of authenticity, which leads to a malnutrition of our spirit. We are starved by our own self-doubt, comparisons and criticism into paralysis and resignation. Craving acceptance, approval and affirmation, we become casualties of our own pursuit of goodness and perfection. Hunting the models and ideals of perfection, we tread the paths that have been well-beaten for us by generations of women who have travelled the same journey. It is a journey that features the inseparable twins of striving and self-negation, conformity and self-denial, comparison and self-judgment, pursuing goodness and never feeling good enough. Worshipping models of perfection is a direct way of diminishing and devaluing ourselves. Pursuing halos is a direct way of pursuing alienation. In pursuing halos we do not always appreciate the degree to which we are running from our own fears of rejection, being unloved and a failure, and our conviction of not being good enough to bear a halo.

It is time we learned, profoundly and deeply, some new lessons in our lives. Perfection is no substitute for authenticity; the models we are exposed to hold no intrinsic authority— we invest them with the authority and power they hold; no-one and no model is qualified to prescribe for us who we should be, appear, produce or become. We need to learn the lessons of acceptance and freedom and undertake the practice of celebrating and honouring. The warrior woman can see the tarnish on the halos and she is not tempted to polish them. It is doubtful that any of us will ever achieve the perfect body, mind or personality. It is probable that none of us will ever be the perfect daughter, mother, executive or disciple. This is not a tragedy, nor a reason to despair—it is an acceptance that enables us to lay down a burden of fear and frees us of the weight of halos that have for too long disabled women. It is a revelation to celebrate, that liberates and enables us to focus upon what is of true significance in our lives and our quests. It is not the perfection of any appearance, role or achievement that brings richness and freedom to our lives. They can never be found within the confines of any halo, no matter how brightly it shines. Richness and freedom can only be found through the sincerity with which we live our lives, the intimacy we nurture with our own being and the interconnectedness with the world which we live in.

The only paths worthy of following in our lives are those that lead to happiness, understanding and freedom. By pursuing halos and the path of perfection we consent to the perpetuation of stereotypes and models which diminish not only ourselves, but all women. Just as we have inherited stereotypes and models from our mothers and grandmothers, suggesting the virtues of compliance or dependence, which we then rebel against or struggle to emulate, so too must we be aware of the haloed models we may bequeath to our daughters. Halos placed upon the paths of success, independence or power equally cast a shadow if they demand perfection. Daughters are encouraged to fulfil their mothers' sacrificed dreams and stagger beneath the weight of expectation. The greatest gift we can offer to ourselves, to our daughters, is to cast off the halos that demand perfection and conformity. The banishment of our halos is directly linked to the degree to which we cease to flee from our own fears of being unlovable, inadequate and unworthy. This is not to resign ourselves to imperfection, nor does it imply ceasing to extend ourselves in our lives and explore what is possible for us. The passion to fulfil what is possible for us, to realise our potential, to reach for freedom, is born of love and not of fear. If we love freedom, peace and dignity, we will seek them in all areas of our lives—not because they bring us applause but because they liberate us to live with authenticity.

As long as excellence is projected into models, goals, images, ideals or attainments then we are sentenced to a life of denial and struggle as we consistently reject all that we deem imperfect within ourselves and within others. If we worship beauty we will fear aging, if we define ourselves by achievement the whole of our life will be a test. To be bound to the dualities of right and wrong, good and bad, perfect and imperfect, dictated by our models and stereotypes is to be equally bound to gain and loss, praise and blame, success and failure. Equally it is to collude in the worship of appearance, production and achievement and the denigration of substance, depth and meaning. The dismissal of the aging women in our culture, the anorexics and bulimics, the hatred women extend towards their bodies, the ranks of the depressed, the legions of women who feel ill-equipped to compete in a male-dominated work culture, and the women who compete but feel it necessary to sacrifice their femininity in order to succeed—all these women bear testimony to the lethal consequences of being bound to models of perfection and the dualities which are their offspring.

The spiritual warrior has forsaken the pursuit of halos; she understands their enticement and their deceptiveness and refuses to spin their web of sorrow any longer. She is no longer willing to sacrifice her uniqueness for the tenuous rewards of conforming to a stereotype. She is no longer motivated by the pursuit of standardised excellence, but is inspired to understand the meaning of greatness—what it means to live with a greatness of heart and mind that is vast enough to embrace the interwoven threads and dynamics of her own being. The wise woman knows in her heart that to be perfect she cannot be whole, integrated or in harmony with herself, for this perfection demands that she ignores, overlooks or suppresses the imperfect within herself. She deeply understands that to be whole, integrated and free she will never be perfect nor will she seek perfection, for such a search will divest her of a life which is meaningful and creative—a life which honours acceptance and authenticity. A warrior woman appreciates that communion is made possible only through the greatness of heart that embraces diversity. Her wisdom guides her to seek freedom rather than excellence, integration rather than fragmentation, harmony over division and acceptance over denial.

The spiritual warrior lives in a spirit of humility—not intent upon overcoming or negating the imperfect but understanding that these imperfections are what bring uniqueness to her life and liberate her own creativity. Her body, with its flaws and its own unique form, is the only body through which she can manifest love, respect and sensitivity—not just for herself but for all the bodies and forms she meets in her life. Through her sexuality she manifests the capacities for intimacy and passion that lie within her. Her mind, with its own unique way of experiencing the world and its capacity for clarity and wisdom, is the only mind through which she can articulate her vision and express in word and thought what she values and honours. In understanding the dynamics of her mind—its struggles and sorrows, its capacity for understanding and depth—she understands all minds. In connecting deeply with the feelings that move her in her life—her yearning for love and peace, her yearning to end fear and pain—she connects with the deepest yearnings that govern all life. The humility, forgiveness and acceptance she is able to bring to the tapestry of her own being empower her to extend those same qualities to all beings and to live a life of integrity and impeccability. The warrior woman knows that through nurturing the gifts and qualities that are unique to her she will find the authenticity and freedom that are possible for her. No model, halo or image can ever provide for her the enduring happiness and integrity she can provide for herself through accepting, honouring and embodying who she is. Freedom is neither feminine nor masculine, neither personal nor impersonal, but our journey to awakening can only be through the vehicles of our own unique bodies, minds and hearts.

The warrior of the spirit knows that her inner life is a tapestry of interwoven threads which include her strengths and weaknesses, her body, mind and feelings, her successes and failures, her capacities for both joy and sorrow. In this tapestry there is profound love as well as the capacity for anger, creativity and despair, empathy and jealousy, compassion and resentment. There is nothing in this rich tapestry which is dismissed as unworthy, contemptible or shameful. Integrity and impeccability, creativity and oneness are found in the willingness to embrace and learn from the whole of the tapestry and never through dividing it into the perfect and the imperfect.

This great openness of heart manifests a true revolution of the spirit which has little support in our culture which is obsessed with perfection. The images and standards of perfection we demand permeate every corner of our lives. We learn to demand perfection in all things—going into a supermarket to purchase fruit we expect to purchase a perfect apple. Responding to this demand, farmers have learnt, through manipulating nature, to produce the perfect apple. Our eyes are met with the sight of row upon row of perfect apples— unblemished, of standard shape, size and colour—perfectly arrayed before us to select. What is also produced is sameness, but we are willing to overlook this sameness because we are able to purchase something that satisfies our ideals of perfection. We are equally willing to overlook the lack of flavour, aroma and quality in the apple we buy and consume; perhaps this seems a small sacrifice to make as long as we are rewarded with the appearance of perfection. The perfect apple we buy has little to do with life or even with nature. Nature produces apples with blemishes and bruises, variations in shape and colour. Within those variations we read the story and life of that apple and it explodes with flavour. The apple of nature teaches about ourselves and the world. Are we truly willing to sacrifice uniqueness, life and vitality in our demand for perfection?

There comes a point for all of us, when life, if not wisdom, awakens us from our fantasies of perfection. The reality of our reflection in the mirror tells us that our wrinkles will never iron themselves out despite the promises of our wonder creams; our body contours are not going to learn the art of levitation; our children have flown the nest despite our attempts to be a perfect mother and the top slot in the office no longer looks so golden as we appreciate the price we may have to pay for it. These moments of awakening are crucial for us—from these awakenings in the present our future begins to unfold.

Faced with the realities of our lives we may be tempted to shroud our imperfect bodies in tent-like dresses, reduce our ambitions, grieve for our lost dreams or spend our hours replaying the mistakes we have made. In choosing this option we have still not fully liberated ourselves from our images of perfection—we have only resigned ourselves to their inaccessibility. The death of fantasy is not an end or a conclusion in our lives; it is the birth of genuine creativity. It offers us the possibility of forming radically different relationships with ourselves and with others. It is a time of nurturing our capacity for intimacy, for befriending our bodies, smiling at our cellulite, wishing our children the best, congratulating our colleagues and getting on with what is truly significant and meaningful in our lives—our understanding of what it means to live with an open heart and mind and what it means to be free.

Pursuing halos is a habit so deeply ingrained in us that we may well have to first learn the discipline of being. There is a time for all of us when undoing is the path for reconnecting with ourselves and renewing our kinship with what we truly value. It is a time of leaving off our make up, putting aside our briefcases, turning off our entertainment systems and listening inwardly. Maybe we need to take a hike in nature; perhaps we need only to turn off the telephone; we may need to join together with other women to share our stories and bond once more with the power of the feminine. We need to do what is necessary to free us of the habit of chasing halos. There is no magical formula for creativity except the capacity to listen to ourselves and discern the messages that speak to us from our bodies, our minds, our values and our aspirations. We do not need experts to teach us the lessons of intimacy—it is enough to put aside our fascination with other people's lives, models and stories and have the patience to attend to ourselves.

The greatest gift of women is their capacity for interweaving and healing. It is their power to do this that will challenge the hierarchies and stereotypes that scar our world and spirit. Endlessly in our lives we are faced with dualities and polarisations which are conventionally accepted as being the truth. Perfection and imperfection, right and wrong, good and bad are polarisations which have the power to torment our lives and spirit. They are the value judgments which are born of more deeply-rooted dualities. The separations that are made between spiritual and worldly, mind and body, inner and outer, I and you, black and white, masculine and feminine, carry the same aura of truth and appear unbridgeable. The acceptance of dualities appears to call us to make value judgments and the value judgments we make create hierarchies, stereotypes and prejudice. Hierarchies tell the story of better and worse, worthy and unworthy—we feel their effect in the feelings of unworthiness, guilt and inadequacy we experience. Feelings which in turn lead us to pursue halos and models of perfection. Asian women continue to earn merit that they may be reborn a man and qualify for liberation. Professional western women may earn merit through striving and power to qualify for promotion. Young girls may suppress themselves into submission to qualify for a relationship. All are chasing an ideal of perfection that demands the denial of the imperfect. Whose value judgment is governing us? Nowhere in the world of polarisations is discovered peace, interconnectedness or liberation.

Hierarchies and the value judgments that are associated with them are the creation of the mind that is exiled from wisdom. The moment that the inner world is divorced from the outer world, the outer world is reduced to a realm of objects holding the power to gratify or threaten us. A hierarchy is created in which there must be a loser. The sacred is separated from the worldly, the spirit from the body, the mind from feeling, and values of inferior and superior ascribed to the polarisations that are created. The casualties of polarisation are easily visible to us—the natural world is exploited, the world of form and body is diminished, emotion and sexuality are treated with contempt. For a woman who feels intuitively bonded with the rhythms of the natural world, who trusts the power of her feelings and intuition to guide her and who disbelieves the separation made between the sacred and the worldly, the polarisations which are conventionally accepted threaten to dispossess her of her own intuition and creativity. She learns to disbelieve in her intuition, to subdue her creativity and feel unworthy and inadequate.

Traditionally women have been the losers of the hierarchies conventionally accepted as sacred. As a woman she is disbarred from spiritual authority because it is considered the domain of men who possess the needed attributes of courage and certainty to guide and govern. Reproduction is deemed less worthy than the productivity that can be measured in objects and achievements. Creativity may be dismissed as a hobby, while emotion is blamed upon unstable hormones.

The warrior's path asks us to abandon hierarchies and their associated value judgments. To discover freedom we are asked to live in the spirit of freedom. In the choices we make in our lives, the paths we follow, the aspirations we cherish, are we pursuing perfection or bringing to fruition the values and qualities of heart and mind that will enable us to live with integrity and freedom? Are our life directions fuelled by feelings of unworthiness that we are attempting to erase or do they embody creativity rooted in acceptance and understanding? Are we captives of hierarchies and value judgments or do we live with the discriminating wisdom that knows the difference between what contributes to well-being and integrity and what undermines it? Are we prisoners of polarisations and dualities that we have accepted as being legitimate? To step off the wheel of struggle we are asked to return to the very fundamentals upon which we build our lives and our paths. Accepting polarisations and hierarchies as truths is accepting the shadows of comparison, judgment, denial and striving. To invest the spirit with sanctity and the body with unworthiness is to be eternally married to a polarisation which results in abuse not only of our bodies, but of all forms of life. To glorify the inner world and denigrate the outer world may lead us to a highly-refined knowledge of the workings of our mind but a vacuum of understanding of how to live in the world in a creative, respectful and sensitive way.

A woman is a weaver; a warrior woman refuses to accord truth to any stereotype, hierarchy or separation. She knows that a life of freedom and integrity cannot be built upon such shaky and false foundations. She knows that she is endangered by the polarisations, hierarchies and models which guide our culture, and declines to consent to them. She understands the transparency of the divisions that are made between body and spirit, inner and outer, the sacred and worldly, and knows that to accept these divisions and their attendant value judgments is to deny the healing of her world and her spirit. Inferior, superior; perfect, imperfect; worthy and unworthy: these words describe our reactions and speak of our imprisonment within our judgments and dualities. They are not words that speak to us of openness, interdependence or the essence of anything at all. The intuition of the spiritual warrior speaks to her of interconnectedness—she affects the world around her with every feeling and action, just as she is affected by it. She sees sanctity in all things and lives her life in a spirit of reverence—not deceived by appearance but respectful and open to receiving the teachings and possibilities of each moment.

A genuine spiritual path is one that invites us not to strive for perfection or engage in yet more earnest pursuits of excellence, but to see the world and ourselves anew with eyes of innocence. We do not need to have a bulging portfolio of spiritual credentials or certificates of worthiness to enter this path—we need only the willingness to set aside the value judgments and separations that have governed our lives. Our world and ourselves are transformed through the simple willingness to withdraw our projections, assumptions and conclusions. Nothing is condoned through this withdrawal, but much is made possible. How would we see our bodies if we were able to put aside all the words, descriptions and judgments we have about them? If we shed the judgments of flawed, imperfect and unworthy, our bodies would become available to us as vehicles for manifesting and embodying the potential for intimacy, affection and love. What would happen to feelings of anger, jealousy and greed if we stripped away the aversion and contempt we extend to them because we have labelled them unspiritual, impure and unworthy? Those feelings too become available to us to explore, understand and heal. What would happen in our relationship to our world if it was no longer seen as being inferior to a life of the spirit? It would be held in the arms of reverence; cared for and respected.

Creativity is not about producing tangible objects—it is born of the openness and innocence of heart and mind that is not confined by its value judgments and polarisations. Reverence is not about worshipping in a church or temple—it describes a life which is lived in a spirit of respect and sensitivity. Reverence cannot be defined by the actions we perform but is evidenced in the quality of respect with which we act. Reverence is not found in what we see but in the spirit of acceptance and sensitivity with which we see. Reverence is clearly not found in achieving any model or stereotype of perfection but is embodied in the openness with which we embrace the faulty and the divine, the flawed and the flawless. Reverence is the thread with which the weaver weaves together the superficial polarisations and dualities which wound our world and our spirit.

We begin to live in a spirit of reverence in setting aside our distinctions between what is spiritual and what is mundane, what is worthy and what is not, and dedicate our hearts to perceiving the immanence of the sacred in all things, in all aspects of our own being. A great Zen teacher once said, 'In making a hair's breadth of difference, heaven and earth are set apart.'

This statement is not an invitation to seek for sameness or to erase the distinctions which manifest uniqueness. It is an invitation to set aside our value judgments and hierarchies and to see the sacred in all things and all moments. When we approach our relationships, our bodies and each connection with our world in the same spirit with which we would enter a sacred place, we begin to understand what it means to live in a spirit of reverence. It is a spirit that awakens us to the mystery of life and which forms the basis of a truly ethical life, a life of honour and respect.

There is a story of an eastern saint, renowned not for the miracles she performs or the lines of wisdom she delivers, but for the great reverence with which she lives her life. Living in a small hut beside an ancient tree, each morning when she awakes she goes to sit before the tree and gazes upon it throughout the day. Unmoving, with a smile upon her lips, she does no more than honour a single tree. At the end of the day, she rises and bows before the tree and speaks but a few words that express her love of life. 'Well done, well done,' she whispers before going to her hut to rest a few hours before repeating the same ceremony the following day. In these few words she delivers her heartfelt gratitude for and appreciation of life. In her willingness to patiently and devotedly attend to the tree's presence she embodies her reverence for life and herself. In the same spirit of patience and receptivity we bear witness to receiving the lessons of our unfoldment. In honouring the wrinkles in our faces and spirit we learn to live with grace. In receiving without contempt or judgment the flawed and the imperfect in our world and in ourselves we learn to live with understanding and compassion. A life of reverence is not available to the mind and spirit that is imprisoned by hierarchies or dualities.

A spirit of reverence also lends a sense of great immediacy to our own spiritual paths. Our lives and everything in them begin to speak to us of the possibilities of awakening, of connecting with the sacred in each moment. We do not have to wait to be perfect, nor do we have to struggle to make ourselves worthy of saintliness. We are not asked to engage in a long and arduous struggle to overcome our imperfections in order to understand what it means to live a spiritual life. A single leaf blowing in the breeze invites us to listen closely and nurture sensitivity. The wilting bloom of a single flower invites us to understand the impermanence of all things and to live with appreciation. The ripple of a feeling in our hearts, the explosion of a thought in our minds, reminds us to attend devotedly to the rhythms of our own spirit without the interruptions of value judgments. The laugh or cry of a child, the tasks that await our attendance, the connections we form with other people—all of the small and large impressions in our lives have the power to startle to wakefulness a receptive and devoted consciousness. All of these moments, received with receptivity, awaken us to the mystery and wonder of our lives and our world.

The heart of the spiritual life rests upon the promise of a way of seeing and living which is not bound by any dualities or value judgments. A spiritual journey is a sacred journey that invites and inspires us to see the immanence of truth, reality, oneness and interconnectedness in all things and in all moments. It is a teaching that speaks to the heart of the weaver, affirming all that she intuitively senses to be true. The teaching of immanence offers a spiritual home to all of us regardless of our circumstances, histories or lifestyle. We are not asked to become ascetics, erase our past or negate anything within ourselves to enter a journey which asserts the immanence of truth. Immanent, truth is not governed by time, circumstance or credentials—it lies within the flawed, the blemished, the imperfect, in all things and all places. We are encouraged to see the sacred in the smallest actions we perform and to live in a sacred way. Driving our car to work, washing the dishes, touching another person are actions as worthy as spending hours on our knees in prayer or months in a monastery, when they are undertaken in a spirit of heartfelt sensitivity, whole-heartedness and impeccability. The actions we do, the connections we make, the directions we undertake are transformed by the openness of heart and mind with which we engage in them. Living in a sacred way has nothing to do with becoming perfect or flawless—it is way of living in which we honour what lies right before us in each moment.

The danger of entering any spiritual path is the temptation to engage in the pursuit of the most hallowed halo of all—the halo of saintliness. The picture we are most frequently presented with is that the qualifications for saintliness lie in excelling in purity, flawlessness and blamelessness. Throughout history, countless women have felt excluded from the spiritual life simply by virtue of their gender. The spiritual heroes who feature in our spiritual legends are made heroic not only through their wisdom and power of integrity but equally through their capacity to overcome and transcend adversity. Transcendence has always been a key message in spiritual mythology—transcendence, not only of delusion and ignorance, but equally of the world, the body, emotion and the heart. Apart from a few rare examples, the stories of the spiritual heroines we inherit describe our heroines by their excellence in purity, meekness, service and devotion. Too many of our stories tell us that the most direct way to saintliness for a woman is through martyrdom. None of these models offer a great deal of inspiration or a spiritual home to a contemporary woman seeker who searches to connect with the immanence of the sacred in a way which does not demand denial.

Women have learnt the lesson that transcendence is too easily translated into a denial of much that distinguishes their femininity and an abdication of responsibility for the quality of well-being in our world. Overcoming, overpowering and surmounting may well be a path to excellence but the warrior woman is concerned less with excellence than with liberation and integration. Contemporary women feel little affinity with the spiritual models that sanctify self-negation or invisibility, no matter how brightly their halos shine. The models of saintliness and martyrdom inherited through our religious stories look attractive and assure us of a place in heaven, but are remarkably ineffective as vehicles for healing the scars caused by dualities in our spirits and in our world. Our stories, the lessons of our lives and the pain of following the paths of conforming to models teach us that halos are no worthy substitute for authenticity and dignity. We have learnt to honour and value our capacities for nurturing, receptivity and open-heartedness as vehicles for awakening and for deepening our understanding of the immanence of the sacred. We have to learn to honour our bodies, sexuality and hearts as vehicles which connect us on an extraordinarily profound level with all life. The warrior woman does not give birth to yet another stereotype through the lessons she has learnt. She is not tempted to define a spiritual woman only by her capacities for receptivity and nurturing. She knows the art of balance—that receptivity enables clear responsiveness; that openheartedness enables creativity and initiative and that the renunciation of all stereotypes enables exploration and investigation.

Countless spiritual traditions and teachers of spirituality have seemingly rediscovered the power of the feminine. Books are written that vociferously proclaim the virtues of femininity—defined as gentleness, receptivity, openness, flexibility and the power to love and nurture. Suddenly, in much of contemporary spirituality, these qualities are proclaimed as highly-evolved spiritual virtues to be sought. Women are advised to reclaim their femininity and men are encouraged to discover the feminine within themselves. For most women, such proclamations are not news, nor do they require the stamp of approval from any spiritual authority to continue honouring their own femininity as a vehicle for awakening. For many women, such proclamations are rightfully greeted with some suspicion and reservation for they seem to promote only a new 'spiritually-approved' stereotype that defines them in an extraordinarily limited way. It is a stereotype that dispossesses once more the warrior woman. There appears to be little room within it for the qualities of boldness, assertiveness, courage and strength as these are defined as being unfeminine. A new halo is promoted with every new stereotype. The warrior woman is not willing to accept such limitation knowing its consequences in denial and restriction.

The weaver of the spirit knows that the discovery of the sacred, the immanence of truth, can lie nowhere apart from in the reality of each moment, each task and each interaction she engages in. Banishing models of perfection from her life, she frees herself from the bondage of halos. With an open heart and clarity of direction she sets aside the dualities of perfection and imperfection and is free to attend to what is of vital significance in herself and in her world—the end of all separation and the discovery of what is sacred. Through her weaving she learns to heal and to live her life in a spirit of reverence. Every warrior is a weaver.

SEVEN

ALONE AND INTIMATE
THE TIGRESS WHO FORGOT HERSELF

There was once a young tigress who was captured by hunters and sold to a circus. In the beginning she paced the floor of her cage, roaring in fury and lashing out at anyone who approached her. Days passed without her being given food or water and her roars became quieter as she weakened. Her training began and for obeying her trainer she would be rewarded with meat and drink. Soon she learned to bare her fangs and look ferocious when the whip was snapped in her face. She learnt to balance on balls and to walk on a tightrope, to stand on her back legs and to turn somersaults on command. The crowds came to see her and cheered at her tricks; she thought only of the meat that would be thrown through the bars of her cage each evening after she had performed well. The months passed and the circus travelled from town to town, crowds flocking to see the performing tigress. One evening some young people, heartbroken by the tigress's plight, crept into the circus and released her from her cage. They bundled her into the back of a truck and drove many miles into the jungle where they set her free. After so many months of living either in a cage or a circus ring, the tigress felt bewildered by so much space. She sniffed the air fearfully and her ears were confused by the profusion of sound. Frightened, she curled up beneath a tree and slept.

When morning came nothing had changed—no-one came to lead her to the ring to practise her routine and, most importantly, no-one came to feed her. As the day passed and her hunger grew she began to do what she knew best. She stood on her back legs and danced, she rolled over and played dead, she roared and bared her fangs and turned the best somersault she knew. Still no-one came to feed her and she began to perform her repertoire of tricks once more. Suddenly she smelled a familiar odour and, turning, she saw a group of tigers looking at her in bewilderment. ' What on earth are you doing?' they asked her. 'I'm waiting to be fed', she replied innocently. 'Don't you know that if you do all these tricks well, someone will come and bring you the juiciest meat you have ever tasted?' The watching tigers rolled on the ground in laughter. 'You simpleton,' they cried. 'Don't you know you are a tigress and not a clown? This is the jungle where you belong. Tigers don't perform tricks. They hunt for themselves, raise their young, and laze in the sun. If you want to stay alive here you must learn to be yourself.'

Mystics and visionaries in every spiritual tradition speak with reverence of aloneness. Being alone is regarded as a sacred space and time; it is the birthplace of vision, renewal and creativity. Being alone is a transformative time, a time of willingly shedding the props of our goals and ambitions, our identities and habits, our assumptions and conclusions, and resting in a fertile inner openness which is the home of guidance, vision and revelation. Spiritual stories abound of shamans and saints who seek seclusion in deserts and on mountains, tales of the countless people who follow the ancient path of going forth into homelessness, not as a rejection of the world but as a way of exploring the richness and joy of inner solitude. Being alone is an invitation to strip ourselves of knowing and to explore the mystery of the unknown. Learning to be at ease in our aloneness, surrendering the desire to discover fulfilment and definition outside of ourselves, is essential to awakening. No-one can substitute for us on this journey to awakening, no-one can provide us with the peace, wisdom and oneness our hearts yearn for. We need to be willing to be alone, to return to ourselves, to take up the invitation of inner solitude. It is a quest to find ourselves and in finding ourselves discovering a quality of profound communion that bonds us with all life.

The reverence given to aloneness is not the territory only of spiritual or religious traditions. Ancient and contemporary tribal cultures honour aloneness both as a time of initiation and as a sacred ritual to mark significant rites of passage. The passage into womanhood and manhood is honoured by undertaking a ritual period of solitude. Entering into marriage, leaving the parental home and honouring the death of a loved one are life changes honoured and marked through entering into a period of seclusion. For young women in tribal cultures, the beginning of menstruation and entering into womanhood is acknowledged as a radical and dramatic event that deserves solitude as a ritual and form of initiation that allows for an integration of this new reality. The seclusion of the young girl is celebrated by the tribe, it honours her emerging identity as a woman and provides the sacred space for introspection and recontacting her own inner depths.

Aloneness demands transformation; it is a catalyst that encourages metamorphosis and renewal. Young tribal girls recount their experiences of solitude and the cycles of change that happen within them. Initially what is encountered is a basic level of fear. Deprived of familiarity, faced with themselves and the natural world that surrounds them, that world is initially experienced as being pregnant with danger and threat. These young women tell the same stories of initially feeling displaced and bereft—their imaginations run riot with the sounds they hear from the outer world, perceiving them as intrusive and filled with peril. Their inner world is equally dark and filled with tumult. Thoughts seem to run out of control, they feel bombarded with memory and the desperation of reaching out with their minds and feelings to hold onto anything that promises order and safety. In the beginning of their period of solitude they cherish the thoughts of it ending. Yet as time passes a subtle change begins to take place—an inner opening to what is heard and felt and sensed, a heightening of sensitivity. They speak of the calmness that begins to saturate their being; a perceptible sense of wholeness that begins to emerge and an inner connectedness that is healing and visionary. Time falls away, the forest speaks to them and they listen to themselves. It is transformed into a precious and unique time in their lives and they are transformed through it. Aloneness is the one sanctuary that can never be lost or taken away from us.

In both spiritual and tribal traditions aloneness is seen as both benevolent and sacred. Seclusion is honoured as an experience that is pregnant with possibilities and richness—it allows us to attend wholeheartedly to the mystery of our own life and being, to be guided by our own emerging wisdom and to integrate the crises and changes which are natural to our lives. Aloneness is embraced like a lover, entering it is akin to entering a womb in which we give birth to ourselves. Learning to be alone with gladness and eagerness is an art important for us to reclaim. It is an art which does not demand geographical seclusion or isolation—all we need for aloneness is an understanding of how to live in a way in which we are never divorced from ourselves. It is the art of inner communion. Reclaiming the sacredness of aloneness is necessary for our survival as women, as warriors and as visionaries. Exiled from being at ease with ourselves we are equally exiled from the art of being together with others in relationships of integrity and wisdom. Uneasy with ourselves, we search the world for someone to provide us with sanctuary, forming relationships of dependency and clinging. Every woman knows the danger of submerging herself into the identity of another and the grief of losing in that transaction her authenticity and freedom. At ease within ourselves, within aloneness we are free to move through the world without opponents or fear.

The cultural conditioning of women leads us to regard aloneness as an alien, unwelcome experience. Women are raised from birth with the assumption that a relationship or marriage is the only sanctuary where they will find identity and freedom from fear. Aloneness is regarded as only a temporary pause between relationships, or as a kind of waiting room or vestibule where we gather together our strategies for pursuing a relationship. For many young women, a temporary period of aloneness may be condoned before they begin their real life's work, signalled by their willingness to 'settle down'—a euphemism for surrendering aloneness and submerging themselves into a partnership. In the light of this conditioning, aloneness can only be perceived as a state that is fraught with terror and signifies failure. Our culture quietly admires and applauds the long tradition of bachelorhood. The image of the rakish bachelor may even be admired for his successful escape from the ties of relationship and for the preservation of his independence. No such approbation is rewarded to single women. Instead she is surrounded with pity, suspicion, blame and anxiety—she is a misfit, an oddity.

The word spinster carries the implication of describing a woman who has somehow failed to meet her destiny. She has been 'left on the shelf', implying that she was unworthy of selection in the marketplace of relationships. Parents, family and friend surround the single woman with concern and anxiety, perpetuating the assumption that no woman can be truly happy alone. For women, aloneness is invariably equated with loneliness, the absence of another. The solitary woman may be vilified and treated with mistrust by other women; it is assumed that if she is alone she is covertly seeking to land a partner. She may be regarded as a hostile or destructive force who will wreak havoc in social conventions. The solitary woman, undefined by a partner, is equally considered to be fair game for predators. A married woman who is a victim of rape will automatically receive greater sympathy from a court, whereas the credibility of a single woman will be doubted simply because her solitary state brings doubt to her victimisation. An independent woman who is comfortable alone, who chooses solitude, is suspected or accused of having to some degree sacrificed her femininity; defining femininity purely by the capacity for relatedness.

The cultural and social messages that join forces in treating aloneness for a woman as an aberration permeate our consciousness throughout our lives. Deprived of the rituals that celebrate and honour aloneness and exposed to the cultural disapproval and censure that surround the solitary woman, aloneness assumes for us an association of abnormality or defectiveness. We become disenfranchised from that most sacred of relationships—the relationship of inner communion. Our lives become dedicated to that most desperate and conventional of searches—the search for definition that relies upon the approval and approbation bestowed by someone or something outside of ourselves. Young girls thrive upon the romantic images of the fairy-tale white wedding—it continues to signify the end of aloneness, a state the successful woman transcends. We become vulnerable to the most traditional ideas of feminine success—the escape from aloneness into relatedness. Fearing aloneness, we join in subscribing to the conventional belief that aloneness and relatedness are states opposed to one another.

Conditioned to fear aloneness, we are inevitably ill equipped to embrace the crises and changes in our lives with grace or with wisdom. Divorce or the death of a partner reduce a woman who can only define herself by something other than herself, to a state of terror and anguish. She feels herself to be cast adrift without an anchor—her world crumbles as her identity which is based upon relatedness dissolves. The pain over loss which devastates her is not only the human grief of being separated from a loved one—it is also the pain of losing herself as she has come to know herself, through the identity of her relationship. Young women fear leaving the parental home and seek the first pair of arms that will open to catch them—to be alone appears to be fraught with danger. Our conditioning teaches us to view aloneness as a problem, a crisis that can only be solved by submerging ourselves into another. Aloneness, from the perspective of such conditioning, is not an invitation to discovery and revelation, but a predicament to be overcome.

Bowed under the weight of the conditioning which condemns and vilifies aloneness, women learn to regard it not as a sacred, but as a malevolent space—a territory to flee from rather than a sanctuary to return to. This is the myth the warrior of the spirit seeks to dispel. The warrior woman understands deeply that aloneness is not a denial of relatedness, nor is it a prescription for divorcing herself from anyone or anything. She welcomes aloneness and is willing to explore its depths. She understands that the most important challenges she faces in her life she will face alone, her deepest learning she will learn alone. In the most tender and fragile places in her psyche and heart she is alone, just as she is alone in nurturing her greatest strengths and wisdom. No-one but ourselves is able to question the reality of the limitations that appear to bind us, no-one but us is able to foster and explore our own resources and capacities for understanding. No-one experiences life in exactly the same way that we do, no-one but ourselves can resolve the conflicts that grieve us or deliver to us peace and grace. No-one but ourselves can bring transformation or freedom to us, no-one but ourselves is qualified to answer the questions of, 'Who am I?' and, 'What is the meaning of my life?' The warrior woman seeks to find amidst the complexity of her own life and relationships the sanctuaries of her own mountaintops and deserts. She is called upon to create her own sacred spaces—spaces of stillness and calm, in which she can listen, learn and be guided by her own wisdom.

Banished from the sacredness and richness of aloneness, we

learn to view solitude as deprivation and impoverishment. After a long training in defining ourselves only by identities of relatedness—wife, mother, daughter, partner—the state of aloneness presents itself as an endless vacuum of nothingness, a black hole that threatens to consume us. We might wonder what would inspire us if we had no-one to serve, answer to or care for. Loneliness and alienation are perceived to lie within the depths of aloneness and we fear we will be swallowed. This fear turns us into contact addicts in our lives—consuming input, distraction and entertainment to protect us from aloneness. Yet the very mechanisms we use to avoid aloneness and the fear it represents serve only to exaggerate the terror we feel. We become increasingly afraid of loss, change, separation, rejection—we are afraid of ourselves. This is the greatest impoverishment we can encounter in our lives—to live in a way in which we desperately seek to be anywhere but with ourselves; anywhere but alone.

We inherit, through our conditioning and through the rosy models of relatedness we are exposed to, a deep fear of aloneness. It is a fear not only of physical solitude, but a fear that infiltrates our psyches to the extent that we come to believe that any form of psychological, emotional or spiritual aloneness is a state to be avoided if we are to avoid deprivation and vulnerability. There is a hidden message in the condemnation of aloneness for a woman—it is a message that teaches us of the assumed weakness of women. We come to understand that relatedness will offer us protection and a safe haven from a world that is essentially more powerful than ourselves. Marriage, membership in a political or spiritual group, or corporate allegiance we believe will offer us a protector powerful enough to keep the world at bay. Finding an identity within them will provide us with the armour to survive in a threatening world. Only through relatedness, we are taught, will we find roles and identities that are accorded respect, safety and sanction.

The assumption of the intrinsic weakness of women is a shadow that haunts and limits our lives. Historically and currently, young women guide their lives into avenues that highlight their auxiliary role. Supporter rather than leader, assistant rather than director, collaborator rather than guide, follower rather than trailblazer, are all positions traditionally allocated to women. They are the outer expressions of the conclusions that our culture draws about women's frailty, fundamentally colouring their aspirations and horizons. They are equally conclusions that further the assumptions of feminine weakness and frailty. In being encouraged to adopt these shadow-like roles women are encouraged to deepen their belief in their need for relatedness to be 'someone' and to find protection. Locked into these shaded identities, a woman's own sense of personal integrity and respect equally becomes a shadow of the respect and accolades rewarded to those whom they support. They bow beneath the responsibility of dedicating themselves to earning success and prestige for those upon whom their identity rests, as their own respect and prestige is seen to be only the derivative of another's. We are familiar with the insecurity that makes a woman exhort her children to great successes and who speaks primarily of her husband's advancements. Her glory relies upon the glory of another; her stature relies upon the stature of another. The same insecurity makes a woman ashamed to speak of her parent's alcoholism or her partner's or children's failures. Inextricably linking her identity to another, her problem becomes both her responsibility and her shame.

There is nothing intrinsically wrong in the role of the supporter or aide. There is a lethal danger in promoting these roles as the only valid positions for women to inhabit—it is a promotion of the myth of feminine frailty and weakness. It is not only our economic structures that must radically change to offer women positions in which they can express the fullness of their creativity without sacrificing their yearning for relatedness—equally the underlying assumptions asserting that feminine creativity can only find expression in relatedness must be dissolved. The economic structures that currently govern our lives demand that women must choose between mothering and professionalism and assume that women will invariably choose relatedness.

Dependency is the price we pay for subscribing to the myth of feminine weakness which implies the need for protection. Ancient forces within our psyche call for us to please others and to make others strong through our own weakness and powerlessness. Women are expected to be dependent and to care for the dependency needs of others. Frailty invites protection and nurtures the desire for dominance and control in others. Frailty allows us to surrender the burden of taking responsibility for guiding our own lives and living in an authentic way.

Sharon was a success in both her studies and her career. In her social life she looked only for 'strong' men to form relationships with. She defined strength as having a life plan, control and assertiveness. She married a man who had a plan that included them both. Everything was plotted—where they would live, the number of children they would have and the kind of friends they would seek. The plan essentially ignored the demands of her career, but she was willing to sacrifice all for the ideal life he promised. The reality was different—living in her ideal home, with her upwardly-mobile husband who needed soothing and care when he returned each day, she realised she was only a fixture that supported the grand plan. She made no decisions, she created nothing of worth and became increasingly numb. She could see the years stretch before her, repeating the same rituals, trapped in triviality. For a time she attempted to distract herself with 'good works'— volunteering her time and skills to others, while protecting the needs of her family. One night, she caught herself reaching for a sleeping pill and realised the extent to which she had sentenced herself to a life she abhorred. Her life began to change, she felt herself make a new beginning as she began to reconnect with what she truly valued.

Upholding the myth of powerlessness it is deemed appropriate to surrender decisiveness, direction, autonomy and self-reliance—to lean upon and look to others for vision, esteem and guidance. Self-reliance is exchanged for self-definition, creativity is exchanged for protection. In these transactions we do not always appreciate the ways in which we debilitate ourselves and further our inclinations towards self-doubt, self-hatred and dependency. Each time we make these exchanges we exile ourselves increasingly from the richness and power that aloneness offers to us. Dependency is a form of self-abuse and it invites abuse from others. If we are willing to lay down in supplication in our lives inevitably we will find someone eager to walk upon us.

Countless women have seen the dangers that lurk in the web of dependency and no longer subscribe to the myth of powerlessness that leads to the seeking of protection. Innumerable women are no longer willing to exchange freedom for safety yet, in stepping out of those transactions, seem to be faced with impossible options. The opposite of dependency is assumed to be independence; a state that appears to imply the sacrifice of relatedness. We know that true independence is not born of separating ourselves from anyone or anything. We know that independence means a profound inner communion where we do not depend upon anyone or anything for guidance, vision, freedom from fear or identity. Our intuition tells us that independence is knowing how to rest within the sanctuary of our own being, to be at ease within our aloneness and to be guided in our lives by wisdom and vision. Yet our intuition struggles with our conditioning that polarises aloneness and relatedness.

We envision a life of aloneness as being a life that is bereft of intimacy; lonely and isolated. Aloneness, distorted by conditioning and by fear, is perceived to demand a sacrifice of communion with others—an emotional and spiritual wasteland. The greatest crisis a woman may encounter in her life is to find the balance between independence and interdependence. It is a crisis that can only be resolved through searching our hearts to discover an understanding of both aloneness and intimacy that is not distorted by conditioning or by anxiety. There are two great yearnings of the human heart that we connect with again and again in our lives. One is the yearning for authenticity, freedom—to know the truth of our own being. The other is the yearning for intimacy—the capacity to touch the heart of another and to be touched.

In our hearts and through our experience we know the power of intimacy. Out of our capacity to dive beneath the superficiality of images and appearances is born the power to heal, to forgive and to sustain a loving relationship with another. Intimacy is the watershed of generosity, openness and compassion, the only basis of an ethical, responsible and dignified life. We know deeply that it is not righteousness, strategies or prescriptions that will heal the sorrows and scars of our divided communities and relationships. They will be healed through the power of open-heartedness and understanding—through our capacity to be intimate with one another we find the means to live in a sacred way.

Our capacity to discover intimacy with another person bears an undeniable relationship to our capacity to be intimate with ourselves. To be together with another in a way that is not distorted by armour, fear or superficiality we need to discover how to be with ourselves; how to be alone in a wise way, free from fear and mistrust. We cannot compartmentalise our lives—to separate the inner world from the outer world is to create an unnatural divorce. The vision that guides the warrior woman speaks to her of the interwoven threads of the inner and outer world. To live in a sacred way, she knows the need to explore aloneness as it was originally defined—to mean 'all one'. To be 'all one' does not imply submerging ourselves into another nor to live like a chameleon absorbing all the colours of the world around us. It means to live with such a radical openness and understanding that we are no longer deceived by appearances but rest in the essence of all things and ourselves.

It does not require mystical vision to understand interdependence, but it does requires a greatness of heart and vision to understand the implications of interdependence. All of life is sustained by interrelatedness. As we read these words with a great and open heart we will have a glimpse of the towering trees that provided the paper, the sun and the rain that allowed those trees to grow and the ways in which this paper becomes compost for yet new growth. As we look into the face of another person we see the faces of the generations of people who came before them, the nurturing that made their lives possible and the ways in which they affect the world around them with their every thought, word and deed. As we look into our own face we see reflected the joys and sorrows, the fears and possibilities, the yearnings and terrors of all life. In everything we see, touch, consume and hear we sense the echoes of the thousand life cycles that made that moment possible. We sense the passage of life that moves through all forms and appearances. There is nothing that is random in this passage; we sense the natural order of life's unfoldment in which we have an intrinsic place and relatedness.

In opening our hearts to the interrelatedness that weaves together all of life we discover an organic kinship. Life manifests in different forms—in stones and trees, in creatures and rivers, in the rhythms of nature's seasons and in ourselves. We are alone in our manifestation, just as all of life finds its own unique expression, yet all are kindred spirits born of life's changes, often mysterious and yet not needing justification. It is our need for explanation and our demand for order that separates one thing from another and demands purpose and definition. It is the moment of setting aside our imperious and controlling mind with all its fears that we begin to sense our depth of relatedness and the joy of being a conscious participant in life's unfoldment. With an open heart we see directly the ways in which all of life's different elements and forms relate to one another and are informed by each other. We learn to listen and be informed—we learn the art of communion, of being all one.

Our lives are made sacred by our consciousness of life. Walking in the woods in a sacred way, the woods speak to us. Each one of life's expressions is to be honoured and celebrated. We live in a noble way—respecting the dignity and freedom of each of life's creatures and forms. We understand profoundly the statement that to harm another is to harm ourselves; to care for another is to care for ourselves. There is no greater isolation than to be banished from this fundamental relatedness; there is no greater intimacy than to live in a sacred way that is rooted in interconnectedness. We are alone in our capacity to nurture the willingness to commune with life and with ourselves. Our essential aloneness offers us an invitation to peel away the armoured layers of our conditioning—to touch the heart of ourselves and of all life.

Learning to befriend aloneness is a primary challenge of the warrior woman. In doing so she reclaims herself and befriends life. Aloneness is the home of the courageous spirit and the great heart—it is where we discover the end of fear. To rest in a quality of aloneness where we fear nothing within ourselves, where nothing is felt to be missing and which is filled with a deep contentment and wholeness, is knowing what it means to banish the demons of dependency and need that impoverish us. To rest in an aloneness that is saturated with inner trust, integrity and courage enables us to live in a fearless way, embracing our relatedness with all life without ever departing from a relationship of intimacy with ourselves. It is in the end of fear that we discover the depth of intimacy with all things that is possible for us.

There is the story told by a young woman who became separated from her friends on a hiking trip in the woods of Alaska. 'I don't know how it happened', she recounted. 'One minute I was following the footprints and the sounds of the person in front of me and the next minute it seemed they were gone. Maybe I was daydreaming, maybe I was thinking of the meal we would prepare together when we stopped. All I knew was that I was alone. At first I didn't worry, I was sure they would come back to look for me at any moment. Then everything became strange. I realised I had no idea of how much time had passed since we had separated. It could have been minutes, it could have been hours. The woods seemed to be filled with noises—none of them were friendly. I imagined I heard bears stalking me, the undergrowth seemed filled with menace. Then those sounds were drowned out by another. I realised it was the pounding of my heart and the sound of my own blood raging through my body. I was sure I was going to die as I sank deeper and deeper into my own panic and terror. I curled up on the forest floor with my arms wrapped around me, lost in the horror of my own darkness. I thought of how awful my own life was—the marriage I was fleeing from, my failure with my children, the people I had hurt in my life. The thoughts of my own inadequacy and darkness seemed endless; everything seemed so pointless. My empty relationships, the degrees I'd worked so hard to win, the love I'd tried so hard to earn—they all seemed so meaningless and were all in vain, ending in my death on this forest floor.

'It seemed like hours that I lay there and wailed and cried—like a baby who lost her mother. My aloneness was like a black and bottomless pool, I was its victim and its creator. I sobbed and moaned and screamed out my hopelessness and terror, I cried out for help and knew it would never come; had never come when I needed it most. At last, exhausted, the tears and the sobs ended and as I lifted my head I realised that the light had changed and a breeze had sprung up. Gratefully, I felt it cool my flushed face and began to look around me. The vast stillness of the forest was still there; it seemed eternal. As I rubbed my swollen eyes I saw the ways that the sun was reflecting off the greenery and the swaying of the branches in the breeze. Silently, hardly moving the branches, she came. A young deer stepped out onto the path in front of me—a path that hadn't even been visible to me when I had cast wildly about in my terror. She seemed born of the woods and stood there lifting her nose to smell the breeze. She was so at home, so complete, so at one with the forest. I was entranced and watched her with a dream-like calm as the doe stepped carefully through the undergrowth. She was alert to danger, constantly raising her head to sniff the air—but totally composed. It came to me that the difference between me and the deer was that fear, for the deer, was an ally—alerting her to danger, connecting her with her world. For me fear was an enemy, driving me out of myself and out of my world. I got to my feet and slowly followed her—the path that was there for her was also there for me. After a time the doe, sensing something imperceptible to me, ran off into the woods. I watched her go, filled with gratitude. Keeping my eyes on the path I was filled with a certainty that it would lead me to safety. To stay with the path, that at times was covered with creeping undergrowth, I needed to be so totally awake that I lost all consciousness of time. My body seemed to lose its boundaries, the branches grazed my face and the sun touched me. A deep peace filled me—I felt I was the forest and the forest was me. It came as a surprise to me when I realised I could smell wood smoke and could hear voices in the distance. When I stepped into the clearing where my friends had made camp they came running with relief and concern etched on their faces. I never could explain to them the journey I had made in being lost.'

There are many times in our lives when we lose our way and flounder in confusion and terror. There are times in our lives when factors outside of our control remind us of our vulnerability. People and circumstances we have relied upon fail us; trust is vanquished; love is withdrawn. There are moments in each of our lives when events and circumstances appear to conspire together to deprive us of all certainty, reliability and order. In those moments we face our own mortality, we face the immutable forces of change that govern our world and our lives and inevitably we face fear. It is moments of crisis that most acutely remind us of our aloneness. Yet it may also be true that many of the changes and shifts we experience in our lives become a crisis because of the ways in which we have become alienated from being at ease and whole within aloneness. We grieve over the death of or separation from those we love. Being at home in aloneness does not mean that we feel loss and grief less keenly. It may mean that we are able to attend to that grief and sorrow with grace and wholeheartedness rather than fear and devastation. Certainties are dissolved through the immutable force of change—aloneness does not leave us untouched or unaffected by anxiety. Knowing the sanctuary of aloneness means that change does not erode or shatter our trust in ourselves.

In moments of uncertainty we have nowhere to turn but to ourselves, to find sanctuary in our own trust, vision and wisdom. Panic is born when we discover that we have become so estranged from ourselves through fear or dependency that no sanctuary is available to us when our external refuges crumble. The cuckoo who always lays its eggs in the nest of another bird lives in constant fear of eviction. Never building her own nest, she neglects the essential foundation of her life and the lives of her young. We cannot afford to neglect the essential foundations of our lives or we too will live with the ongoing fear of eviction.

The one thing we can never divorce ourselves from is the quality of our own being. Whether we live in community or on a mountaintop, the quality of our inner world, our relationship with ourselves is our constant companion. It is the enduring thread that informs our relationship with every facet of our lives. Our thoughts, our feelings, our memories and hopes, our sense of possibility and vision travel with us on every journey we make in our lives. We must learn the ways of befriending ourselves and befriending our aloneness. Unless we are willing to do this, fear and estrangement, grasping and dependency will also be our constant companions in the journeys we make.

The demand for order, predictability and certainty from the world and other people is the forerunner of bereavement, panic, desperation and dependency. To make similar demands upon ourselves is to invite the same chaos into our hearts and minds. Like the woman lost in the forest we need to learn the art of transforming fear into an ally that bonds us with the world and guides us, rather than regarding it as an enemy to be fled from, that sends us rampaging through the world in search of certainty. Surrendering the demand for order and certainty entails opening to our own wildness. Like the deer, we too must learn to live with our senses acutely honed to our inner and outer world. Learning to open to the multiple facets of our own being demands a keen receptivity and responsiveness. Too often we exclude from our consciousness many of our feelings, thoughts and sensations out of our craving for order, manageability and certainty. A woman accustomed to agreeability may not welcome rebelliousness if it threatens to disturb the placidity of her days. A woman who has invested her identity in an image of compassion and care may find herself reluctant to acknowledge feelings of anger or resentment. To be all one, we must be all one with all of ourselves without conditions. Anger, greed, jealousy—we need to make room for them in our hearts, just as we embrace empathy, compassion and love. Fear is a feeling to be explored and befriended, just as we open our hearts to joy and sensitivity. Jealousy, anger, or greed that are shut out of our hearts because of judgment are jealousy, anger or greed that increasingly become opponents to be feared.

During the time of the Buddha, when it was traditional for monks and nuns to gather together in communities, it came about that there was one particular monk who consistently avoided gathering together with his brothers, preferring to separate himself. A number of the monks came to the Buddha complaining, asking if this was the true way to travel the path and to be alone. The Buddha answered that the fulfilment of aloneness was never to be found in pursuing isolation. The fulfilment of aloneness, he said, is to be found in letting go. To know aloneness, the Buddha answered, we must explore what it means to relinquish the past, all that has already gone by; to hunger not for the future, for what is yet to come; and to be free from all grasping and resistance in the present. It is not the virtues of physical solitude that are praised in these statements. What is spoken of is the richness of inner solitude, a quality of aloneness that does not rely or depend upon past history, present companions or future dreams for self-definition.

It is not difficult for us to renounce the world and our relationships when they are filled with disharmony and conflict. We become enthusiastic advocates of solitude and withdrawal when we have been wounded or disillusioned by our world or the people in it. Leaving a destructive relationship, we welcome the possibility of being alone. To know how to live in the world free from enmity, dependency and fear is a profound challenge. To relate with others wholeheartedly without ever renouncing aloneness requires ever-renewed wisdom. To accept and learn from our personal histories and past experiences without defining ourselves by them is to learn the art of letting go that liberates us. To live in the world without ever being confined by self-images and beliefs is to live in the spirit of freedom. No longer abandoning ourselves or our connection with this moment through preoccupation with future fantasies and promises, we learn the wisdom of aloneness. The warrior's quest does not demand that we sacrifice our learning from the past, negate the future or surrender our relatedness to the present. It is a quest that invites us to surrender dependency and the confinement that is the only possible offspring of clinging.

There is one constant and enduring factor that draws together the relationships we form with other people and our world and the relationship we have with ourselves—it is the factor of personal identity. The quality and depth of intimacy that is discovered in any relationship hinges upon the clarity with which we hold our own sense of identity. Understanding identity is the key to being at ease in aloneness and equally at ease in relationships of intimacy and closeness. There is nothing in our lives—our ways of seeing, acting, choosing, defending, opening our roles and lifestyles—that is not flavoured by the sense of identity we hold. Our sense of identity in this moment is profoundly flavoured by our personal histories, our stories and experiences from the past. The impact of authorities in the past; our encounters with pain and sorrow; our experiences of joy and closeness; the expectations we have been exposed to and the feedback we have received, all play a part in forming the identities we have come to inhabit. Many of the descriptions we hold about ourselves have an extraordinarily long history, conditioned by what we have lost or gained, possessed or been denied; experiences which in turn condition our relationship to the world and to ourselves. They equally condition our capacity for intimacy.

Identities that are dependent upon the credentials or descriptions derived from the past are essentially fragile because of their dependency upon what has already gone by. Fearsome independence rooted in the wounds of past dependency or chronic dependency rooted in the pain of past disempowerment may be identities we protect and cherish, yet both deny true intimacy with ourselves and others. To know ourselves only by what has already gone by is to confine ourselves to existing within a museum. All that we are able to communicate through those identities is our re-enactment of what has already passed. Our wounds, memories and past experiences are replayed over and over in life and continuity is given to what has finished, yet not been completed, through our continuing identification with it.

In the days of the wandering nuns in India, a great mystic was passing through a village one day, tired and dusty from her travels. Seeing a young girl by the village well, she requested of her a cup of water to drink. The young girl said to her, 'Oh, great teacher, I'm unworthy to offer you water. Please do not ask this of me for I would only cause you impurity. I am a child of the lowest caste of this village.' The wandering teacher looked at her with eyes of compassion and said, 'I did not ask you for your caste but for a drink of water.'

Identities which are deeply rooted in the memories of the past are invariably rigid and inflexible and they inform our relationship to the present and the future. The rigidity of them denies to us new ways of seeing ourselves and new vision for our lives. It is like the story of the famous author who desired an audience with a Zen master. She arrived at his home and presented the master's attendant with her business card which stated her name followed by a long list that mentioned all of her degrees and successful publications. The Zen master pondered the card for a time and then tore it up saying, 'Such a learned person has no need to visit with such a poor person as myself. Send her away and give her directions to the most famous master in Kyoto.' When the attendant relayed the message to the woman, she realised her error and, taking a blank piece of paper from her bag, she wrote upon it a simple request for a meeting and signed it with her name. When this message was delivered to the master, he took one look at it and exclaimed, 'Ah, I have been waiting a long time to meet with this person. Please send her in.' Identities, adopted through fear and uncertainty, become rigid and decree a rigidity in the way in which we perceive and relate to the world. If we see ourselves only in the form of an image, we inevitably perceive the world and other people only in the form of an image, based upon appearance and the descriptions and judgments we place upon those appearances. There is no intimacy in the world of appearances nor any genuine relatedness.

Identities adopted out of fear and uncertainty manifest the deepest levels of need and dependency. The need to be able to say 'I am' with certainty as a means of providing inner authority and gaining approval from others ensures that we become increasingly dependent upon the descriptions we have adopted for ourselves. Yet the Siamese twin of dependency is fear. Aloneness becomes an uneasy experience because it highlights the fragile nature of our adopted identities—there is little feedback forthcoming in aloneness that affirms the identities we rely upon.

Aloneness offers us revelations we do not always welcome. Taken out of the familiarity of our worlds we are faced with the degree to which we have invested our sense of identities in roles and appearances. A course was offered for women seeking a renewal of direction in their lives. Preparing to leave, one woman found herself packing her suitcase with photo albums that recorded her family's life. On arrival, she filled her room with pictures and filled every conversation with references to her children. Another woman participating in group discussions would begin every dialogue with the words 'I am a therapist'. Having established her credentials she would proceed to offer all of her expertise. Both women came with an armour that denied intimacy. As the days passed and the women listened ever more keenly to each other, they began to appreciate how very redundant the armour of their identities was. They did not need to prove their worth or protect themselves. In doing so they understood the degree to which they were denying the very intimacy they sought.

Intimacy is uneasy if we approach relationships with adopted identities at the forefront of our consciousness—there lurks within us the fear of being disrobed and divested of our identities by another. We know that beneath our façade of competence, niceness, independence and winsomeness there lies a whole world of hidden feelings, thoughts and forces. Unaccepted by ourselves, we doubt that they will win us any credits in the world of relationship. Waking up in our lives is about not hiding from anything. Hiding nothing from ourselves, we are no longer compelled to hide anything from another. The barriers and armour we use to camouflage who we are or who we fear ourselves to be, dissolve in the light of an awareness that is vast and generous enough to embrace every facet of our being.

To be identified with any image, description, role, appearance or definition means that 'I' can never be alone. The endless monologues flow through our consciousness stating 'I am', 'I used to be', 'I must have', 'I will become' and 'I need'. It is the 'I need' that reaches its tentacles out to the world and to other people to affirm the 'I am' and to cast us into the perpetual exile of dependency. The satisfaction of need always appears to lie outside of ourselves, to be gained or won from another. The 'I' that depends upon the satisfaction of need for affirmation can never be alone—it relies upon having a companion and the companion is found through clinging. The sense of self that is exiled from aloneness feeds and thrives upon consumption, gain, experience, possessions and contact—seeking to find a reality for itself. Yet anything that can be gained, experienced, contacted or possessed can also be lost; realities are dissolved and the 'I' wanders on perpetually seeking security and rest.

Our own life stories and experiences tell us of the destructive force of neurotic dependency upon relatedness. There is no growth or creativity in a relationship that is governed by need and dependency because the primary demand of dependency is for order, sameness and predictability. Change, from the perspective of dependency, is not seen as the fertile ground for new growth, but as a threat which spells danger not only to our relatedness but equally to the identities which are invested in our relationships. We need only to look at nature, our world, our relationships, ourselves, to know that anything that cannot change, that is not open to change, is doomed to wither or to endless repetition which inevitably results in frustration. This message is relayed to us on a microcosmic level in our lives; it is revealed to us again and again on a global level in our world. Endless battles and wars are fought which replay ancient hatreds that never heal because of the unwillingness to let go and open to new possibilities. Aloneness is denied through the demand for sameness, through dependency and through fear.

Learning to be alone is learning the art of intimacy—to be present in the presence of all things, to live with a heartfelt communion. It is learning to unlock the doors of the prison of fear. We are not asked to erase the past but to transform our relationship to it—to surrender our clinging to the past as a way of gaining self-definition. We are not asked to sacrifice direction in the present—but to renounce identities that are rooted in fear. We are not asked to deny thoughts of our plans for the future—but to discern the difference between creativity and the search for security. Letting go is not concerned with negation but with transformation.

Abandoning clinging does not demand that we abandon identity. Countless women have extended endless effort to discovering an identity they can honour. Courage, perseverance and determination have brought them out of invisibility and powerlessness. Learning how to be a woman, how to be themselves, how to live with dignity and honour, are hard-won lessons. Appreciating the trials of our path, we are reluctant to take any steps that would mean relinquishing the integrity we have discovered. Letting go is not to reduce ourselves to nonentities. Each one of us makes an appearance in the world, inhabiting roles and identities that offer us the possibility of communicating in clear and wise ways all that we honour and value. Identities are vehicles of expression—through them we touch the world and other people and manifest integrity and wisdom. Identities which serve us as vehicles of communication differ radically from identities that are clung to out of fear or dependency. They are never rigid or inflexible, but ever open to learning. Because they are means of embodying the wisdom that is close to our hearts they bring joy and creativity. Free of clinging, they need no defending or proving. They are appropriate—a mother in one set of circumstances in our lives does not sentence us to attempting to mother the world. An employer in our office does not mean having to organise every situation we enter. There is a remarkable fluidity and freedom in our being in the absence of clinging—we can move through this world and our relationships without dragging behind us the shadows of the past or the burden of need that so distorts the present.

To be all one with ourselves we need no longer fear vulnerability. In this profound inner communion there is a trust in our own wisdom and being that can never be stripped away from us. To be all one means being able to let go of the desperation of seeking outside of ourselves for the warmth, sanctuary and openness our hearts yearn for—it is present with us in all moments. To be all one with this moment in our lives awakens a deep sense of possibility. This moment is our next moment's personal history. To cling or to let go, to resent or to forgive, to distance ourselves or to connect, to further hatred or to extend love—these are the possibilities that each moment offers to us. The choices we make in this moment inform the quality of the next moment. To explore these possibilities in a way that deepens freedom and intimacy we must clarify what it is we are committed to and honour. If we are committed to freedom and intimacy we must manifest an equal commitment to letting go of dependency and learning the wisdom of aloneness. Commitment to intimacy asks us to let go of anything that dishonours or distorts the fundamental interconnectedness that marries us to all life. It is a renunciation of hatred, images, demands and dependency. Commitment to freedom asks us to renounce anything that dishonours our intrinsic dignity and aloneness—the clinging to roles, descriptions and our notions of need. To cease to cling to anything does not introduce us to bereavement but to a vast intimacy with all things, with ourselves.

There is a profound generosity of spirit that is embodied in our willingness to let go. Renunciation is a greatness of heart that fully embraces another person as they are—accepting their failings and imperfections as equally as we accept their strengths and virtues. It is the same greatness of heart that allows us to accommodate all of who we are in the same spirit—that shows us how to be alone. Renunciation is the gift of freedom we are able to offer ourselves and the world in each moment. It is a gift that fosters intimacy and relatedness.

Zen master Dogen once said, 'To be enlightened is to be intimate with all things.' It is actually much harder to be distanced from all things than it is to be intimate. Intimacy is sparked by love, there is nothing in this world that is not enriched by the touch of love. Distance requires suspicion, fear and resentment—there is nothing in this world that is not impoverished by the touch of all of these. Intimacy asks compassion and acceptance—they are qualities that open our hearts and ignite responsiveness. Distance relies upon clinging to resentment, images and the past—they can serve only to harden our hearts and to live with reactiveness. Intimacy with ourselves asks of us trust and a profound generosity of spirit—a greatness of heart that deepens wisdom and sensitivity. Alienation demands judgment, denial and avoidance—qualities that can only erode well-being and inner communion. Intimacy asks for honesty; distance requires dissembling. Love is a major ingredient of intimacy just as defensiveness perpetuates distance. It takes no great expertise to see where the paths to healing lie and where the paths to the furthering of separation and alienation are found.

The warrior woman knows that intimacy is not a static state she reaches with anyone or anything. Like a growing plant it asks for nurturing. The nurturing that sustains and deepens intimacy in our lives is in the commitment to it that we renew again and again. In exploring the depths of her own consciousness and spirit she journeys without fear or resistance. The courage she learns means that there is nothing in the world that will imprison her. She seeks communion and lives with an abiding faith that communion with all things, all people, is possible and accessible to her. Her journey is one of creation—consciously participating in the creation of each moment in her life, in the healing of her world. She is alone but never lonely. She knows a profound joy in her aloneness but there is never a moment when she is not conscious of her relatedness with all things. At ease with herself, she lives in a world without opponents.

EIGHT

THE FEMINIST MYSTIC

Envision a woman who walks the earth with grace and dignity; who lives her life with integrity and compassion; a woman who sees the presence of the sacred in all things—she is a mystic. Envision a woman who knows a profound inner freedom and embodies it in her every thought, word, action and choice; a woman who is dedicated to seeking and understanding the deepest truths about herself and her world, whose life is given dignity and nobility through manifesting those truths—she is a mystic. Imagine a woman whose heart and spirit are filled with compassion born of her unshakeable understanding of interconnectedness; a woman who sees the transparency of separation and celebrates her freedom in joy—she is a woman who is impatient with division and limitation. She is a mystic. She is a woman who sees the special in the ordinary and the ordinary in the special. Autumn leaves speak to her of endings, just as every sunrise reminds her to greet the beginning of a day with the same reverence with which she would greet her lover. Profound experiences of joy are embraced with the same balance she brings to anger. The life and world of the mystic are touched and transformed by her dedication to understanding what is true. She is a woman who rejects nothing but prejudice and falsehood, she is at home in aloneness and silence yet moves with ease in the world. A mystic is a woman who is awake.

Envision a woman who seeks to travel a path in her life

where she lives, loves and creates in and through all that makes her a woman—she is a feminist. She is at ease within the body of a woman; creates with the hands and heart of a woman and sees with the eyes of a woman. She is a woman unwilling to surrender wisdom or vision; she lives with dignity and impeccability. Envision a woman of courage, who seeks to fulfil all that is possible for her, who consents to no definition or structure that seeks to confine her—she is a feminist. She is a woman guided by inner authority; open to learning and embarked upon a journey of discovery upon which there are few sure signposts. She is a woman who seeks to be awake. A feminist mystic is a woman who has discovered the art of weaving together vision and action; wisdom and expression; her spirit and her life, into an indivisible tapestry.

At first glance a vast gulf appears to separate the feminist and the mystic. The mystic, we assume, will be solely occupied with matters of the spirit, intent upon the heavens, whereas the work of the feminist seems to be rooted in the world of structures and institutions—focussed upon change and the nurturing of respect and integrity. The paradox lies not within the spirit of these women but within our associations. To understand their essential unity, we are asked to dive beneath our associations and images and understand the spirit and the truth in which the feminist and the mystic merge. The word mystic evokes for us images of remote, bearded men entrenched upon mountain tops from where they deliver their prophecies and commandments. We may hold romantic and idealised images of women dressed in black praying before altars upon bended knees. In a similar way, the word feminist may evoke images of strident activists marching behind banners or articulate women arguing their case for equality. Our culture has succeeded in producing a wealth of stereotyped images portraying feminists as angry, embittered women intent on denigrating men; images which serve only to trivialise the wisdom that lies within the heart of the feminist. All of these images act only to camouflage the truth and the spirit of the feminist and the mystic.

A mystical life cannot be qualified by the wearing of a uniform, adherence to a religious system or withdrawal from the world. The life of a feminist cannot be qualified only by her allegiances, her identification with a sisterhood or her education in the history and crimes of patriarchy. Neither the mystic nor the feminist will be known by their uniform or their credentials. They will be known by the compassion, courage and integrity they bring to their words, actions, relationships and choices. A mystical life can be qualified only through the love and wisdom with which we live our lives and touch our world. An authentic mystic is not confined to the heavens by her vision—the heart of mysticism is concerned with freedom. She is as likely to be found in the supermarket as in the nunnery. The life of the mystic cannot be defined by any particular lifestyle—but only by the freedom of her spirit from which she is never separated. There are countless mystics in the world who have never been associated with any movement. They are women who have learnt through their own experience and stories that wisdom, freedom and dignity cannot be delivered to them by anything or anyone outside of themselves. They have discovered their own footpath through the wilderness of voices that seek to confine them and learnt to walk that path with wisdom.

The birth of the mystic is a mysterious process and the feminist mystic may be found in the most unlikely of places. A young woman speaks of the awakening gifted to her through the birth of her severely disabled child. The first days after the birth she spent in a twilight of grief, anger and denial. She found it difficult to hold her baby or to look into her face without being overwhelmed by sadness and terror. All the dreams she had cherished of a beautiful, lively child who would share her days replayed themselves over and over in her mind. She felt shame and blamed herself. All that the future seemed to offer her was endless years of hospital visits and caretaking. One morning, as she was trying to feed her crying baby, it came to her that this tiny infant cherished no thoughts of past or future, she had not chosen her body nor could she change it. All that her baby asked of her was for the loving touch and affection that only she could provide in that moment. She realised that her baby's gift to her was innocence—an opportunity for her to love without conditions or expectations. She also knew that to enter that innocence she needed to have the willingness and greatness of heart to set aside her world of dreams and regrets. Unless she could do this she would always be separate from her child, imprisoned in a world of regret and lost dreams. She spoke of the relief she experienced as she dropped the burden of pain and the joy of embracing her child, just as she was.

Mystical awakening, mystical vision is born of the openness of heart through which life touches us. It is born in the hospital bed of the elderly woman who in the last days of her life seeks to live with greatness of heart. It is found in prisons beneath the shadows of brutality. The possibility of awakening lies in each moment that we are present, seeking to understand what is true. The mystic trusts the possibility of transformation and liberation and knows that she holds in her own hands and heart the realisation of that possibility. Any woman who seeks to understand the nature of pain and conflict and their causes, who ventures to explore the deepest levels of her own psyche is a mystic. She is intent upon awakening, upon nurturing wisdom, upon transformation. The mystic knows how to listen inwardly, how to attend to the guidance of her own intuition. She knows that a life of compassion, love and integrity is the only meaningful way to live.

The feminist mystic is unlikely to conform to our stereotypes of saintliness. A woman who refuses to accept limitation does not easily wear the mantle of self-effacement or meekness. In allowing nothing to stand between herself and freedom she will be willing to challenge the structures and institutions that seek to divest her of authority. In her search for transformation she knows in her heart that there is no place for passivity, but that vitality and creativity are the keys to embodying wisdom. A mystic values above all else love, compassion and freedom. She is a woman of wisdom who knows that to live her life in a truthful way she must find the courage to live her life in a radical way.

There are many women mystics who have their roots within the institutions and structures of organised religious traditions and institutions that offer them the language and forms through which they can express and articulate their vision. Many of these institutions and structures are terrified by the presence of the feminist mystic who has appeared in their midst. Two thousand five hundred years ago dire prophecies predicted the death of Buddhism when women were admitted into the ordained orders. The same prophecies are repeated today in the Church of England. The structures of our spiritual paths are invited to respond to the vision and wisdom of the feminist mystic. Too often they shame themselves with shallow arguments that seek to convince the mystic that her home is in service and silence but not in awakening and celebration. The mystic is blessed with the intrinsic authority that is born of profound wisdom—she is disinterested in argument, unswayed by authority that is rooted in ancient prejudice. Needless to say she is not always popular or venerated, but glory and applause do not rank highly on her list of priorities.

The feminist mystic who has her roots in traditions such as Buddhism or Christianity must be a pathfinder and a trailblazer. The contemporary mystic is no longer willing to shroud the authority of her vision in silence, but seeks to create forms for its expression. Inevitably her passion for truth and her determination to create vehicles for its expression bring her into contention with the institutions and authorities who have previously held the right of authority within their hands. She invites the structures and institutions that have offered her a spiritual home to look anew at what genuine authority is and where its source lies. The feminine mystic is unwilling to accept that history, custom, ancient hierarchies or tradition can claim the sole right to dispense authority. For a woman of wisdom, the right of leadership lies not in the past, in hierarchy or credentials, but in insight, dedication and authenticity. She challenges the assumption that the rightful place for the feminist mystic in religious tradition lies solely in the roles of a disciple or devotee who follows preordained paths outlined for her by the authority of tradition. Leadership, for the feminist mystic, can no longer be equated with having 'authority over', nor is it acceptable to her that leadership is manifested only through the dispensations of decrees and rules. She knows that true leadership never deprives anyone of freedom, creativity or vision, but instead encourages it. The contemporary mystic eagerly welcomes the debates that currently rock our churches and monasteries. This is a crucial time for the feminist mystic—it is a time of necessary transformation. It is a time, unlike any other in the history of our religious structures, for the feminist mystic to manifest the power of her own vision and wisdom in a way that cannot be ignored or denied.

There are few precedents for such expression and, understandably, existing structures and hierarchies feel threatened in the face of challenge. There was a time when, visiting an eastern monastery, I was invited by the abbot to give a talk to the resident monks on renunciation. I gladly agreed, not knowing the difficulties that would follow. According to the rules, as a woman I was disbarred from giving the talk from the podium that the speaker would traditionally sit upon, because this would elevate me physically to a position above the monks, forcing the monks to look up to me. A woman, according to tradition, could only occupy a position lower than the monks, anything else threatening their stature. In the face of this seemingly insurmountable problem a great variety of strategies was offered. Perhaps I would be willing to sit in the abbot's hut and give the talk through the PA system; would I be willing to stand at the side of the hall where the monks would not see me and use a microphone; perhaps I could tape the talk and then the tape could be replayed in my absence— the suggestions became more and more ingenious and elaborate. As the arrangements and discussions went on, it was easy to forget that the core of all of this argument was an exploration of renunciation.

There is a great paradox that exists in the spiritual life in that the forms and structures that exist to give life and nourishment to the spirit and to awakening equally have the power to suffocate the life of the spirit through fear and protectiveness. The feminist mystic knows in her heart and through her experience that the forms and institutions of the spiritual life exist to serve the truth and as a vehicle of expression, and not to serve themselves. To venerate our institutions, forgetting that they are symbols reminding us to awaken, is akin to admiring a picture frame and ignoring the portrait it holds. The courage of the mystic means that she does not shrink from debate, if debate will bring transformation, but equally she knows that she comes to the spiritual life as a woman and must travel her path as a woman, honouring and utilising all of who she is as a vehicle of awakening.

The feminist mystic knows that confinement and limitation do not lie inherently in any form, institution, lifestyle or model. Confinement is found equally in the attempted imposition of the institutions and in the consent to that imposition. A woman may be commanded to silence, but silence ensues only when she agrees to muzzle her voice. The mystic knows that to rest within a true understanding of freedom and wisdom within her own being means that there is nothing in the world that can imprison her.

The feminist mystic may never have set foot in a church or a temple, she may be entirely bereft of religious education. Her awakening may be born of tragedy—pain has a remarkable power to startle us to wakefulness and enquiry. Her awakening may be born of a single moment of being touched by life's mystery; the laugh of a child or the touch of the wind upon her cheek received with an open heart and receptive spirit hold the power to move her to look at her world and herself with a sense of wonder and possibility. The mystic lives within the heart and the life of any woman, anywhere, who senses the possibility of transformation, who refuses to accept imprisonment, who trusts in her capacity to rest in a quality of inner freedom and compassion that is without restriction.

There have always been mystics—the woman who first sought blessing from nature as she planted the Spring's first seeds knew of the need to live with reverence and gratitude upon the earth. The woman who ritually cleansed herself before going on a hunt and then honoured her kill manifested the spirit of communion with the creatures upon the earth who would nurture her. The woman who sought time for solitude and reflection in the midst of her clamouring family knew of the need to nourish her spirit. The woman who could forgive her rapist sensed that only she could free herself of the prison of pain that had been inflicted upon her life. The aging grand-mother who whispers visions of possibility into her grand-daughter's ear and encourages her to reach for greatness passes on the priceless gift of seeking. Mystics are real women, living real lives, holders of ancient wisdom.

There was a woman whose baby died soon after its birth. She had never known such pain was possible, her heart was broken. No-one, it seemed, could comfort her. Her husband, her friends, her family—all were shunned. Days passed and she returned home from the hospital and buried her baby. Day after day, she would sit in her darkened house—unwilling to share her grief; sure that no-one could understand her pain. She began to hold her anger, bitterness and pain close to her heart as she would have held her baby. Soon people began to stop trying to reach her, hurt by her rejection. She no longer had the energy or wish to care for herself and lay in bed, her hair greasy, her body uncared for, her bitterness and loneliness hardening. One morning she heard a child playing outside her window and she began to get up—intending to shout at the child to go away and stop disturbing her. Something happened in her heart as she began to drag herself out of her bed. She saw all of the women in Africa who helplessly watched their babies die of hunger. She saw the countless women who had received the broken bodies of their children killed in wars they had not chosen. She saw the slave women whose babies were torn from their arms, to be sold, never to be seen again. She saw the young girl, forced to have her baby adopted because she could not provide a home for her. Image after image came into her mind and she began to cry the tears of all of those women. She felt the pain and the desolation which bonded her with all those women and her heart opened. Something changed in her from that day. She began to call her friends and spoke to them of her care for them. She reached out to her husband with love, and happiness filled her home again. She experienced in her life a renewed gentleness and sensitivity. A great knot had been untangled in her heart and she felt an eagerness to live that she had never felt before.

The feminist mystic is vulnerable, open and receptive. She feels the pain and the grief of her world echoing in her heart. She knows the futility of attempting to drown those echoes in distractedness, numbness, or through distancing herself, and is willing to embrace the challenge of transformation. The ordinary mystic who lives in the world, like her sisters in the convents and the religious life, inevitably finds that she, too, will struggle with the institutions and structures of her culture, her relationships and her conditioning that expect of her limited fulfilment and possibility. Young girls will struggle with the models that tell them it is better to be appealing than intelligent. Young women will meet the expectations that remind them of the impossibility of combining mothering and a career. Women in their middle years will meet the institutions that define feminine responsibility as caring for others. Aging women will struggle with the cultural expectations that equate aging with a lack of worth. The feminist mystic knows that she must challenge the external imposition of any form of structure that attempts to confine her and limit her possibilities. She equally knows that she must call forth from within herself the courage to challenge her own consent to imposition, if she is to live a life of integrity.

The contemporary mystic, unlike the mystics of our images, has little appetite for traditional interpretations of transcendence. Historically, our spiritual conditioning has spoken of the need to leave the world in order to realise the transcendent. The feminist mystic of today is acutely aware of the price that has been paid for the divorce of the spiritual from the worldly. Generations of seekers have sought a place in the heavens while ignoring the very real pain and conflict of their immediate world. Closet mystics delight in their insight, while abdicating responsibility for healing their planet, their communities and their societies. There are too many contemporary spiritual visionaries who justify their lack of integrity and impeccability in their relationships and their world by professing their transcendence of them. The feminist mystic, who is rooted in the wisdom of her relatedness with all life, is not intent upon following the traditional paths of transcendence. Abandonment of the world is tempting primarily to those who feel consciously or unconsciously abandoned by the world, bereft of relatedness. It is easier to feel contempt for the world if we have received contempt from the world. A woman established in a vision of interconnectedness is intrinsically unable to abandon the world in her pursuit of a disembodied spirituality. A wise woman knows that transcendence may allow her to live as a saint, but if her ascendancy relies upon abandonment, her saintliness will be lived against a backdrop of a world which increasingly sinks into destruction and conflict. Knowing that heaven and earth, the inner life and the outer life, the body and the spirit, the world and herself are all interwoven threads in one tapestry, she does not seek to flee from anything but to find the deepest wisdom and compassion within herself to embrace that tapestry.

The feminist mystic holds and embodies a radical vision of freedom and this is the gift she offers to the world. She seeks to discover the transcendent within the worldly and heaven upon the earth. She seeks to discover the sacred at the heart of the world of appearances and to live with nobility and compassion amidst a world of chaos and confusion. The feminist mystic who seeks not to flee from the world but to discover the immanence of freedom within each moment knows that the path she must forge is the path of transformation. She is called to live in a spirit of freedom, challenging the decrees and structures that perpetuate division. She calls for radical transformation in our perception of what defines spirituality and refuses to consent to any commandment that decrees that she must divest herself of her femininity in order to achieve a spiritual life.

Joseph Campbell stated: 'The task of the warrior is to shatter established order and create new community.' The feminist mystic will be a warrior. She is a woman who is acutely aware of the choices between creation and destruction that are offered to her in each moment. She knows that to consent to any path that emphasises dominance, control, subjugation or denial is to consent to destruction and the furthering of pain. Consenting to any structure that demands the subjugation of her femininity is to choose destruction; consenting to any relationship that demands subservience or the sacrifice of integrity is to choose destruction; to live in a way that ignores her relatedness to all of life is to collude in destruction. In choosing the path of transformation and creation a woman who is a mystic will be a feminist.

219

The mystic and the feminist meet in their shared commitment to freedom, authenticity and creativity. Like the mystic, a feminist is unwilling to abandon the possibilities of her femininity in order to support ancient prejudices, preordained roles and identities. Spiritually she is unwilling to accept that asexuality is a pre-requisite to saintliness. Professionally she is unwilling to don the qualities of domination and control as the price for advancement. She shuns relationships that demand passivity and suppression as the foundation for relatedness. A woman of dignity faces daily the choices between creation and destruction. Countless women know that their willingness to subdue their femininity, to be silent, to consent to regarding their bodies as an ornament in the marketplace of relationship, to adopt sanctioned roles and to constrain their dreams and vision will garner a harvest of approval, safety and acceptance. Countless women equally know that in this transaction they are consenting to a path of destruction, an inner erosion of their spirit, a path which they are no longer willing to travel. The path of creation asks a woman to learn how to honour all that makes her a woman—her body, her heart, her aspiration, her power to transform, her creativity. Every woman who chooses the path of creation is a feminist.

Like the mystic, the feminist is no longer willing to accept the constraints of stereotypes or models imposed upon her by any external authority. She knows that to free herself of the shadow and power of externalised authority she must discover the wisdom of her own inner authority. No longer amenable to accepting the limitations of imposed images and roles that decree her place and value in the world, she knows the necessity of listening inwardly to discover the path of exploring her fullest potential as a human being—to be an awake and free woman. In that exploration the feminist is not desirous of discarding her femininity, becoming asexual in her quest for visibility and liberation, but seeks to utilise her mind, body and feelings as the vehicles for transformation.

The feminist, like the mystic, honours freedom and knows that she must embody her vision in every choice, action and word if she is to live a life of truth and integrity. It is a life which calls not for the abandonment of her femininity, but for the abandonment of compliance, malleability, the desire to please and for approval. A woman of wisdom knows too the need to balance the abandonment of her inclination towards compliance with an acute receptivity and willingness to listen both inwardly and outwardly to the wisdom and guidance that will enrich her path. A feminist is a woman who no longer equates the guidance and wisdom of others with an authority that is empowered to define her or her path.

The feminist, like the mystic, will be a warrior. She is steadfast in her determination to allow no structure, institution or authority to stand between her and what is true. Neither the feminist nor the mystic seeks war or battle; they are called upon to be warriors through the intractability of the structures that refuse to heed their vision and their wisdom. Countless women, by choice and necessity, work to share in supporting their families only to return home to discover that their roles within their homes remain unchanged. Endless tasks still remain within the realm of 'woman's work'. The vast majority of churches and temples are sustained through the service and devotion of their women supporters. They are considered eminently capable of raising funds, caring for the sick and lonely, but incapable of celebrating their faith in a visible way. The warrior spirit is not concerned with reversing positions of dominance or creating new hierarchies but with transformation of values, assumptions and structures that perpetuate dominance, subjugation and exploitation. The warrior spirit is required not only to transform outer structures but equally to meet with courage our inner structures and values that confine us.

The feminist and the mystic merge in their determination to bring to an end the old orders that govern our world and decree that power over self-betterment, oppression or mastery are significant values to hold and meaningful goals to aspire to. The feminist and the mystic seek for change—in their own experience of the pain of denial, constraint and subjugation they feel the echoes of the same pain rippling through generations of the invisible and the oppressed. They hold within their hearts the grief, rage and pain of the countless victims of sexism, racism and exploitation. They know in their wisdom that the forces that countenance sexism and racism are no different from the forces that destroy the planet that nourishes us. Passivity, indifference or powerlessness are abandoned by the feminist and the mystic. They are women of courage and truth, unwilling to consent to any order or authority that colludes in violating the integrity and spirit of any life.

There are those who proclaim that the work of the feminist is done; who state with some relief that we have now entered the post-feminist era. These proclamations rarely emerge from the heart of a woman who is awake to the pain and conflict that continue to scar our world. Rightfully, women can celebrate the extraordinary changes that have brought them greater equality and visibility. Yet the feminist mystic knows that as long as any woman is forced to live a life of subservience, is demeaned by the structures and authorities that govern her life, her voice is still needed. The warrior woman knows that as long as we live in a world that still countenances pornography, excuses rape, justifies inequality or turns a deaf ear to the suffering of exploitation, her courage is needed. As long as any living being lives in fear, deprived of freedom and dignity, there is a need for wisdom, healing and transformation. The feminist mystic is not satisfied with cosmetic changes or the postponement of freedom and integrity; she is steadfast in her call for transformation.

The union of the feminist and the mystic is a merger that has given birth to the warrior woman. She is a woman who knows that radical transformation can only emerge from a radical change of heart. To transform the world in an enduring and wise way, there must be a simultaneous inner transformation. The wisdom that emerges in the heart of the feminist and of the mystic bond them together in their dedication to the end of suffering and division. The mystic, rooted in the truth of her revelation of interconnectedness, seeks for a form to celebrate her vision. In this quest she cannot countenance the separation of her vision from her sexuality, politics, economics or structures of authority. The feminist, in her quest to live a life which honours her femininity, is called upon to find inner vision, a spiritual basis for her life. The essential quest that bonds the feminist and the mystic lies in their dedication to healing, creating and awakening. These women know that to heal the schisms that wound our planet and our communities, creating hierarchies and dominance, they must learn to heal the schisms that lie within their own hearts. It is a healing that inevitably calls us to dive deeply into the depths of our own psyches to discover the inner institutions, structures and divisions that lead us to live in fear. To be awake and free in the world we need to be awake and free within ourselves. To be empowered to heal and transform we need to know the unshakeability of an inner authority that is rooted in wisdom and truth.

We cannot deny the relatedness of inner and outer transformation. A woman profoundly dedicated to disarmament told the story of a march she had participated in to protest against a new bomber base. The demonstration that started peacefully went awry and the police plunged into the marchers, kicking with their boots and flailing with their batons. The woman recounting the story spoke of the fury that rose within her as the woman beside her was hit in the face with a nightstick. 'In that moment', she said, 'I found myself reaching down for a rock and threw it into the face of the policeman before me. As I saw the blood spurt from his mouth, I also realised that we shared a marriage of rage and hatred. We were no different in the way that we touched the world. We both wounded it.'

A woman who spent many years in a monastery in the east spoke of the contentment and peace that filled her days. 'So little was asked of me—apart from a few chores to perform, I was free to spend my life in meditation, refining the calmness and happiness my path offered me. One day I set out to travel to another monastery to visit with a great teacher. As I left the gates I was faced with a tiny girl, hand outstretched, face pinched, begging for food. As I sat on the bus and looked out of the windows it seemed that everywhere I looked I saw the face of hunger and hopelessness. I saw the young girls who would pass from serving their fathers to serving their husbands, their faces blank, their bodies already bowed with work. I saw the widows left to beg, stripped of dignity on the death of their husbands. I saw the baby girls, their birth greeted with dismay because of the burden they would place on their family. I saw myself removed from this suffering, yet in their faces I saw myself. I could only wonder at how much protection I sought in peace, rather than compassion.'

The feminist mystic knows that to honour and value her own integrity and freedom, she must honour and value the integrity and freedom of all life. Artificial divisions between inner and outer, us and them, black and white, enemy and ally must be abandoned. They are the sanctuary of the fearful, who build upon those divisions the hierarchies and prejudices that demean and condemn our world. A woman rooted in wisdom may not leave behind her a legacy of grand deeds, fame or renown, but her life will be a living testimony of impeccability. She knows that there is nothing that is irrelevant; every word she utters and gesture she performs touches the world and has the potential to contribute to creation or destruction. She will be careful and vigilant in her life without being self-conscious. She will be patient but equally knows that the time of waiting for transformation has passed. She will be fluid and receptive yet ever guided by a steadfast direction and vision. She will be loving and compassionate and yet know how to say no without trembling or living in fear of censure. She is a woman of balance; in her heart resides the sensitivity of the benevolent grandmother and the boldness and courage of the warrior.

A life that honours the interrelatedness of all life must be founded upon an inner communion that embraces our minds, bodies, feelings and vision. A spiritual life which attempts to divorce itself from any of these cannot heal the world but will perpetuate the same practices of abandonment—practices which cannot heal but are only able to harvest further division. A spiritual journey that is rooted within our bodies is rooted within the earth and will honour, with respect, that heritage. A spiritual journey that is founded upon respecting the power of our hearts to create or destroy will be able to draw upon the power of compassion and love that lies within our hearts. A spiritual journey that embraces the potential creativity of our minds will utilise that creativity to dissolve the assumptions and structures that attempt to limit communion. The feminist mystic will never attempt to bypass any aspect of her being in her search for wisdom. She is not, nor attempts to become, asexual; her femininity is a precious gift that teaches her how to care, to give and receive, to heal and to awaken.

Her own life stories and experiences inform the journey of the feminist mystic. She does not seek to forsake her stories but to learn from them. Beginning her journey, she does not reach for some fanciful plateau of spiritual awakening, but looks to the sometimes harsh and sometimes joyous realities of her life and world to guide her. She knows in her heart what saddens and wounds her and what empowers and heals her. Her stories teach her about where she will find alienation and separation and where she will find co-operation and wholeness. She knows what brings numbness and what awakens her. Through the willingness to learn from her stories and experiences, the feminist mystic discovers a path that is uniquely her own. Here she learns the most challenging lessons of her life—

what she needs to nurture and what she needs to renounce; what she needs to challenge and where her consent is required. No-one outside of herself is qualified or able to define this path for her; no-one has lived her life before.

The feminist mystic is a woman at home within the body of a woman, she speaks the language of a woman and carries a woman's history. She bears within her a heritage of belittlement, powerlessness and rage. She bears within her too the joy of creating and nurturing life, the communion born of her sexuality that connects her with the earth and the lives and deaths of all living beings. She carries within her the frustration of confinement and there lives within her the ancient wisdom that tells her that no-one and nothing actually possesses the power to contain her spirit. She is a woman of balance—honouring her receptivity and vulnerability, yet freely able to access her courage and creativity. Her intrinsic sensitivity and receptivity mean that she receives into her heart the grief of her world. She grieves that the children of her world will never see the fertile forests and clear rivers of her childhood. She is grieved that she is unable to walk the streets without suspicion, over the violations that wound the integrity of her sisters. She grieves for the tortured, the exploited, the maimed and the starving. On a cellular level she has known the pain of deprivation, subjugation and hopelessness. She defies a culture that attempts to camouflage or excuse the perpetuation of pain in the name of progress, ambition, inevitability or competition. She is steadfast in her determination to be a conscious participant in the creation of each moment; equally determined not to be a conscious or unconscious participant in destruction.

The feminist mystic is no stranger to grief; she is also intimately acquainted with joy. She knows the joy of creating and nurturing; the gift of bonding with the heart of another in love and empathy. Joy is found in her gift for community, in her capacity to heal and to embrace with compassion the pain of another. She feels in her own body's rhythms the rhythms of nature and knows a kinship that deepens her understanding of connectedness. She knows the joy of embodying her wisdom in her life, relationships and work and the joy of being empowered to transform her world. The feminist mystic finds joy in her aloneness knowing that she is never set apart from anyone by it.

The warrior woman is not passive in her grief or her joy. She is empowered to speak her truths, to embody her understanding and to be visible within her world. She knows the power that silence offers her to deepen in intuition; she equally knows that the power of transformation lies within her speech, her actions and her willingness to make her vision visible. Interconnectedness is the most important and essential spiritual truth. It is the reality that compels us to see the sacredness and preciousness of all life; that inspires us to live in a noble and ethical spirit. Interconnectedness is equally nature's first and primary law. It is the incontestable reality that marries the spirit and the world—it is a reality that challenges all concepts of personal worlds, separate and apart from one another. The reality of interconnectedness teaches us that we cannot cherish 'self' over 'other' nor harm any 'other' without harming 'ourselves'. A life that honours this essential reality must challenge any structure that supports dominion or subjugation for this is a structure that, in demeaning life's essential principle, can only sow pain and division. The feminist mystic can conceive of no life that is not lived in accord with her understanding of interconnectedness. It is an understanding that demands change—both inner and outer, if peace and freedom and are to be discovered.

The Hindu Goddess, Kali, portrayed as the cosmic mother, illustrates the essential unity of creation and destruction. She brandishes the sword of death or truth in one hand even as she offers reassurance and protection with the other. Her stance is one of fearlessness and dedication—she embodies the interwoven threads of creation, preservation and destruction. The feminist mystic is called upon to be a weaver of opposites, a healer of polarisations. She marries inner and outer, us and them, the profound and the mundane. She will never wreak destruction solely to manifest her own power, but only as a means of creating new forms, paths and structures that are founded upon respect and integrity. In her heart she knows that death must precede birth. Hierarchical structures, unauthentic identities, fears that bind her to conformity—all of these false gods must die if she is to give birth to herself and a world that is free of division and struggle. Creation of new forms and language that embody her vision and dedication will rise out of the ashes of the forms, structures and identities that have served only to wound and alienate. The feminist mystic, like Kali, is committed to preserving—the preservation of life which is sustained only through the willingness to change.

There is no area of our life which remains untouched and unscarred by the honouring of separateness. Racism, sexism, intellectual elitism, the exile of the poor and invisible from our hearts and the abuse of nature are all expressions of a profoundly-held belief in separation. It is a belief that divorces one person from another, just as it exiles us from any true sense of relatedness with our earth. Through this belief we objectify life and learn to see other people as competitors or adversaries in our quest for self-enrichment, gratification and personal gain. In a vision of separation, all forms of life, all people, the world that appears to exist outside of the sphere of our separate individuality, are perceived to be objects endowed with a particular promise. They are invested with the power to enhance or further our own ambitions or desires for gratification or are seen to hold the power to interfere with or threaten our personal self and its quest for fulfilment. It is this belief in separateness that is the foundation for all exploitation, cruelty and oppression. This is the schism that the feminist mystic is called upon to heal.

Every woman knows the pain of being objectified, the

humiliation of being dismissed and deemed irrelevant on the basis of her femininity. In that process she is deprived of respect and integrity: engaging in that process herself through denying her femininity she colludes in self-abandonment. The pain of being objectified is repeated in endless moments, experienced in the hearts of countless lives in our world. The elderly, the mentally ill, the poor are reduced to ciphers on statistical charts. Nature becomes a potential profit earner. Whenever we objectify anyone or anything we demean their spirit and do a disservice to ourselves. The world is not filled with predators, dedicated consciously to destruction and exploitation, but perhaps we have lost the art of living in a sacred way. The belief in separateness shadows our hearts, leading us to forget how to live in a way that honours our relatedness.

Upholding the belief in separateness is to sentence ourselves to a life of fear and mistrust, potentially a life of greed and hatred. Only when blinded by a belief in separateness can we carelessly and knowingly plunder and wound our planet, bequeathing to our children and our children's children an inheritance of destruction and imbalance. Only when lost in a belief in separateness can we banish the poor and the invisible from our hearts or support structures that enrich us while impoverishing another. It is a belief in which there is abandoned all that which is most true within ourselves. To support this belief we are called upon to abandon compassion, integrity and our own potential to create and heal. A North American Indian shaman confronted this belief in saying, 'We live in a way that is most unnatural to our true selves and our true selves know it.'

To heal the endless schisms born of the mythology of separateness the feminist mystic is called upon to be spiritually visible, to speak the truths revealed to her and to embody those truths in her life. The enactment of a belief in separation outwardly cannot be divorced from the schisms and divisions that reside within our relationship to our own being. That most intimate relationship in our lives, our relationship to ourselves, is the microcosm of every other relationship. In our ways of seeing and holding and interacting with our world we enact and embody the patterns and habits of our relationship to ourselves. The contempt or respect we extend towards ourselves will govern the ways in which we receive and relate to the world we live in. The love, compassion and acceptance or the self-abandonment and denial we offer to our own being will inevitably influence our vision of others. We hold within our own hearts the capacities to extend to ourselves trust and sensitivity or to wound ourselves with suspicion and insensitivity—none of these possibilities will be confined to ourselves, but will spill over to bond us with or banish us from the world and all of the life it holds.

Blinded by separation, our choices and our sense of possibility become limited. Believing in separation we will live a life of separation—a life of fear and mistrust, surrounded by enemies. Discovering the truth of interconnectedness we will be inspired to embody it in every moment of our lives—living in a sacred way, with compassion and dignity. It is time to learn new and profound lessons and to live them in our lives. Neither we nor our world can afford any longer to live in a way that is untrue to ourselves and that upholds a belief in separateness. We need to learn the healing power of compassion and the wisdom of interconnectedness. The lessons that empower us to live in a sacred way are learned within our bodies, minds and hearts; they can only be learned in the moment we are present in. Every moment of judgment, of self-denial or belittlement offers us the possibility to continue with a path of abandonment or to open our eyes to the healing power of forgiveness, trust and compassion. The lessons that we need to learn do not lie in some far-off spiritual dimension which we reach after transcending ourselves—they lie in the moment-to-moment realities of our lives.

Several of the most dedicated nuns came to their abbess for

guidance. 'There are those, among the novices, who continue to fall asleep during services. They bring shame upon us and we pinch them to make them stay awake. Should we punish them further?' The abbess replied, 'You would do better to offer them your knee to rest their heads upon.'

The calling of the feminist mystic is to unravel the knots of alienation and delusion that breed division. She nurtures and awakens her own wisdom and integrity so that she is empowered to heal and transform her world. The mythology of separation isolates humankind from the earth, self from other, the mind from the body and the spirit from the heart. Through all of these divisions runs the thread of alienation. From each of the chasms created by division rises a storm of destruction.

Historically, spirituality has separated itself from the world, deeming it to be inferior, worthless and contemptible. Involvement in social and political transformation is seen to be a distraction, an impediment to spiritual fulfilment and the world is abandoned in pursuit of holier goals. Abandoned too are all those in our world who have no voice to speak with, no power to transform the pain of their realities. It is truthfully said that it is easier to love 1,000 people at a distance than to love one person intimately. It is undoubtedly easier to shelter in an abstract love and compassion for all life than to live in a way which embodies love in all of our interactions, speech and deeds. The alienation of the spiritual from the worldly is the first of the schisms the feminist mystic is called upon to heal. She renounces all models of spirituality which hold the world in contempt, for she knows that to subscribe to any such model is to subscribe to the perpetuation of suffering and division. A genuine spirituality can never be a disembodied spirituality—the casualties of disembodiment are our earth, our bodies and our hearts. No such sacrifice is demanded by a spiritual path which is rooted in healing, compassion and wisdom.

To see the sacred in all things, the special in the ordinary and the ordinary in the special—this is a vision of healing and freedom. It is a vision that is unmarred by any sense of division or aversion. There are nuns in Calcutta who have dedicated their lives to caring for the poor and dying. The dying are brought to the shelter, their bodies covered with the lesions of leprosy, racked with tubercular coughing, dirty and emaciated, yet within those tortured bodies the nuns seek the face of God. Day after day, countless people are brought to the nuns; many die, but in their last hours they are touched by love. The nuns do not seek martyrdom or transcendence, they seek to discover the sacred beneath appearance.

The feminist mystic learns to touch her world and herself in the same spirit. She has inherited a conditioning that tempts her to abuse and despise her body, to devalue her feelings and to mistrust her mind and intuition. Politically her femininity has left her powerless, socially her femininity has attracted invisibility, and spiritually her femininity has reduced her to being a scapegoat and a victim. From the beginning of creation women were blamed for sorrow. Mythology continues to offer the fiction that the delusion of women led to the banishment of humankind from the sacred. Much of this history has been disowned by women, yet a legacy of inner alienation continues in the hearts of too many women who have still to find a home of peace and sanctuary within their bodies, their hearts and their minds. The mythology that surrounds women bequeaths to us a chronic legacy of inner mistrust. This is the primary knot of alienation the feminist mystic is called upon to heal.

To continue to abuse or hold in contempt our bodies in any way is to uphold the path of destruction and alienation—the feminist mystic withdraws her participation. To honour and respect our bodies as vehicles for embodying sensitivity and compassion is to follow a path of creation; a path which seeks to discover the sacred in all life. The passion of our feelings bonds us with the world—enabling us to hear the sounds of pain and grief and to respond with love. A path of destruction is one that leads us to mistrust that passion. A path of creation is one that knows that it is passion that allows us to penetrate and transform a world of indifference and heedlessness. Our minds are not the possessors of wisdom, nor the ultimate judges of right and wrong, but are the vehicles through which we are able to articulate vision and wisdom. Alienated from our hearts, our minds travel the familiar pathways of judgment and confusion. Bonded with our hearts, our minds are powerful vehicles of transformation, enabling us to communicate to the world the authority of our wisdom.

The feminist mystic will allow nothing to stand between herself and her understanding of what is true, no matter how much history or authority a person or institution may appear to possess. She is a woman of passion, but calm within chaos. She is contemplative, but at ease in assertiveness. She knows how to weave together the qualities of courage and empathy, effort and surrender. She is determined, but lives with serenity. She embraces fear with courage. She lives with an open heart but is never removed from discriminating wisdom. Above all, the feminist mystic is a woman of compassion.

In the Buddhist tradition, the feminine deity Kwan Yin is the embodiment of compassion. Translated, 'Kwan Yin' means 'one who hearkens to the sounds of the universe'. Listening to the sounds of the universe, the feminist mystic knows that compassion is the key to transformation, healing and liberation. In listening to herself she listens to the world, in listening to her world she listens to herself. Compassion is her offering, her response, her life. She is a woman of grace and fire.

CLOSING

The quest of the warrior woman is the path every woman travels as she learns to awaken inwardly and touch her world with compassion and wisdom. It is an ancient path, travelled by countless mystics and healers through the centuries. The vision of the mystic is alive within us, calling us to reclaim the freedom intrinsic to us. The wisdom of the mystic whispers to us through our lives, reminding us not to be deceived by our shadows and demons, but to learn to embrace them with a heart of compassion. The mystic sees her own face reflected in the faces of joy and sorrow she meets in her every day. She is alone and intimate; a seeker devoted to understanding what is most true in herself and her world. The warrior woman is a healer. She gazes upon her world, fraught with conflict and division, and responds with a greatness of heart that seeks healing and not blame. Dedicated to the end of sorrow, she challenges hatred and anger. Above all, the healer knows how to love; she is possessed of a boundless sensitivity and commitment to the end of pain. The warrior woman is a visionary. She is forging new paths, overturning complacency and structures that deny profound wisdom and transformation. She is guided by the wisdom of her intuition.

Travelling the path of the warrior woman, we are asked to find an ocean of patience, the courage of a tigress, the steadfastness of a mountain and the compassion of a Buddha. Patience is needed to be present and awake in the moments we

may falter, in learning how to nurture a finely-honed atten-
tiveness and to discover the willingness to begin again when
we have lost our way. Travelling the warrior's path, we are
challenging the habits of a lifetime that tempt us into numbness, fearfulness and avoidance. The warrior is in quest of
meaning, understanding, openness and wisdom. It is the warrior's patience that refrains from the temptations of superficiality, dullness and confusion. The warrior is in search of
greatness—greatness of love, heart and wisdom.

Courage and steadfastness enable the warrior to remain
firm and committed in the face of her demons and shadows.
Every woman who travels this path will encounter anxiety,
insecurity and the ancient pulls of conformity and passivity.
The warrior has made a commitment to dignity, integrity and
freedom. To live in their spirit and embody them in her life she
calls on courage to transform her demons and withstand the
pulls of fear. Above all, the warrior learns to travel her path
with a heart of compassion. Dedicated to peace and healing, she
seeks the end of all war and struggle. She knows the wisdom of
forgiveness, acceptance and love. They guide her to welcome
her life and welcome her world free of resistance or denial.

Learning the art of being still and listening inwardly, the
warrior learns the art of transformation. She receives her
demons and the struggles of her world with the same sensitivity and understanding. She is a woman of peace, creativity and
balance. The warrior lives in every woman who seeks to live
her life with profound peace, in a spirit of freedom.

INDEX

Our world and ourselves are transformed through the simple willingness to withdraw our projections, assumptions and conclusions.

Meditations For Women Who Do Too Much

ANNE WILSON SCHAEF

• • • • • • • • • • • • • • • • • •

Daily meditations to help women break the cycle of doing too much – for workaholics, rushaholics, and careaholics.

Many of today's women are overextended – addicted to working, rushing, taking care of *other* people's needs. With wisdom, insight, and humour, these 365 meditations – combined with quotations from women of different ages, cultures and perspectives – will help women recognize that cycle. A welcome antidote to the mad rush of modern living. Schaef's concise meditations will open new doors to new ways of living.

For all women who do too much – regardless of where they do it or how – these meditations will provide sustenance and inspiration and create possibilities for positive change in their lives.

The Awakening of the West

STEPHEN BATCHELOR

•••••••••••••••••••

Buddhism is now one of the most influential spiritual movements in the Western world, yet for more than two thousand years the religious traditions of East and West developed in ignorance of one another. In *The Awakening of the West* Stephen Batchelor tells the story through the lives of its key personalities: historical founders and modern exponents of the Theravada, Tibetan, Zen and Nichiren schools, as well as the Western pioneers who travelled to Asia and returned to create the first Buddhist centres. This encounter between East and West involved not only Colonialists' rational categorization of Asian culture but also Romantic fantasies of the Orient, and culminated in the 'hippy trail' of the 1960s, which opened doors between the two cultures as never before.

The Awakening of the West offers a clear introduction to Buddhist thought and practice and an overview of the major traditions active in the West today. Stephen Batchelor reveals Buddhism as a living spiritual tradition being transformed by its very interaction with the West. He suggests how with tolerance, compassion, humour and wisdom the two cultures may move closer together while respecting each other's diversity.

The Heart of Buddhism

GUY CLAXTON

•••••••••••••••••

At the heart of Buddhism is a Buddhism of the heart. The religion for a secular age, it offers a practical, comprehensible way to achieve more peace of mind and generosity of spirit. Concerning itself primarily with improving the quality of everyday life, it requires no adherence to obscure or magical beliefs, and offers a penetrating diagnosis of the human condition as well as a powerful and proven set of techniques for overcoming the rigours of today's world, both at home and at work.

Guy Claxton explains why Buddhism is so appropriate to our personal, social and global predicament and goes on to describe how we can help ourselves individually, with a teacher, or in a group, through understanding, meditation, communication and discipline.

'Written with humour, lightness of touch and an affection for the human condition with all its faults, this book is a blessedly easy and reader-friendly account of what Buddhism has to offer. But it is also a serious book and nothing of the basic teaching is left out.'

ANNE BANCROFT, *RESURGENCE*

The Heart of Buddhism	185538 274 1	£7.99	☐
Meditations for Women Who Do Too Much	0 06 254 866 2	£7.99	☐
The Awakening of the West	185538 343 8	£12.99	☐
Woman Changing Woman	185538 224 5	£7.99	☐

All these books are available from your local bookseller or can be ordered direct from the publishers.

To order direct tick the titles you want and fill in the form below:

Name: _____

Address: _____

_____

_____Postcode: _____

Send to: Thorsons Mail Order, Dept 3, Harper*CollinsPublishers*, Westerhill Road, Bishopbriggs, Glasgow G64 2QT.
Please enclose a cheque or postal order or your authority to debit your Visa/Access account –

Credit card no: _____

Expiry date: _____

Signature: _____

– up to the value of the cover price plus:
UK & BFPO: Add £1.00 for the first book and 25p for each additional book ordered.
Overseas orders including Eire: Please add £2.95 service charge. Books will be sent by surface mail but quotes for airmail dispatches will be given on request.

24 Hour Telephone Ordering Service for Access/Visa Cardholders – Tel: 041 772 2281